YET ONCE MORE

YET ONCE MORE

VERBAL AND PSYCHOLOGICAL
PATTERN IN MILTON

by

EDWARD S. LE COMTE

Columbia University

1953
LIBERAL ARTS PRESS
NEW YORK

31190

CONTENTS

PREFACE

OVERWHELMINGLY MUCH has been said about Milton's borrowings from others. Nothing, or next to nothing, has been said about his borrowings from himself. There is not even an article, not to say a book, on this subject. Inevitably, various editors, in the course of their annotations, have drawn attention to an occasional parallel, made here and there a cross-reference. The editions of Henry John Todd, in the nineteenth century, and Merritt Y. Hughes, in the twentieth, are especially valuable in this respect. Charles R. Sumner, in notes added to his translation of *De Doctrina Christiana* in the Bohn edition of the prose, pointed to numerous verbal parallels between that treatise and Milton's other works, especially *Paradise Lost*. The nearest to a collection in one place of various parallels has been the three columns on pages 1276–1277 of the Index to the Columbia *Milton*, and these are swelled by other than verbal parallels. Hundreds of Milton's repetitions have gone unrecorded and uncommented on; there has been no attempt to find the sum and assess it. The only general remark I have met with was made by Hugh C. H. Candy in the course of his special pleading, entitled *Some Newly Discovered Stanzas written by John Milton on Engraved Scenes illustrating Ovid's "Metamorphoses"*,[1] "he did in a sense plagiarize himself, as, in fact, Milton had rather a habit of doing." This is so to a degree unrealized by the commentators, as is evidenced not only by their silence but by the actual misstatements that some of them, and these not the least eminent, have let drop. I am not referring here to the assertion made by the latest of Milton's biographer-critics, Rex Warner:[2] "He never repeated himself"; for I have no disposition to quarrel with the truth in that statement. But, as Mr. Warner himself points out, Milton's peculiar greatness lies in the extent to which he is a tension of opposites, and this means, among other things, that his critics can—and certainly they do—make opposing statements about him: that he is classical and that he is romantic, that he is

a Puritan and that he is a humanist, that he is a revolutionary
and that he is an aristocrat, that he is highly original and that he
borrows from everybody, and so on. I have, in the present study,
set out to demonstrate how much psychological and literary
truth there is in *this* opposite statement: "Milton constantly repeated himself." And I do not mean anything vague by that, for
there is an abundance of riches to gather by being literal.

In gathering material, I have incurred a debt to three works
that can hardly be overstated: John Bradshaw's *Concordance to
the Poetical Works of John Milton* (London, 1894); Lane Coop-
er's *Concordance of the Latin, Greek, and Italian Poems of John
Milton* (Halle, Germany, 1923); and the *Index to the Columbia
Edition of the Works of John Milton,* compiled by Frank Allen
Patterson, assisted by French Rowe Fogle (New York, 1940).
The first two are, of course, exhaustive in their respective areas,[3]
and they ought to have assured my not missing any repeated
phrases within the English poetry or within the Latin poetry.
The Patterson *Index,* with its "more than 170,000 entries," is a
prodigious achievement; I speak from no casual acquaintance. It
amounts to a selective concordance. Indeed, the only objection
that could be made to it as an index is that it is too literal, and
that was precisely its usefulness to me. It is an alphabetical
anthology of Milton's words (or those of his translators), but
naturally more an anthology of nouns than of modifiers and
verbs. For all its help, it turned out to be no substitute for reading and rereading and, in a very definite way, trying to remember
the collected works of Milton in the original languages, with the
discovery by that process of a goodly number of parallels within
the prose and between the prose and verse not to be found
through any reference book—enough, I hope, to save me from
exclusive classification among the species Milton scorned, "the
ferrets and mousehunts of an index."

The references to commentators are highly specialized and are
not meant to add up to a bibliography. It follows that objections
I may have expressed are also specialized; indeed, I am sometimes in the ungracious position of mentioning very distinguished
critics and scholars only to tilt with them on a particular point,

which is—let me be the first to say—like the spoiled child who bites the hand that has fed him for years because, on just one occasion or two, the food is not to his liking. The standard editions I seldom cite, but have had them by me, open, all the while; and I hope it will not be assumed that I must be ignorant of what they say because I do not repeat from them.

Some of the material in Chapter VII appeared as an article in *Publications of the Modern Language Association* (LXII, December, 1947).

The text has been modernized in spelling and editorial style. Over and above the fact that Milton deserves the treatment regularly accorded the King James Bible and Shakespeare, it would have been impracticable for a book critically concerned with identical or similar combinations of words to pause, each time, over trivial differences in spelling, italics, and the like. Those who have occasion for them can get them instantly, for all citations from Milton's prose are located by a capital Roman numeral, followed by an Arabic numeral, referring to volume and page number in the Columbia University Press edition of *The Works of John Milton* (New York, 18 vols., 1931–1938). *Paradise Lost,* which is naturally the work most frequently cited, is referred to simply (without title) by a small Roman numeral, standing for the book number, followed by the line number (Arabic). *Paradise Regained* is *P.R.*, followed by book and line number, both in Arabic numerals. The other poems are cited by title, or easily understood abbreviation of title, and line number. I have usually followed the Oxford World Classics edition of *The English Poems* (imprint of 1940), with Merritt Y. Hughes' edition of *Paradise Regained, The Minor Poems, and Samson Agonistes* (New York, 1937) supplying a convenient text for the Latin poems. Those who look up references in the 1673 text of *Comus* should note that I used the 1645 text, which results in a difference of one in line numbering after line 167, "Whom thrift keeps up about his country gear," that line having been dropped from the 1673 text.

E. S. L.

YET ONCE MORE

"A mind not to be changed by place or time."
(*Paradise Lost,* i, 253)

"Word for word, . . . as an author borrows from himself."
(*An Apology for Smectymnuus,* III, 320)

CHAPTER I

CONNECTIONS

I T IS USUAL to divide Milton's career into three parts. There is, first, the young Milton, closest chronologically and poetically to the Renaissance, the Milton of the Nativity Ode, "L'Allegro" and "Il Penseroso," *Comus,* and "Lycidas," the Milton of Cambridge, Horton, and the Italian journey. This period of preparation and innocence and perfection in little closes in 1640 with "Epitaphium Damonis." The second period got under way after Milton, having received "the melancholy tidings from England of the civil war" (VIII, 125), gave up his plan of going on to Sicily and Greece, and instead returned home, where for twenty years, from 1641 to 1660, from *Of Reformation touching Church Discipline in England* to *The Ready and Easy Way to Establish a Free Commonwealth,* he exchanged "a calm and pleasing solitariness fed with cheerful and confident thoughts" for "a troubled sea of noises and hoarse disputes" (III, 241). The third and last period, of course, is that of the three major poems [1] which, in his blind old age, he brought out of the palpable ruins that "encompassed him around."

The feeling has been that these three parts of Milton are quite distinct. Thus it is possible, with some latter-day critics,[2] to admit the Milton of the first period into the realms of grace, while shutting out the Milton of the third period as a show without substance, a kind of automatic writer, of divided sensibility, an orotund dogmatist—in short, another author altogether. He *is* another author, or rather, three other authors. His extraordinary versatility will always call for the most careful discrimination in handing out praise or blame. But, as will be shown, his later self

3

borrowed in detail from his earlier. And as early as "At a Solemn Music" he foreshadowed both the theme and the style of *Paradise Lost*. Sin, he wrote,

> Broke the fair music that all creatures made
> To their great Lord, whose love their motion swayed
> In perfect diapason, whilst they stood
> In first obedience, and their state of good.   (21)

"Of man's first disobedience . . ."—it is this poem and "Lycidas" that cause Sir Arthur Quiller-Couch to declare that "Milton, before his Italian journey, had fairly mastered his style, fairly mastered the organ-music of speech." [3]

Quiller-Couch is remembering Tennyson's "God-gifted organ-voice of England," and that tag leads us to think of another that came to Milton through Matthew Arnold and has since been inseparable from him: "the grand style." [4] The poet in his youth not only anticipated *Paradise Lost*, but also this now standard description of its style. "Quid tam grande sonat distento spiritus ore?" he exclaimed in his Fifth Elegy (21), and again in "Epitaphium Damonis" (155), "nescio quid mihi grande sonabat Fistula." Moreover, he said it in prose, too, as he was preparing to write "Lycidas": "sinito paulisper apud te grandia loquar" (XII, 26).[5] It is a direct and far-reaching prophecy.

The second period, that of the controversial prose, would seem to be the most distinct. Some scholars have specialized in it, but for the general reader it is a bleak period, except for some occasional sonnets, *Areopagitica,* and perhaps a curious glance at *Of Education.* For Mark Pattison these are the years of waste, when Milton gave to party what was meant for mankind. "Our wish for Milton is that he should have placed himself from the beginning above party." [6] To which Richard Garnett properly retorts, "We think, on the contrary, that such a mere man of letters as Pattison wishes that Milton had been, could never have produced a *Paradise Lost.*" [7] Whether in prose or in verse, in *Paradise Lost* or the *History of Britain* or the *Doctrine and Discipline of Divorce,* Milton thought of himself as the counselor and teacher of his countrymen. He told Oldenburg in 1654: "I am far from thinking that I have spent my toil, as you seem to hint, on matters of inferior consequence" (XII, 65). He included *Of Education* in the 1673 edition of his shorter poems. While it remains undeniable that his prose is not verse, we shall presently see how nearly the two coincide at times, word for word.

There is overlapping both of an out-of-the-way sort which will be the special object of study here and of an obvious sort which is often forgotten. Critics often speak of *Paradise Lost* as if it were a composition wholly of the third period, whereas some of it—it may well be as much as half of it [8]—was written before the Restoration. With a like disregard for period classification, Milton returned to pamphleteering the year before he died with *Of True Religion*, even as it has been said with warrant that "It was at Cambridge that he became a controversialist." [9]

The division of Milton's lifework into three parts is certainly more convenient than such divisions frequently are. It has an obvious neatness and a general validity that are unassailable, provided it is not insisted on too much, dogmatically. Milton's development—poetically, politically, theologically—has been the subject of innumerable articles and books and notes. Time brought sharp changes in some of his major opinions. Brought up as a possible future bishop, he passed through an unattached Puritanism to Presbyterianism to Independency, and finally to what Hanford calls "pure individualism." [10] He believed in the Trinity when he wrote *Of Reformation*,[11] but not when he wrote *De Doctrina Christiana*. Chastity once meant virginity to him; then it meant marriage. Much can be pointed to on the side of change. But when all has been said, Milton's consistency as reflected in his open or latent recurrences on a small or large scale, his tenacity in regard to certain attitudes and modes of expressing himself, makes a remarkable, perhaps unique, record on the other side. It is time, not by any law of reaction, but in the interests of the whole complicated truth, that some reminders and some discoveries be set down testifying to a fixity of idea and emotional stand and verbal pattern that crosses the boundaries of periods and form, as well as of language and subject.

Broadly speaking, however, how many subjects did Milton

have? One might contend that, in his major work, he had but
one: the distinction between liberty [12] and license. Or, to narrow
the field to his five great poems, the initial fact is that four of
them deal with the theme of temptation. It is not the same kind
of temptation in every case,[13] which is one large reason the poems
are as different as they are, but the fact is nevertheless impressive. And even the one poem of the five which is an exception
contains the lines:

> Were it not better done, as others use,
> To sport with Amaryllis in the shade,
> Or with the tangles of Neaera's hair?
> ("Lycidas," 67)

A surprising number of editors, influenced by Warton's discovery
that the names Amaryllis and Neaera occur in some Latin amatory verses by George Buchanan, have asked us to believe that
Milton is here alluding to the composition of erotic poetry.[14] The
context not only does not encourage, it does not permit so oblique an interpretation. "To scorn delights," the poet goes on to
say. Amaryllis and Neaera stand for the natural pleasures. They
are symbolic, but they are also girls. Milton was his own best
commentator (this is often the case) when, after stating in *Tetrachordon* that "no worthy enterprise can be done by us without
continual plodding and wearisomeness to our faint and sensitive
abilities"—in earlier words, "live laborious days" ("Lycidas," 72)
—he added:

We cannot, therefore, always be contemplative, or pragmatical abroad,
but have need of some delightful intermissions, wherein the enlarged
soul may leave off a while her severe schooling, and, like a glad
youth in wandering vacancy, may keep her holidays to joy and harm-
less pastime: which as she cannot well do without company, so in no
company so well as where the different sex in most resembling un-
likeness, and most unlike resemblance cannot but please best, and be
pleased in the aptitude of that variety.   (IV, 86)

Indeed, while on the subject of "the tangles of Neaera's hair,"
we are close to a favorite conception of Milton's, that of "the
amorous net." He dealt with it in prose and verse, in three lan-

guages, and in all three "periods." He began by proclaiming, in the First Elegy, that he was by no means immune to the charms of the British maidens, "virginibus . . . Britannis." Often he had been made aware of their waving tresses, golden nets which deceitful Love sets out:

> tremulosque capillos,
> Aurea quae fallax retia tendit Amor. (59)

In the Italian sonnet to Diodati he speaks of himself as one who used to mock Love's nets—"suoi lacci," where a good man sometimes gets entangled, "s'impiglia." Not tresses of gold, "treccie d'oro," but this time a dark foreign beauty has dazzled him (Son. iv, 2). This is light, or at least demonstrably imitative, Petrarchan, but the time was to come when there could be no doubt of his earnestness. In the *Doctrine and Discipline of Divorce,* after his own bitter taste of marriage, he would pity the man who "sees himself, without fault of his, trained by a deceitful bait into a snare of misery" (III, 405). ("The bait of women," *P.R.*, 2, 204, trapped "wisest Solomon.") Marriage too often presents the sorry spectacle of "two ensnared souls" (III, 427). In controversy with More, however, twelve years later, he was to be sarcastic about the picture of the latter as a man tangled in a feminine net, "homo nassa muliebri indutus" (IX, 244; cf. 242, quotation, and 246). Adam grimly and prophetically gives the plural of this, "female snares" (x, 897). Finally, *Paradise Lost* and *Paradise Regained* bring in "the amorous net." Michael gives Adam a vision, based on Genesis, vi, 2, of men "in the amorous net Fast caught" (xi, 586). And Belial proposes to tempt Jesus with "daughters of men the fairest found" who have the ability to draw "Hearts after them tangled in amorous nets" (*P.R.*, 2, 162). Such is the wily evolution, the decreasing innocence, of "the tangles of Neaera's hair." That Milton was already thinking of the tangles as an entanglement, as something of an enveloping net,[15] is evidenced by his having written "Hid in" (I, 465) before he changed to "Or with."

There are many particular spans of unity. Much, for instance, has been written about Spenser's influence on Milton, especially the young Milton. Everyone remembers that in *Areopagitica* the author (he was then thirty-five) went out of his way to pay tribute to "our sage and serious poet Spenser" (IV, 311). No one [16] seems to recall that in *Comus* this very phrase occurs and is the other side, as it were, of an equation: "the sage And serious doctrine of Virginity" (786)—i.e., which Spenser taught.

Comus is himself a light sketch for the Satan of *Paradise Lost,* even as the Attendant Spirit is a precursor of the guardian angels: like Uriel he comes down "swift as . . . a (shooting) star" (80; iv, 556). There comes a curious confirmation of the former fact when both tempters use the same words of flattery to their intended female prey: "Hail, foreign wonder!" exclaims Comus to the Lady, and identifies her with a "goddess" (265, 267). "Thou . . . art sole wonder," glozes the serpent to Eve in his opening speech, which closes with the assertion that she should be "a goddess" (ix, 533, 547). Both key words of praise, "wonder" and "goddess," were used by Ferdinand in addressing Miranda,[17] but whatever (if anything) Milton owed to Shakespeare the first time, he was clearly doubling back on himself the second. He was doubling back, too, when he used the same description of a supernatural plant in both poems. Haemony, in *Comus,* is a small unsightly root, "But of divine effect" (630).[18] Eve tells Adam the forbidden fruit is not dangerous, "but of divine effect" (ix, 865) to open eyes. The difference here is between starting a line of blank verse with the words and ending one, and between the truth and a lie (or a half-truth).

Three years before he assembled lesser devils, such as Moloch, in the Nativity Ode, Milton, at eighteen, composed an epic, a little epic, an epyllion, "In Quintum Novembris," in which the dominating figure is Satan, who, like his great successor in *Paradise Lost,* swims through the air with his wings ("In Quintum Novembris," 45; cf. 208), and, like the Satan of *Paradise Regained,* comes disguised, as a gray eremite ("In Q.N.," 79 ff.), on a mission of temptation. The author of *Paradise Lost* was quoting the Cambridge undergraduate when he alluded to the "eyes That sparkling blazed" (i, 193) ("Ignescunt oculi," 38); compare too vi, 848: "every eye Glared lightning and shot forth pernicious fire"—of the "Artificer of fraud" (iv, 121) ("fraudumque magister," 17). Both Satans inaugurate an insidious conspiracy at night (the one is "Prince of Darkness," x, 383, the other, "niger umbrarum dominus," 78), rousing a subordinate with the question, "Sleep'st thou?" (v, 673) ("Dormis?" 92 [19]), and each puts himself in position "to behold The fellows of his crime, the followers rather" (i, 605) ("Dinumerans sceleris socios, vernasque fideles," 10). God above is moved to laughter: "Laugh'st at their vain designs and tumults vain" (v, 737) ("Vanaque perversae ridet conamina turbae," 168).

No piece of advice in the great epic is more famous than Raphael's words to Adam: "Be lowly wise" (viii, 173). The young Milton, in 1637, before he had written "Lycidas," said precisely the same thing in Latin: "humile sapiamus" (XII, 26). It may be very well, with one or two recent commentators,[20] to cite Sylvester's Du Bartas, "Be sober wise," but this closer parallel [21] in Milton himself ought not to be neglected. The danger of paying too little attention to this kind of evidence is shown by a recent article speculating that the poet had read a book published in 1640, Robert Crofts' *A Paradise Within Us, or the Happy Mind*.[22] The reason for wondering if he did so lies in the verbal coincidence of Michael's final statement in Book xii:

> then wilt thou not be loth
> To leave this Paradise, but shalt possess
> A paradise within thee happier far. (585)

But there was not a little inspiration for the line within Milton's previous writing. In Book iv, with reference to Satan, he had spoken of

> The hell within him; for within him hell
> He brings.... (20)

In a poem so full of balances, so conscious of its double theme, it would be incautious to say that Milton was not thinking of this passage when he wrote the later one. For a second inspiration we may refer to a statement about the possessors of knowledge (Michael had been bestowing a special kind of knowledge on

Adam) in Milton's Seventh Prolusion. In grand style the Cambridge student declared: "illi apud se regno fruuntur, omni terrarum ditione longe gloriosiori" (XII, 268).[23] Considering how easily Milton passed from Latin to English, the relevant words here —that those who have mastered knowledge "enjoy a kingdom within themselves far more glorious" than a worldly one—furnish a verbal inspiration in some respects closer than "A Paradise Within Us, or the Happy Mind," for though the adjective of commendation is a different one, it is in the comparative degree and modified by the Latin equivalent of "far" (*longe*). Centuries of commentators have spoken of Milton's Latinate style. It is to be pointed out that in many cases he is actually translating from his own Latin.

Whatever may be the uninvestigated facts in regard to other major writers [24] (who perhaps are not to be approached in this way), Milton's work abounds in autoplagiarisms, whether bilingual or not, and these form the subject of the present book.[25] Certain distinctions need to be made early. This is not necessarily a study in imagery, of the kind that has been so popular in literary criticism of the past twenty years and that Milton has not failed to receive at the hands of G. Wilson Knight,[26] Malcolm Mackenzie Ross,[27] and Theodore Howard Banks.[28] Many of the verbal recurrences with which we shall be concerned do not embody images. On the other hand, some images or ideas return in completely different words and do not constitute what is here meant by an autoplagiarism. Professor Maurice Kelley has reviewed the many coincidences of thought between *De Doctrina Christiana* and *Paradise Lost* which do not involve coincidence of language.[29] For further instance, there is Milton's preoccupation with the view that he lived in a climate too northerly to be favorable to the production of great works of the mind.[30]

> Me, of these
> Nor skilled nor studious, higher argument
> Remains, sufficient of itself to raise
> That name, unless an age too late, or cold
> Climate, or years, damp my intended wing
> Depressed.   (ix, 41)

For we Englishmen, being far northerly, do not open our mouths in the cold air wide enough to grace a southern tongue.   (IV, 281)

> Haec ergo alumnus ille Londino Milto
> Diebus hisce qui suum linquens nidum
> Polique tractum (pessimus ubi ventorum,
> Insanientis impotensque pulmonis,
> Pernix anhela sub Iove exercet flabra),
> Venit feraces Itali soli ad glebas.
> ("Ad Salsillum," 9)

For the sun, which we want, ripens wits as well as fruits.   (X, 325)

But if from the industry of a life wholly dedicated to studious labors, and those natural endowments haply not the worst for two and fifty degrees of northern latitude .... (IV, 296)

quo magis illum mentis tuae vigorem plane aethereum et quasi purissimam divinae aurae partem in illas ultimas regiones delapsam admiramur; quam neque caelum illud triste ac nubilosum ullis frigoribus extinguere aut gravare ... potuit.   (VIII, 106)

... if to the instinct of nature and the emboldening of art aught may be trusted, and that there be nothing adverse in our climate, or the fate of this age, it haply would be no rashness, from an equal diligence and inclination, to present the like offer in our own ancient stories.   (III, 237)

> Ridet Hyperboreo gens barbara nata sub axe.
> (" In Q. N.," 95)

Eight times different words have been found for the same idea. Another time, however,

> Manse pater, iubeo longum salvere per aevum,
> Missus Hyperboreo iuvenis peregrinus ab axe.
> Nec tu longinquam bonus aspernabere Musam,
> Quae nuper, gelida vix enutrita sub Arcto,
> Imprudens Italas ausa est volitare per urbes.
> (" Mansus," 25).

Milton slightly echoed the line last quoted, "Hyperboreo . . . sub axe" and "Hyperboreo . . . ab axe" occupying the same position in the Latin hexameter, so that on this, as on other occasions, the exigencies of meter invited repetition.

To give an illustration in another category: "On Shake-speare" contains a conceit,

> Then thou, our fancy of itself bereaving,
> Dost make us marble with too much conceiving; (13)

which is like the conceit about the songs of Circe and the Sirens in *Comus,*

> ... they in pleasing slumber lulled the sense,
> And in sweet madness robbed it of itself; (260 [31])

but there is no verbal parallel, unless (which is dubious) "of it-self" constitutes one.

It is true that a single word, if individual or crucial enough, may make a verbal parallel between passages (e.g. the flattery of addressing a woman as a "wonder"). The earlier version of "sage and serious" was "sage and solemn":

> And if aught else great bards beside
> In sage and solemn tunes have sung,
> Of tourneys, and of trophies hung,
> Of forests, and enchantments drear,
> Where more is meant than meets the ear.
> ("Il Penseroso," 116)

The first thought is still Spenser.[32] And if "sage" without "seri-ous" can introduce Spenser, so can "solemn" without "sage": "I betook me among those lofty fables and romances, which recount in solemn cantos the deeds of knighthood" (III, 304). To give another illustration of the magnetism of a single word in the right surroundings, "Il Penseroso," 79–80,

> Where glowing embers through the room
> Teach light to counterfeit a gloom,

anticipates *Paradise Lost,* i, 63,

> No light, but rather darkness visible,

without adopting Bentley's emendation: "No light, but rather a transpicuous gloom." "Helpless" plus synonyms makes a paral-lel within *Comus:* "a single helpless maiden" (402), "one virgin, Alone and helpless" (582). *Comus,* 448, "Minerva, . . . uncon-quered virgin," [33] is close enough to "Palladis invicta virtus"

(XII, 124). Obviously, there is more than "gray" between the arrival of evening in *Comus:* "the gray-hooded Even, Like a sad votarist in palmer's weed" (188), and of morning in *Paradise Regained:* "till Morning fair Came forth with pilgrim steps, in amice gray" (4, 427; cf. iv, 598). Then there is the dancing wine: "this cordial julep here, That flames and dances in his crystal bounds" (*Comus,* 672); "the dancing ruby, Sparkling outpoured" (*Samson Agonistes,* 543).

The verb "tax" bridges the following quotations from the *Doctrine and Discipline of Divorce* and *Samson Agonistes,* quotations that would in any case be akin for identity of counsel to those who have been rendered desperate by a bad marriage:

of all those wild words which men in misery think to ease themselves by uttering, let him not open his lips against the providence of Heaven, or tax the ways of God and his divine truth.   (III, 496)

> Tax not divine disposal.   Wisest men
> Have erred, and by bad women been deceived.
> (*S. A.,* 210)

But it is seldom that Milton borrows from himself one word only. Even here the adjective "divine" was in attendance in the earlier passage, as was, besides "wonder," "goddess" in the *Comus-Paradise Lost* parallel. Metrical considerations apart, the Latinate "divine disposal" was used where some variation was necessary, for not only had "the ways of God" been used twice in *Paradise Lost* (i, 26; viii, 226): it was, eighty-three lines further on, to be used in *Samson Agonistes.* (And at the end of the drama we are given this echoing reason why the divine disposal should not be taxed: it is "the unsearchable dispose . . . ever best found in the close," 1746.)[34]

Henceforth, the parallels to be studied will comprise a combination of two or more words. Of course the combination must be sufficiently striking. There are difficulties here, for the modern reader may mistake as individual what was in fact a commonplace at that time. "Christian liberty" and "right reason" *were* common references[35] (too common for us to cite). Everyone must know that "thrice great Hermes" ("Il Penseroso," 88), "Ter magnus Hermes" ("De Idea Platonica," 33) is a case of a fixed epithet, not of a newly invented tribute, but how many know that the "golden" of "the Golden Chersonese" (xi, 392; *P.R.*, 4, 74) is also—"Aurea Chersonesus"—a fixed epithet? [36] "Filthy lucre" would be passed over as a still common echo from the Bible (I Tim. iii, 3; Tit. i, 7, 11; I Pet. v, 2): we should be interested only if Milton repeated some variation, such as "the filthy love of gain" (V, 45) (he does not: we get only "the excessive love of gain," X, 363, "spem quaestus uberiorem," VIII, 28, etc.). We are interested in cases where a point of style is involved. It is scarcely a point of style when the historian reports that Boadicea wore "a great golden chain" (X, 69) or that the jennet of the emperor of Russia had "a great chain of plated gold about his neck" and two of the emperor's attendants "chains of gold hanging to their feet" (X, 379, 380). This is Milton as a reporter (and we get him as a translator at VI, 275). But he is more than a reporter when he tells of "This pendent World" "fast by, hanging in a golden chain" (ii, 1051); "Hung o'er my realm, linked in a golden chain" (ii, 1005), even though he has a source for this, too, a source to which he himself has pointed: "Homerus etiam per auream illam Jovis catenam de Caelo suspensam . . . ," (XII, 150).

Some of the quotations to be made here are of the diction of the time or borrowings from preceding authors.[37] For "hard assays" (*Comus,* 972; iv, 932) Todd in his Canterbury, 1798 edition of *Comus* cited Fairfax, Spenser, and other old writers. "Adamantine chains" can be found in Spenser and other Elizabethans, but we shall always think of it as Milton's: "there to dwell In adamantine chains and penal fire" (i, 48). He tried it out in Latin first, "catenis adamantinis subduxit se Briareus" (XII, 122), and then applied it to the bonds of matrimony: "and give it such adamantine chains to bind with" (III, 425). Indeed, to vary slightly the procedure of looking into Spenser for Milton's phrases, we can turn, for illustration, to Fairfax's Tasso.[38] There, in the second stanza of the first book, is an invocation to the "heavenly Muse," but Milton made the "heavenly Muse" his, his uniquely, the more his for having repeated the reference (i, 6; iii, 19; Nativity Hymn, 15; *Comus,* 515). In the eleventh stanza we find "Heaven's Eternal King," which has the indubitable Miltonic ring. After using it once in the Nativity Hymn (2), the poet broke it up and repeated the parts: "Heaven's King" (ii, 751; ii, 992; iv, 111; 973; *P.R.*, 1, 421), "Eternal King" (iii, 374; vi, 227; *P.R.*, 1, 236). This is what we are interested in: that which Milton, exercising choice, made his, and liked enough consciously or unconsciously to repeat. There are many "orient pearl(s)" (iv, 238; v, 2; X, 354) outside Milton, but, for once, we should not let that concern us too much.

We must not pass over the very interesting case where a combination as undistinctive as "I waked" is made distinctive by context. The two passages are the ending of the poignant sonnet in memory of the poet's second wife,[39]

> But O, as to embrace me she inclined,
> I waked, she fled, and day brought back my night,

and the lines where Adam fears his vision of Eve will remain only a dream:

> She disappeared, and left me dark; I waked
> To find her, or for ever to deplore
> Her loss, and other pleasures all abjure.   (viii, 478)

The emotion that came to the blind poet in 1658 when, according to the traditional interpretation, he saw in a dream her whom he had never seen in actuality, that "late espoused saint" with whom he had made his happiest marriage, has returned to color Adam's unfounded anxiety over Eve. Needless to say, the darkness in each instance is more than physical, even as it is less than permanent: Adam has light, presently, to see his newly created wife; Milton will hope for "full sight" of his "in heaven without restraint." Yet, how unfounded, after all, is Adam's fear of loss? The passage prepares for his finding her truly lost, soon after this declaration to Raphael, and for the tragic chivalry by which he, falsely deciding "to lose thee were to lose myself," (ix, 959) falls too. If we proceed to examine the two preceding lines in the sonnet,

> Love, sweetness, goodness, in her person shined
> So clear, as in no face with more delight,

and the four preceding lines in the epic,

> And in her looks, which from that time infused
> Sweetness into my heart, unfelt before,
> And into all things from her air inspired
> The spirit of love and amorous delight,

we come upon further connections, for besides the "in her person"—"in her looks" parallel, three principal words, "love," "sweetness," and "delight" have been drawn into the same orbit. This illustrates a tendency (which has been impressively noted in Shakespeare [40]) toward the formation of word clusters (sometimes, though not this time, better described as image clusters). It may or may not be surprising, then, that in the following book, ix, 454, Milton again combines "in her looks" and "delight"— "and in her looks sums all delight:"—and adds "sweet" two lines later. In the above instance, the bond is emotional rather than logical. ("Sweet" and "sweetness" are words that this poet reserves, almost always, for music,[41] for paradise, and for the originally perfect affection between Adam and Eve. As he had indicated as early as in "At a Solemn Music," to be unparadised is to lose music and love: "disproportioned sin Jarred against nature's chime," "with harsh din Broke the fair music." [42] The sinful may no more hope for an ideal marriage than to hear the music of the spheres.[43]) By contrast, a logical bond would be the association of "I waked" with "find" and "found":

> I waked
> To find her . . .

> but O, how glad I waked
> To find this but a dream!   (v, 92)

> whereat I waked, and found
> Before mine eyes all real.   (viii, 309)

> As new-waked from soundest sleep,
> Soft on the flowery herb I found me laid.   (viii, 253)

This is nothing more than part of the pattern of dreams and portents in this epic, among others, dreams that turn out to be true in the long run, if not immediately—the dream of the fall, or of creation. So, too, the sonnet "On his deceased Wife" and the parallel passage in *Paradise Lost* both commence with the words, "Methought I saw" (viii, 462).

The presumption is that the verbal echoes, when they cross from one work to another, are mostly unconscious (a circumstance which by no means reduces their interest). The most conspicuous exception is the relation, the chronology of which is uncertain,[44] between the sonnet beginning,

> O nightingale, that on yon bloomy spray
> Warbl'st at eve, when all the woods are still,

and two lines in Elegia V,

> Iam philomela tuos, foliis adoperta novellis,
> Instituis modulos, dum silet omne nemus, (25)

an artful translation, if ever there was one. But, to take another bilingual example, when it comes to comparing a line in Elegia VII (45),

> Nec te, stulte, tuae poterunt defendere Musae,

with two lines in "Lycidas," written ten years later,

> What could the Muse herself that Orpheus bore,
> The Muse herself, for her enchanting son, (58)

and both passages with the lament for Orpheus in *Paradise Lost*,

> . . . nor could the Muse defend
> Her son, (vii, 37)

—we are already in the doubtful and fascinating realm of unexplicit connection. Love or womankind destroyed Orpheus, with whom the English poet throughout his life felt affinities, while the adolescent Latin poet was also speaking of love and himself and the not always protecting muses, and our recurring question has to do with what associations or turns of mind underlie the surface resemblance.

Only in the case of the Latin poetry can one say with some assurance that economy is dictating the repetition. Most striking of many instances [45] is the reappearance scarcely changed, in "Mansus" of lines from "Ad Patrem," "Victricis hederas inter laurosque sedebo" (A.P., 102) becoming "Victrices hederas inter

laurosque sedebis" (Man., 6) and "Heroumque actus imitanda-
que gesta canebat" (A.P., 46) becoming "Heroum laudes imi-
tandaque gesta canebant" (Man., 43). There is obvious thrift
here, but one of Milton's chief subjects, too—the crowned poet,
sitting with his victory wreath,[46]

> Yet once more, O ye laurels, and once more
> Ye myrtles brown, with ivy never sere . . . .
> (" Lycidas," 1)

he whose function it is to sing of heroic action. This is not Milton
just repeating himself. It is Milton being true to himself.

Then, amidst the hymns and hallelujahs of saints, someone may perhaps be heard offering at high strains in new and lofty measures to
sing and celebrate . . . .[47]   (III, 78)

to celebrate in glorious and lofty hymns the throne and equipage of
God's almightiness, and what He works, and what He suffers to be
wrought with high providence in His Church, to sing the victorious
agonies of martyrs and saints . . . .   (III, 238)

(Here is another cluster: "hymns," "saints," "high," "lofty,"
"sing," "celebrate.") It is no accident but a law of character that
four times in prose and once in verse Milton alluded to "matchless deeds" (IV, 17; V, 41; 69; 270; *P.R.*, 1, 233). (Do "egregia
facinora," XII, 262, "egregium facinus," VII, 50, "facta egregia,"
VII, 550, "egregie facta," VIII, 2; 254, raise the sum to ten?)
This is what he was meant to be, the celebrator of matchless
deeds: the ambition stirred within him often and early.

Those verbal echoes, on the other hand, that occur within a
single work—notably *Paradise Lost*—are more likely to be deliberate, and to these we turn first in the following chapter.

CHAPTER II

EPIC REITERATION

OF DELIBERATE REPETITION Milton was—all would grant though few discuss it—a past master. From his earliest original English poem, "On the Death of a Fair Infant Dying of a Cough "[1] (which he withheld from publication in 1645), through "Lycidas" and beyond, his development in this particular art of language can be impressively traced. Surely only the blind, or rather the deaf, can fail to notice the increase in skill from

> Young Hyacinth, born on Eurotas' strand,
> Young Hyacinth, the pride of Spartan land;
> ("Fair Infant," 25)

which is no better than its model, Spenser's

> Young Astrophel, the pride of shepherds' praise,
> Young Astrophel, the rustic lasses' love,[2]

to

> For Lycidas is dead, dead ere his prime,
> Young Lycidas, and hath not left his peer.
> ("Lyc.," 8)

It is the difference between apprenticeship and mastery. That apprenticeship got under way, in exercises that do not survive,[3] at Saint Paul's School as a regular part of the boys' pursuit of the trivium. Milton must often have written Latin compositions in which he was required to use the tropes and schemes to be found in such textbooks as those by Talaeus and Butler and Farnaby, to say nothing of that by the headmaster himself, Alexander Gill's *Logonomia Anglica*.[4] As Erasmus had said a hundred years before, and the tradition remained unbroken:

So at some time or other the boys practice the elementary exercises of rhetoric, taking them up separately, one at a time. That is the

19

plan Aphthonius followed in his *Progymnasmata*. At one time praise, blame, fable, similitude, comparison. At another time figures, or description, division, disputation, classification, characterization.[5]

Milton, even as Shakespeare before him,[6] had such training as a schoolboy as would have made him instantly aware—unlike his editors, who never mention the fact—that the above two lines of "Lycidas" illustrate the figure of repetition called "epanalepsis," combined with another figure of repetition called "epizeuxis." There are many examples throughout Milton's work. "O dark, dark, dark amid the blaze of noon!" (*Samson Agonistes*, 80) is "epizeuxis," too, and the two places, so many years and poems apart, are connected, since this darkness is feared as a kind of death, an end of usefulness, just as "Lycidas" was engendered by, or at least derives much of its passion from, a fear of the cutting off of usefulness. Ultimately the technical terms do not matter, but the art does, and it is important to have some realization how early training in rhetoric and logic directed poetical genius in those days, as it does not now.[7]

Milton's repetitive devices range from a simple parallelism, which has more to do with grammar than with rhetoric,

> Jehovah's wonders were in Israel shown,
> His praise and glory was in Israel known,
> ("Paraphrase on Psalm 114," 5)

> So little is our loss,
> So little is thy gain,
> ("On Time," 7)

to the use of refrain, the lines occurring twice on two occasions— "Such a rural Queen/All Arcadia hath not seen" (*Arcades*, 94, 108), "Listen and save" (*Comus*, 866, 889), many times on two other occasions—once under Hebrew influence, once under Greek. At fifteen, when he would have been commencing the study of Hebrew in the last form at Saint Paul's,[8] he paraphrased Psalm 136, turning what the King James version gives (in each of the twenty-six verses) as "for his mercy endureth for ever" to (twenty-four times):

> For his mercies aye endure,
> Ever faithful, ever sure.

In "Epitaphium Damonis," pursuing the well-known principle of unity in variety, the grieving poet bade the sheep go home unfed seventeen times,

> Ite domum impasti, domino iam non vacat, agni,

which is oftener, though only a little oftener, than any comparable refrain occurs in Theocritus or Moschus. It has been well said that the effect is one of "almost impatiently" thrusting aside the cares of the present.[9] Here, in two senses of the word, is a *burden* from which to turn at the beginning of each paragraph. Thyrsis has become a bad shepherd in his sorrow. "The hungry sheep look up, and are not fed" ("Lyc.," 125).

> ovium quoque taedet, at illae
> Moerent, inque suum convertunt ora magistrum.
> ("E. D.," 66)

It is odd, this return of a situation that was matter for stern reproof in "Lycidas."

All other artful repetitions in the shorter poems are examples of various kinds of emphasis. It is obvious, for instance, what is being emphasized in the same elegy when the poet writes:

> Nil me blanditiae, nil me solantia verba,
> Nil me, si quid adest, movet, aut spes ulla futuri. (91)

Less obvious is

> Illi tibi vota secundo
> Solvere post Daphnin, post Daphnin dicere laudes
> Gaudebunt. (30)

Why is so much made of Damon's secondary position after Daphnis in the esteem of shepherds? Could not Milton's friend have been made equal, as Virgil made his: "Ut Baccho Cererique, tibi sic vota quotannis Agricolae facient"?[10] The answer seems to be that Milton is not making Damon less, but himself as poet. He is thinking, not of the mythological Daphnis at large, but of Daphnis as memorialized in Theocritus' First Idyl and Virgil's Fifth Eclogue, with which modesty forbids putting "Epitaphium Damonis" on a par.

Repeating imperatives is perfectly understandable. The "Carmen Elegiacum" found with the Commonplace Book opens and closes with these lines:

> Surge, age, surge! Leves, iam convenit, excute somnos!
> Lux oritur; tepidi fulcra relinque tori.

One may be reminded of "Corinna's Going A-Maying": "Get up, get up, for shame, the blooming morn. . . ." In either case the sleepy or sluggish must be stirred by iteration. But the difference between Herrick's hedonistic *carpe diem* and Milton's moral and hygienic approach is important and keeps the poems apart. Milton is addressing a man, and bidding him attend to his duties. (The Cambridge students had to be ready for chapel at 5 A.M.[11] Milton's Latin Grammar and a prolusion of his contain the saw, "Diluculo surgere saluberrimum est," VI, 330; XII, 288.[12]) Similarly, when "Surge, age! surge piger" (in prose, "surge igitur, surge deses," XII, 288) begins a line of "In Quintum Novembris" (97), the business is serious—in this case evil. All these passages get ready for Adam's aubade to Eve, on arousing her from her troubled sleep: "Awake! the morning shines, and the fresh field Calls us; we lose the prime" (v, 20).

This poet is not altogether incapable of Herrick's kind of appeal, as witness Elegia V "On the Coming of Spring," in which the wanton Earth ("Tellus lasciva," 95) woos Phoebus, thrice in nine lines inviting him: "Huc ades," the second and third time following these words with an explicit plea for light and love: "Huc ades, et gremio lumina pone meo" (88, 94). For such excitement one had been prepared early in the poem with the announcement of the bridegroom's coming:

> Delius ipse venit—video Peneide lauro
> Implicatos crines—Delius ipse venit, (13)

—which, whether called "epanalepsis" or "diacope," is a splendid use of repetition to convey the rising of emotion. Elsewhere it is the rising of certainty that Damon is among the heavenly inhabitants:

> Tu quoque in his—nec me fallit spes lubrica, Damon—
> Tu quoque in his certe es.
>
> ("E. D.," 198)

Or it is the insisting on the divine influence on Leonora's singing, "serpit agens" ("Ad Leonoram Romae Canentem," 6, 7), or on the bounty of spring, "munere veris adest" (El. V, 6, 7) for Milton's own inspiration.

These are tricks, to be judged on their individual merits in context. A theme easily leads to a small, a technical variation. Having said that Damon dwells in the pure ether, "purum colit aethera Damon," Milton at once has before him the question, Why? and instantly answers it, "Aethera purus habet" ("E.D.," 203)—because Damon is himself pure. (This leads into the remarkable closing lines on Damon's virginity, which has won him honor in heaven.) There is sometimes a brilliant, sometimes a wan, convenience in thus allowing words to beget words.

> Carmine scire velis quam te redamemque colamque.
> Crede mihi, vix hoc carmine scire queas.
>
> (El. VI, 5)

The formula sticks out here, even as it does in the unsuccessful, conceited poem "Upon the Circumcision," where again a question is asked and rather too mechanically answered:

> O more exceeding love, or law more just?
> Just law indeed, but more exceeding love!

Richardson's suggestion that Milton was recollecting two lines in Virgil's Eighth Eclogue (49–50), "Crudelis mater magis, an puer improbus ille? Improbus ille puer: crudelis tu quoque mater!" is interesting, for it helps us to see that "cruel" was not far from Milton's thought when he wrote "just." Hughes notes that "The antithesis of Law with Love recurs in Michael's prophecy of Christ satisfying 'high Justice' ":

> The law of God exact he shall fulfill
> Both by obedience and by love, though love
> Alone fulfill the Law; (xii, 402)

so that we have another odd return across the years, not very inspired this time, albeit based on Scripture.

Another trick is to follow the indicative with a wish. Diodati (Damon), a medical student, used to show Milton (Thyrsis)

various healing herbs: let them perish now, since they could not
heal their master:

> ... Quasque habet ista palus herbas, artesque medentum.
> Ah! pereant herbae, pereant artesque medentum. (152)

Or there can be the opposite wish of continuing the present:

> Et sua quisque sibi numina lucus habet.
> Et sua quisque diu sibi numina lucus habeto.
> (El. V, 132)

There are shades of schooldays here, certainly. It is like those
paradigms in which the Latin verbs are put through their paces
—indicative, subjunctive, imperative. Milton also used antimeta-
bole, the syntactical reversal of a sentence: "Carmen amat Bac-
chum, carmina Bacchus amat" (El. VI, 14).

The most musical and the most subtle iteration before *Paradise Lost* is contained in "Lycidas." Signaled in the first line,
"Yet once more, O ye laurels, and once more," it pours out in
compelling abundance:

> For Lycidas is dead, dead ere his prime,
> Young Lycidas, and hath not left his peer.
> Who would not sing for Lycidas? he knew
> Himself to sing.
>
> Begin, then, Sisters of the sacred well
> That from beneath the seat of Jove doth spring;
> Begin, and somewhat loudly sweep the string.
>
> Together both, ere the high lawns appeared
> Under the opening eyelids of the Morn,
> We drove afield, and both together heard
>
> But oh! the heavy change, now thou art gone,
> Now thou art gone, and never must return!
> Thee, Shepherd, thee the woods, and desert caves,
>
> What could the Muse herself that Orpheus bore,
> The Muse herself, for her enchanting son,
>
> He asked the waves, and asked the felon winds,
>
> Last came, and last did go,
> The Pilot of the Galilean Lake;

Stands ready to smite once, and smite no more.
  Return, Alpheus, the dread voice is past
That shrunk thy streams; return, Sicilian Muse,

Looks toward Namancos, and Bayona's hold.
Look homeward, Angel, now,

  Weep no more, woeful shepherds, weep no more,
For Lycidas, your sorrow, is not dead,
Sunk though he be beneath the wat'ry floor.
So sinks the day-star in the ocean bed,

. . . .

So Lycidas sunk low, but mounted high,

. . . .

Where, other groves and other streams along,

. . . .

That sing, and singing in their glory move,

. . . .

Now, Lycidas, the shepherds weep no more;

And now the sun had stretched out all the hills,
And now was dropped into the western bay.

This is, whatever else it is, a technical delight in its combination of various forms of verbal repetition—of which anaphora, epanalepsis, and polyptoton are the most notable—with the smaller internal repetition of end rhyme, alliteration, assonance, and consonance (to say nothing of meter). It is no wonder that so often the critics think of music when they read "Lycidas," for never, short of crudity, has a poet carried the analogy further. As Arthur Machen puts it, " 'Lycidas' is probably the most perfect piece of pure literature in existence because every word and phrase and line is sonorous, ringing and echoing with music." [13] Iteration is the *sine qua non* to this end. The effect of the repetitions quoted above is to charge the poem with emotion. More specifically, their effect is one of lamentation: they are Milton's poetical equivalent of that wringing of hands and moaning that Dr. Johnson, in his notorious criticism of "Lycidas," seemed to be asking for when he found it, because of its art, "not to be considered as the effusion of real passion." [14] Actually that critic, like tenderer ones to be met in classrooms today, was confusing sincerity with spontaneity. Admittedly spontaneity, even the practically final drafts of the Cambridge Manuscript testify, is a charge which it is this poem's glory to keep at a distance. "Procul o, procul este, profani!" including the seekers after "unpremeditated verse." However "easy" the "unpremeditated verse" (ix, 24) of *Paradise Lost*, anadiplosis is still the mold into which the passion is poured in the following most personal lines,

> I sing with mortal voice, unchanged
> To hoarse or mute, though fallen on evil days,
> On evil days though fallen, and evil tongues; (vii, 24)

but no one has ever doubted the existence of the passion there, and there is no reason to doubt its existence in "Lycidas" for the latter's being less transparently autobiographical.

On turning to *Paradise Lost* we ought first to consider the passage that stands out above all others as Milton's masterpiece of repetitive art, which is to say that English poetry can produce no equal to it. It is Eve's tribute to Adam, and incidentally to paradise, after she has told him,

> With thee conversing, I forget all time,
> All seasons and their change; all please alike.
>
> Sweet is the breath of morn, her rising sweet,
> With charm of earliest birds; pleasant the sun,
> When first on this delightful land he spreads
> His orient beams, on herb, tree, fruit, and flower,
> Glist'ring with dew; fragrant the fertile earth
> After soft showers; and sweet the coming-on
> Of grateful evening mild; then silent night,
> With this her solemn bird, and this fair moon,
> And these the gems of heaven, her starry train:
> But neither breath of morn, when she ascends
> With charm of earliest birds; nor rising sun
> On this delightful land; nor herb, fruit, flower,
> Glist'ring with dew; nor fragrance after showers;
> Nor grateful evening mild; nor silent night,
> With this her solemn bird; nor walk by moon,
> Or glittering starlight, without thee is sweet. (iv, 641)

So it ends, returning to the word with which it began, an exqui-
site weaving and unweaving, the negatives marking the principal
points of detachment as the shuttle, going now in reverse direction, unravels the fabric. It is unique,[15] and yet a sure means of
appreciating it is to put something beside it—not Cowper's parody,[16] but a stanza by Traherne which may or may not have been
influenced by it:

> Where are the silent streams,
> The living waters and the glorious beams,
> The sweet reviving bowers,
> The shady groves, the sweet and curious flowers,
> The springs and trees, the heavenly days,
> The flow'ry meads, and glorious rays,
> The gold and silver towers?
> Alas! all these are poor and empty things!
> Trees, waters, days, and shining beams,
> Fruits, flowers, bowers, shady groves, and springs,
> No joy will yield, no more than silent streams;
> These are but dead material toys,
> And cannot make my heavenly joys.[17]

Here are some of the same words, a similar subject, and a comparable rhetorical device (known to Puttenham as *collectour,* or
"the recapitulator"), and Traherne is above his own average
here. But what the stanza does is make one glad that Milton
avoided in his lines "the jingling sound of like endings" and that
he proceeded at his own deliberate, in this case daringly deliberate, pace, instead of flinging his effect at the reader in a nervous
flurry of nouns. Of course, we should bear in mind the difference
in intention, that the one poet is praising "heavenly joys" at nature's expense, while the other does not mean to be violent in
designating Adam the most important part of paradise. But Milton has the better of it also in his epithets; not that any of his
are surprising—it would spoil his purpose if they were, for this
is the traditional paradise—but that some of Traherne's ("shady
groves," "flow'ry meads") have no excuse for being in an out-
moded tradition. They are just stereotyped resting places for a
flagging imagination or perception. But it does not matter that

Milton's "silent night" goes back to Virgil's "nocte silenti," if
not to Homer's νὺξ ἀβρότη,[18] any more than it matters that he tried
out the Latin himself twice, "nocte silente" (El. IV, 114), "silenti nocte" ("De Idea Platonica," 27). Milton is the magician
(song is indeed "charm" with him), holding us fascinated by his
incantation and his rhythmical movement. He knows just the
right amount of variation, as in the change from "this fair moon"
to "walk by moon" (the latter perhaps suggested by a neighboring phrase, "Our walks"—changed to "walk" in 1674—"at
noon," iv, 627)—a skill which contrasts with his 1634 translation
of Psalm 114 into Greek, where he repeated lines wholesale, or,
at most, following the original, turned statements in the third
person into questions in the second.

It is the difference between being independent and having a
model. As everyone knows, Milton usually has a model. The
other piece of large and concentrated repetition in *Paradise Lost*
is on the "Greek Psalm" pattern, lines being returned to un-
changed or with a shift of pronouns. Adam is urging repentance:

> "What better can we do than, to the place
> Repairing where he judged us, prostrate fall
> Before him reverent, and there confess
> Humbly our faults, and pardon beg, with tears
> Wat'ring the ground, and with our sighs the air
> Frequenting, sent from hearts contrite, in sign
> Of sorrow unfeigned and humiliation meek?
> Undoubtedly he will relent, and turn
> From his displeasure; in whose look serene,
> When angry most he seemed and most severe,
> What else but favor, grace, and mercy shone? "
>   So spake our Father penitent; nor Eve
> Felt less remorse: they, forthwith to the place
> Repairing where he judged them, prostrate fell
> Before him reverent, and both confessed
> Humbly their faults, and pardon begged, with tears
> Wat'ring the ground, and with their sighs the air
> Frequenting, sent from hearts contrite, in sign
> Of sorrow unfeigned and humiliation meek. (x, 1086)

But whatever there may be here in the reiteration and in the subject to remind one of Hebrew poetry, Homer looms large, too, and ultimately in Milton's epic reiteration Homer looms largest.

For it is Homer rather than Virgil, that sophisticated varier,[19] from whom Milton gets precedent for this important trait of his style, that "Homer, whose two poems" (Toland reports [20]) "he could almost repeat without book." Milton's first editors, Patrick Hume in 1695 and Richard Bentley in 1732, found more repetition in *Paradise Lost* than was to their taste; needless to say, both the schoolmaster and the great classical scholar recognized the poet's model, even if they did not forgive him for following it. The former says of the following passage:

> him, through their malice fallen,
> Father of mercy and grace, thou didst not doom
> So strictly, but much more to pity incline.
> No sooner did thy dear and only Son
> Perceive thee purposed not to doom frail Man
> So strictly, but much more to pity inclined—(iii, 400)

"A Repetition affected after the Homeric manner, who often uses the same Verses and Words, in which Commands were given, or Messages sent, as supposing it not possible to change them for better." But as a modern defender expresses it, "Milton here is not lacking in invention, but evidently wishes to emphasize the words as sounding the keynote of the passage." [21] The fit audience will recall such a case (to take the most conspicuous) as the false dream in the second book of the *Iliad* (11 ff.). First Zeus calls the Dream to him and tells him what to say. Then the Dream goes to Agamemnon and says it. Finally, in the same words, Agamemnon confides the Dream's message to his council. Five or six consecutive lines thus make an appearance three times within an area of sixty lines. In like spirit, and to stress the fallen pair's didactically important repentance, Milton brought his tenth book to a close.

The fact is, "out of the total 27,853 lines which make up the *Iliad* and the *Odyssey,* about one-third—9,253—are repeated or contain repeated phrases." [22] The repetitions in *Paradise Lost* are fewer and smaller (it being a literary or secondary epic as distinguished from a folk or primary epic), but they amount to far more than even a very careful reader is likely to realize. To say nothing of the scores of repetitions involving single words, with which we are not concerned ("With ruin upon ruin, rout on rout, Confusion worse confounded," ii, 995), everyone, of course, can observe, and almost everyone can appreciate the repetitions of the "though fallen on evil days, On evil days though fallen" type, repetitions occurring within one or two, or at most four, lines. Of approximately fifty strewn through the poem, we may single out for quotation twelve, one for each book:

> Say first—for Heaven hides nothing from thy view,
> Nor the deep tract of Hell—say first what cause (i, 27)

> and feel by turns the bitter change
> Of fierce extremes, extremes by change more fierce, (ii, 598)

> " Then thou thy regal sceptre shalt lay by;
> For regal sceptre then no more shall need;
> God shall be all in all. But all ye Gods," (iii, 339)

> " Know ye not, then," said Satan, filled with scorn,
> " Know ye not me? Ye knew me once no mate
> For you, there sitting where ye durst not soar!
> Not to know me argues yourselves unknown,
> The lowest of your throng; or, if ye know," (iv, 827)

> now ere Night,
> Now ere dim Night had disencumbered Heaven, (v, 699)

> " To manifest thee worthiest to be Heir
> Of all things, to be Heir, and to be King " (vi, 707)

> With thousand lesser lights dividual holds,
> With thousand thousand stars, (vii, 382)

> and closed mine eyes.
> Mine eyes he closed, but open left the cell
> Of fancy, (viii, 459)

> " Tempting affronts us with his foul esteem
> Of our integrity: his foul esteem
> Sticks no dishonor on our front, but turns
> Foul on himself;" (ix, 328)

> " O voice, once heard
> Delightfully, ' *Increase and multiply*; '
> Now death to hear! for what can I increase
> Or multiply but curses on my head? " (x, 730)

> "All thy request for Man, accepted Son,
> Obtain; all thy request was my decree: " (xi, 46)

> " In me is no delay; with thee to go
> Is to stay here [in Paradise]; without thee here to stay
> Is to go hence unwilling." (xii, 615)[23]

Such turns as these were old devices with Milton, as we have seen, years before *Paradise Lost:*

> Was I deceived, or did a sable cloud
> Turn forth her silver lining on the night?
> I did not err: there does a sable cloud
> Turn forth her silver lining on the night.
> *(Comus,* 221)

Room is found for the like even in *Paradise Regained:*

> Now missing him, their joy so lately found,
> So lately found and so abruptly gone,
> Began to doubt, and doubted many days,
> And, as the days increased, increased their doubt. (2, 9)

What the reader likewise cannot fail to notice and what is peculiar to the epic is the recurrence of the grandiose nominative of address, "Thrones, Dominations, Princedoms, Virtues, Powers." It is employed by God, by Satan, and by Abdiel, in the fifth book (601, 772, 840), as the rebellion takes shape and the celestial hierarchy chooses sides. Satan returns to it in the tenth book (460), to open his last speech, than which none is prouder, before the jeering metamorphosis of all the devils into serpents. Thus, to reverse the French proverb, the more the line is repeated the more it changes, and finally becomes preposterous.

One cannot forget, either, the "serpent, subtlest beast of all the field." It outdistances in every way the comparative of the Authorised Version, "the serpent was more subtile than any beast of the field" (Gen. iii, 1), and Milton's own positive in

"In Quintum Novembris," "Subdolus . . . serpens" (90). It has become an authorised version itself, like so much in the poem. (For example, the commentators are fond of pointing out it is from Milton, not from Genesis, that we derive the idea that not just a serpent, but Satan in the serpent, was the tempter in Eden.) When we have twice met the line introduced by the definite article, "The serpent, subtlest beast of all the field" (vii, 495; ix, 86), it has an almost punning effect when Eve says, "Thee, Serpent, subtlest beast of all the field/I knew" (ix, 560). Milton is, indeed (like Homer in the *Odyssey*), given to puns— a natural consequence of his single-minded dedication to the aural. (T. S. Eliot, writing on Milton,[24] and Harry Levin, writing on Joyce,[25] have more than once paired the poet and novelist who, unable to see, pre-eminently *heard*.)

To pass on to the less conspicuous, there is Satan questing through unknown space:

> thither he plies,
> Undaunted, to meet there whatever Power
> Or Spirit of the nethermost abyss
> Might in that noise reside. (ii, 954)

When he reaches the kingdom of Chaos, he begins, " 'Ye Powers And Spirits of this nethermost abyss . . .' " (ii, 968). There is an old and simple satisfaction in such fulfillment of an anticipation. We get it again when the Creator delivers to Adam sovereignty over the earth, "In sign whereof, each bird and beast behold After their kinds" (viii, 342); then, seven lines later, "As thus he spake, each bird and beast behold Approaching two and two." At an interval of sixteen lines, "Creator from his work . . . returned" is repeated. First there is the statement marking the close of the sixth day: "Yet not till the Creator, from his work Desisting, though unwearied, up returned" (vii, 551). He is welcomed back by celestial voices: "Open, ye Heavens, your living doors! let in The great Creator, from his work returned" (567). Within eleven lines of Book x the "fruit" or "fruitage" that dangles before the devils is "fair" and "like that which grew"

(550, 561) in two other places. In Book ii Milton catches a stitch in a long sentence by repeating "Into this wild abyss" (910, 917). God emphasizes to the Son that the war in heaven has gone on long enough:

> two days are passed,
> Two days, as we compute the days of Heaven,
>
> . . . .
>
> Two days are, therefore, passed; the third is thine.
>
> (vi, 684, 699)

How many readers are aware that when Michael tells Adam in Book xi, lines 259-62,

> But longer in this Paradise to dwell
> Permits not; to remove thee I am come,
> And send thee from the garden forth, to till
> The ground whence thou wast taken, fitter soil,

the archangel is repeating God's words, lines 48 and 97-98?

> But longer in that Paradise to dwell . . .
> And send him from the Garden forth, to till
> The ground whence he was taken, fitter soil.

The satisfaction may operate below the level of complete consciousness.

This becomes an important point when a student of the poem, having marked a concordance, discovers there are hundreds of repeated phrases scattered through *Paradise Lost* of which at most the reader is but dimly aware, because they are small and far-flung, and most of them occur but two or three times. To take samples suggested by quotations already given or referred to, "dim night" occurs not once but three times (ii, 1036; v, 685, 700), and this is the total for "regal scepter" (iii, 339, 340; v, 816) and "new laws" (v, 679, 680; xi, 228). "Thousand thousand" comes in twice (v, 588; vii, 383), "fierce extremes" once more (vii, 272), and Milton is not done with "to pity incline" either, for it returns seven books later (x, 1061). "His wondrous works" is back five books later (iii, 663, 665; viii,

68). Without reference to the serpent, "beast of the field" begins one line in the seventh book (522), ends another in the tenth (176).

One can scarcely open a page that does not contain something to be found on another page. Most common, and least interesting, are the expressions commencing or closing a speech.[26] They correspond to Homer's formulae for discourse. More indicative of Milton's style are his equivalents for Homer's fixed epithets. (We can find a patronymic in *Comus*, "virgin, . . . daughter of Locrine," 827, 922.) They are, of course, less persistent than the ancient poet's and accordingly attract very little notice. Deity, as might be expected, receives the greatest number. God is "the Almighty Father" (iii, 56, 386; vi, 671; vii, 11), "the . . . Eternal Father" (v, 246; vi, 96; vii, 137, 517; x, 32; cf. "Father Eternal," x, 68), "the Omnipotent/ Eternal Father" (vii, 136, 516), "mighty Father" (v, 735, 836; vi, 890). Either the Father or the Son is "the great Creator" (ii, 385; iii, 167, 673; vii, 567; "their great Creator," iv, 684), "God, creator wise" (ix, 938; x, 889), "great Maker" (v, 184; viii, 278).[27] The Savior is "King anointed" (v, 664, 777) or "anointed King" (v, 870; vi, 718; xii, 359), "begotten Son" (iii, 80, 384; v, 835; vii, 163), "Son beloved" (vi, 680; x, 70), "the filial Godhead" (vi, 722; vii, 175), "great Messiah" (v, 691; xii, 244), "Presence Divine" (viii, 314; xi, 319). There is nothing comparable for the Holy Ghost, except possibly "Heavenly Muse"[28] (i, 6; iii, 19) and "Spirit within" in two (xii, 488, 523) of its three (viii, 440) uses.

From the point of view of the fallen angels, God is "so great a foe" (ii, 202, 722), "our grand foe" (i, 122). From the point of view of "frail man" (iii, 404; iv, 11; vi, 345), Satan is "our grand foe" (x, 1033), "the grand foe" (vi, 149). To Sin and the guardian angels he is "the subtle fiend" (ii, 815; x, 20). To the fallen angels he is "their mighty chief" (i, 566; x, 455).

"Our (two) first parents" (iii, 65; iv, 6) are not without their titles. Adam is our "great progenitor" (v, 544; xi, 346). Eve is but too much "fair Eve" (iv, 481; viii, 172), "his fair spouse" (iv, 742; v, 129), "fair creature" (iv, 468), "creature so

and glittering array in heaven and on earth that it is hard to decide whether to classify them as characters or as setting. The blind poet stressed their brightness, as he did that of everything, *Paradise Lost* being a study, not in colors, but in darkness and light.[33] He gives us "orders bright" (i, 737; v, 587), "brightest Seraph(im)" (iii, 381, 667), "angel bright" (iii, 645; x, 327), "guardians bright" (iii, 512; xi, 215), "in bright array" (vi, 801; xii, 627). Adam compares the "glorious shape" (v, 309, 362) of Raphael to "another morn Risen on midnoon" (v, 310). The other stress is on rank, function, place of origin; "Cherub and Seraph" (i, 324; vii, 198), "angel guest" (v, 328; ix, 1) "cherubic watch" (ix, 68; xi, 120), "angelic guards" (iv, 550; x, 18), "the angelic throng" (v, 650; vi, 308), "heavenly host" (ii, 824; xi, 230), "heavenly spirits" (iv, 361; vi, 788; viii, 615; cf. ii, 824), "sons of Heaven" (i, 654; v, 790), "heavenly guest" (vii, 69; viii, 646), "heavenly stranger" (v, 316, 397). In most of these iterations we are made very much aware of the unique privileges of Adam and Eve, denied since to the "(whole) race of man (men, mankind)" (ii, 382; iii, 161, 280, 679; vii, 155; xi, 13, 782, 786).

The great descriptive poet fixes heaven and earth and hell with many a repeated phrase. To take Satan's "nether empire" (ii, 296) first (Adam has one, too, below the mount, iv, 145), what mostly characterizes "the house of woe" (vi, 877; x, 465), the "ill mansion" (ii, 462; vi, 738), is depth and darkness. These are combined in such phrases as "the dark abyss" (ii, 1027; x, 371) and "in(to) utter darkness" (i, 72; v, 614). It is part of the definition of hell that it is "far removed" (i, 73; ii, 211, 321; vii, 272) from heaven. To "the lowest deep" (ii, 392; iv, 76), "to deepest hell" (iii, 678; v, 542), the fiends were cast, "down they fell" (ii, 771; vi, 593), "fell . . . from heaven" (i, 491, 740) "to . . . eternal woe" (ii, 161; iv, 70), "to waste eternal days in woe" (ii, 695). The darkness of "this (the) infernal pit" (i, 657; ii, 850; iv, 965; x, 464) is not the less for the momentary interruption of "sudden blaze" (i, 665; iv, 818; x, 453) or "raging fire(s)" (ii, 213, 600). (Milton passes from the literal to the figurative in his three uses of "inflame(d) with . . . rage": first it is Phlegethon, ii, 581, then Death pursuing his mother, "more, it seems, In-

flamed with lust than rage", ii, 791, finally Satan, bent on re-
venge, iv, 9.) We are not permitted to forget "the burning lake"
(ii, 576) ("Chained on the burning lake," i, 210; ii, 169), the
"liquid fire" (i, 229, 701). A kind of "dry land" (i, 227) remotely
comparable to earth's (vii, 307; xii, 197) hell may have, "easy"
may be the "ascent" (ii, 81; iii, 524), but the consulting devils,
afraid, prefer the "gems and gold(en)" (i, 538; ii, 271) appurte-
nances to which Mammon can point. Sometimes we feel the den-
sity, as in "many a row of" (i, 709, 727) and "thick swarmed" (i,
767; x, 526). We get the sense of a prison by the very emphasis
on the gates and locks, "the mouth of hell" (x, 288, 636; xii, 42),
"hell gate" (ii, 725, 746; x, 415), "bars of hell" (iii, 82; iv, 795),
"forever shut" (ii, 776; iii, 333), "the fatal key" (ii, 725, 871).
The only times "hell trembled" (ii, 676, 788) were at the stride
and name of Death, by the gates. Death's mother

> opened; but to shut
> Excelled her power: the gates wide open stood. (ii, 883)

There the grim pair wait, to be found eight books later, after the
fall of man:

> Within the gates of hell sat Ṣin and Death,
> In counterview within the gates, that now
> Stood open wide. (x, 230)

A little later,

> Through the gate,
> Wide open and unguarded, Satan passed. (x, 419)

There is a parallel emphasis on "the gate(s) of heaven" (iii,
515; v, 253; i, 171), "heaven gates" (i, 326; ii, 996), "to (from,
at) heaven gate" (v, 198; vii, 618; x, 22, 88), "opened wide, . . .
On golden hinges turning" or "moving" (v, 255; vii, 207). If hell
trembled twice, so twice heaven "had gone to wrack" (iv, 994; vi,
670), had not Paternal Deity interrupted war. To the darkness of
hell is opposed "celestial light" (i, 245; iii, 51), to the lowest deep
"highest heaven" (i, 517; iii, 657; viii, 178; x, 889). Heaven is

less describable than hell: Milton depends largely on the word itself,[34] or he produces many connections between earth and heaven, ever keeping in mind what a blessed bright and fruitful place earth *was*.[35]

The "marriage rites" (viii, 487; xi, 591) are not unconnected with Adam's fall. When the crisis comes, Adam can only reiterate, "I feel the link (bond) of nature draw me" (ix, 914, 956) and of course he means Eve, "bone of my bone" (viii, 495; ix, 915), Eve, that "heavenly form" (ix, 457) that makes the Evil One himself hesitate, found "too heavenly form" (x, 872) for Adam's good. Milton finds a ready way of emphasizing the union: "So hand in hand they passed, the loveliest pair" (iv, 321); "Thus talking, hand in hand alone they passed" (iv, 689). Their hands are still joined at the end: "They, hand in hand, with wandering steps and slow . . ." (xii, 648). Nothing could better give us the tenderness. Adam bends over her as she wakes, "Her hand soft touching" (v, 17). It is poignant as well as wrong that she leaves her husband's side, to be tempted and fall: "Thus saying, from her husband's hand her hand Soft she withdrew" (ix, 385). We cannot be sure in either instance whether "soft" is an adjective or an adverb; the doubt, far from doing harm, is advantageous.

But Eve is associated with evil (Milton's pun—"in evil hour," ix, 780, 1076) in several phrases. She and Satan both lay claim to "firm faith" (ii, 36; ix, 286) in situations where we can appreciate the irony. She echoes the Serpent when she tells Adam to "freely taste" (ix, 732, 988). Sin preceded her as a possessor of "attractive grace(s)" (ii, 762; iv, 298). She shares "act(s)" that are "graceful" (ii, 109; viii, 600) with Belial, "peril great" (ix. 922; x, 469) with Satan. She was Adam's "sole delight" (x, 941). "Ever to do ill" is the fiends' "sole delight" (i, 160). Similarly "amorous ditties" (i, 449; xi, 584) (Milton did not write any) has pejorative connotations, with reference to pagan or illicit love: "In amorous ditties all a summer's day." (Incidentally, Mulciber fell "A summer's day," i, 744, but that was probably chosen without prejudice for maximum duration.)

There is hardly enough here to draw any conclusions about

Milton's conscious or unconscious prejudices. It is true that there is nothing comparable for Adam, but Milton repeats many expressions indifferently—that is, without a tendency.[36]

It may, finally, be noted how Milton, far from absent as a personality acting and acted upon, keeps before us the inspiration and difficulties and uniqueness of his epic. The inspiration, of course, is the "heavenly Muse" (i, 6; iii, 19) (invoked by him in his youth, too, as we have seen). Adam is in one sense the first, in another the last of "heroes old" (i, 552; xi, 243), and Milton is prone to take advantage of both facts, saying in almost the same breath, "It is like this" and "Nothing is like this." He has to tell of what is "beyond compare" (i, 588; iii, 138; ix, 228)—such as the Son of God, Adam's love for Eve, the prowess of the army in hell (yet similes help, and so the poem is thick with them). He must somehow render it intelligible to "human sense" (iv, 206; v, 565, 572; ix, 554, 871; xii, 10). He feels and conveys a majestic satisfaction on reaching the precincts of light in Book iii: "thee I revisit" (13, 21). To tell of "war in heaven" (i, 43; vi, 897) or of the fall of man is a "sad task" (v, 564; ix, 13). Without excessive self-consciousness here is a poet who is openly moved by his own poem, and these invocations compel us, as if he had already done what he is going to do.

The last book of *Paradise Lost* tells us, among other things, of the escape of the Israelites from Egypt through "the wild desert" (xii, 216). The scene of *Paradise Regained* is "the . . . desert wild" (*P.R.*, 1, 193; 2, 109), and the style of this brief epic is relatively bare, as befits not only the scene but the austerity of its hero. The pomp, for instance, of the two councils—that in heaven and that in hell—is telescoped in a phrase: "in full frequence" (*P.R.*, 1, 128; 2, 130). There is little occasion for repetition, but some Milton does allow himself, such as the formulae for discourse.[37]

The poem is almost entirely made up of soliloquy (Jesus' "holy" or "holiest meditations," 1, 195; 2, 110) and discourse. Some of the repetition is the natural bandying of words between two interlocutors: "my offered aid" (4, 377), "thy offered aid" (4, 493), "offered with my aid" (4, 468). We get it in *Paradise*

Lost when Raphael, referring to Eve, says, "An outside; fair, no doubt" (viii, 568), and Adam takes him up, "Neither her outside formed so fair . . ." (596). The Savior asks, " 'Shall I seek glory, then, as vain men seek?' " (*P.R.*, 3, 105). The Tempter instances "thy great Father: he seeks glory" (3, 110). Then comes from the Savior, "But why should man seek glory?" (3, 134). This is comparable structurally to the conversation of the brothers in *Comus:*

> she has a hidden strength,
> Which you remember not.
>   *Second Brother.*   What hidden strength,
> Unless the strength of Heaven, if you mean that?
>   *Elder Brother.*   I mean that, too, but yet a hidden strength,
> Which, if Heaven gave it, may be termed her own.   (415)

So it is with the Biblical phrase, "the kingdoms of the world" in two of its three appearances (4, 89, 163, 182). Jesus' opponent says, "The kingdoms of the world to thee I give," and is answered, "The kingdoms of the world to thee were given."

Nothing receives so much emphasis as the matter of Christ's identity. Having "Heard thee pronounced the Son of God beloved" (4, 513), Satan wishes to learn

> In what degree or meaning thou art called

> The Son of God, which bears no single sense;
> The Son of God I also am, or was;
> And, if I was, I am; relation stands:
> All men are sons of God. (4, 516)

Again and again the scene "at the ford of Jordan" (1, 328; 4, 510) is alluded to, when

> in likeness of a dove
> The Spirit descended, while the Father's voice . . . (1, 31)

> The Spirit descended on me like a dove;
> And last, the sum of all, my Father's voice (1, 282)

—gave recognition to "his beloved Son" (1, 32, 285) ("my Son beloved," 1, 85, "the Son of God beloved," 4, 513, "to be beloved of God," 1, 379). A phrase varied in a manner we have seen before (see above, p. 32) is, "called the(e) Son of God" (1, 136, 329; 4, 516). There is much reference to "David's throne" (1, 240; 3, 153, 169, 357; 4, 108, 147, 379, 471), "thy father David('s)" (3, 153, 282, 353), "in the fields of Bethlehem" (1, 243), "in Bethlehem field" (4, 505), before the final revelation in the fourth book of "the Lord thy God" (177, 561).

How the prophecies can be "best fulfill(ed)" (3, 177, 182; 4, 381) is the question before Jesus, what "High actions" (2, 411; 4, 266) he is to perform, "many a hard assay" (1, 264; 4, 478). Is he, for instance, to lift the "Roman yoke" (1, 217; 3, 158)? Meanwhile, for the "forty days" (1, 303, 352, 353; 2, 243, 276, 315), two of his ordeals are hunger—"nor tasted human food" (1, 308), "human food nor tasted" (2, 247)—and exposure, especially the storm of the last night, with which the succeeding "morning fair" (4, 426), "fair morning" (451) is in contrast.

Recently the accusation has been leveled at *Samson Agonistes* that "in this work Milton repeated beyond his wont." [38] In the first place, this statement is very imperfectly documented as regards phrases: actually more than a score of instances can and will be given. In the second place, it is unlikely that the statement would have been made if Milton's "wont" had been carefully studied. The writer of the article is out to show that the drama never received final revision, but if "the repetition of idea and word" [39] is to be used as evidence for that, what shall be said of *Paradise Lost?* Besides, the "repetition" so disapprovingly pointed to is mostly a natural thematic development or emphasis, or an unnoticeable matter of vocabulary.

Being a drama, *Samson Agonistes* has that bandying of words between characters that we have found elsewhere. Harapha refers to "when they took thee As a league-breaker, and delivered bound" (*S.A.*, 1184). Samson opposes the argument that he had acted as "a private person, whom my country As a league-breaker gave up bound" (1209). Samson says to his father, "This only hope relieves me, that the strife With me hath end" (460). Manoa takes him up, "With cause this hope relieves thee" (472). Samson denies to Dalila that "weakness" is a "plea" (834, 843). Or he impatiently tells Harapha, "Boast not of what thou

wouldst have done, but do" (1104) and is shortly after led to
threaten, "Thou oft shalt wish thyself at Gath, to boast Again in
safety what thou wouldst have done" (1127). It is mostly debate,
external or internal, an example of the latter being the brooding
of Samson, in the beginning, over the "Philistian yoke":

> Promise was that I
> Should Israel from Philistian yoke deliver;
> Ask for this great deliverer now, and find him
> Eyeless in Gaza at the mill with slaves,
> Himself in bonds under Philistian yoke. (38)

"Great deliverer" (applied to Gideon) comes back (279): so,
twice, does "at the(ir) . . . mill" (1327, 1393). Indeed, this is
the key passage dramatically, for it has the promise, has the past
accomplishment—Samson *was* a great deliverer—and gives us
the agonizing present. There are recurrences for each of these
phases: for the promise, "birth from heaven foretold" (23, 525),
"Israel's God" (1150, 1527), "sacred trust" (428, 1001); for the
past, "with . . . trivial weapon" (142, 263), "worthiest deeds"
(276, 369), "in strength all mortals . . . exceed" or "excelled"
(523, 817), "a common enemy" (856, 1416); for the present, "to
sit idle" (566, 1500), "old age" (used only here in Milton's poetry, 572, 700, 925, 1487), "eyes put out" (33, 1103). In this hard
present there is much consolatory appeal to the actions and views
of "wisest men" (210, 867, 1034), particularly to "wisest and best
men" (759), "wisest men and best" (1034), as they have been
deceived by bad women (a subject—indeed a phrase, with which
we are by no means finished). Then comes the climax as Samson
feels "strength again . . . with . . . hair" (1355, 1496) returning, grasps "those two massy pillars" (1633, 1648), returns to
"high exploits" (525, 1492) on this day of "a solemn feast" (12,
1311) (a Biblical phrase, but cf. "sollenes epulas," El. VI, 9).

That sensitive but sometimes mistaken critic, Walter Raleigh,
was never more wrong than when he wrote, after citing a French
critic's hostile attitude to Homer's repetitions:

Milton felt none of this contempt for Homer, but he discarded the
practice. His epithets are chosen to perform one exploit, and are dismissed when it is accomplished. As with single epithets, so with

lines and phrases; he does not employ conventional repetitions either for their lyrical value or for wafting the story on to the next point of interest . . . . He arrests the attention at every word; and when the thing is once said, he has done with it.[40]

We have put in review in text or notes hundreds of individual refutations of this assertion. Milton *does* have his equivalent for Homer's conventional repetitions and fixed epithets, but the expressions are less set and occur less often, as is to be expected in a shorter and "secondary" epic. Whether deliberately or instinctively, the poet has, with some frequency, introduced small variations, especially by altering the position of the modifier and the position of the phrase in the line. At iii, 74, of *Paradise Lost* he wrote of "the bare outside of this world," which returns at x, 317-318, as "the outside bare Of this round world." "Inversion of the natural order of words and phrases" is the first in a catalogue of traits of Milton's style presented by Raymond D. Havens in his *The Influence of Milton on English Poetry*.[41] The same analyst does not fail to give as another trait "Intentional repetition of a word or a phrase," [42] but this has been omitted from the more widely consulted summary in Hanford's *A Milton Handbook*.[43] Yet, in 1740, the eccentric Francis Peck listed as characteristic thirty-one of Milton's style, "return of the same, or very near the same, words and lines"—and gave *two* examples! [44] It is time that reiteration be placed high in every such catalogue, reiteration far more than is to be found in any other English poet of stature, not excepting Marlowe, whom Raleigh quotes.

There are those who will argue that what a reader is not fully conscious of in a poem can be of no importance. If most of the recurrences are latent, so scattered and small that an expert reader like Raleigh or Professor Stoll (who finds only two recurring phrases in *Paradise Lost*—hardly enough to be called what he calls them, *leitmotivs!* [45]) does not divine their presence, in what way do they matter? The answer is that they do work, however inconspicuously, for the unity and solidity of the poem. There is bound to grow in us, as we read, the feeling (however little we seek to verify it) that we have been here and here before. In this quite simple way Milton makes the world (in *Paradise Lost* the universal setting) and the style of his poem familiar. There are things that are the better said for being said more than once, a practice which is consonant both with purposes didactic (he has much to teach, much that we have forgotten or never knew to describe) and architectonic: not every joist and lath and filigree can or should be different. The poem stands firmly, is mortised and tenoned, at fixed points.

CHAPTER III

FROM POEM TO POEM

WHATEVER the rationale for repetition within a single poem, there are numerous surprises in store for us when we proceed to consider Milton's borrowings from poem to poem. Embedded in his various English poems are about three hundred duplicated phrases that connect them in sometimes very odd ways and open up possibilities of increasing our knowledge of not only how the poet wrote but how he thought.

Aproximately one hundred of these phrases connect *Paradise Lost* and *Paradise Regained*. To this group we naturally turn first, since, the Quaker Ellwood's perhaps too naive story apart, Milton himself clearly regarded his short epic as a sequel to his long one (which is not to say, as some critics fear, that *Paradise Lost* is incomplete). We have as initial evidence not only the title but the opening lines, modeled after those that the early editions of the *Aeneid* gave Renaissance readers to understand Virgil had prefixed to *his* epic:

> I, who erewhile the happy garden sung,
> By one man's disobedience lost, now sing
> Recovered Paradise to all mankind,
> By one man's firm obedience fully tried ....

The self-echoing begins in the first line, with "the happy garden" (iii, 66). That it continues, despite the great difference in style between the two epics, is of course largely to be attributed to this position of *Paradise Regained* as a sequel, in which the same forces of good and evil are pitted against each other, on an earth the topography of which *Paradise Lost* has sometimes used the same words to describe. In Milton's words, here again are "devilish machination(s)" (vi, 504; *P.R.*, 1, 181), here again is "the prince of darkness" (x, 383; 4, 441), "the subtle fiend" (ii, 815; x, 20; 1, 465; 2, 323), who, "fraught with envy" (v, 661), "with

48

envy fraught" (1, 38), sallies out in "hoped success" (iii, 740; 4, 578). It is a limited objective, "all hope" (iv, 105; 3, 204) of escape from damnation or recovery from the "fall from heaven" (xii, 391; 4, 620) being lost. It emerges from a council, "in council sat" (x, 428; 2, 118), at which Satan receives the usual "loud acclaim" (ii, 520; 2, 235) when he offers to take all risks: "The rest commit to me." It is a gloomy consistory, "Within thick clouds and dark tenfold involved" (1, 41). In the first consistory, Mammon had derived some consolation from the fact that God could be likewise dark:

> How oft amidst
> Thick clouds and dark doth Heaven's all-ruling Sire
> Choose to reside, his glory unobscured,
> And with the majesty of darkness round
> Covers his throne ... (ii, 264)

Satan is the hypocrite of old: "and Satan, bowing low" (iii, 736; 1, 497). "Stood awhile" (vi, 556; 3, 2) points to his hesitations in the presence of the opposition. In both poems he pretends to admire the "good or fair" (1, 381), the "fair and good" (ix, 605, 606; x, 618) of creation.

Adam was not "of woman born" (xi, 496); Christ was (1, 65). This poem shows the fulfillment of the prophecies ("prophets old," iii, 36; 3, 178, means poets) about "the woman's seed" (xi, 116; xii, 327, 543, 601; 1, 64) with which the former poem ended. It was the woman's seed, but Mary has told Jesus that he is not the son of "mortal man" (1, 234; plural, i, 51; iii, 268; xii, 248), that his father is the "Eternal King," "Heaven's King" (see above, page 15). Jesus is "by merit . . . Son" (1, 166; iii, 309). There is some awareness of a "great purpose" (vi, 675; 2, 101). The "voice divine" (vii, 2; 1, 35) has been heard. "Heaven opened" (vii, 205; 1, 30, 281). The question is where Jesus' empire is to extend. Beelzebub had prophesied that God ineluctably would "over hell extend His empire" (ii, 326). In the desert the last temptation is: "as thy empire must extend, So let extend thy mind o'er all the world" (4, 222). The association is thus one of worldly knowledge with hellish. This temptation involves learn-

ing, among other things, "the secret power of harmony" (4, 255).
Sin had told her parent that her heart, "by a secret harmony"
(x, 358), moved with his. But the scorner of "dignities and powers" (i, 359; 3, 30) emphatically rejects distorted, pride-inducing
human lore as well. Yet "all . . . ethereal powers" (xii, 577; 1,
163) are hovering around him, and there is shortly to be a manifestation of "a fiery globe Of angels" (4, 581). The emperor of
hell retained "A globe of fiery seraphim" (ii, 512).

It is the same, but different. The "great emperor" was Satan
(i, 378). Now it is Caesar (4, 81). Formerly Hecate, now Herod,
is identified with the shedding of "infant blood" (ii, 664; 2, 78).
Satan's "fiery darts" (vi, 213; xii, 492; 4, 424) contribute to a
surprising imitation of hell in the wilderness, during the storm.

By "desert wild" (see above, page 42) Milton means, after
all, deserted wilderness, not barren sands without topographical
variety. There is, in fact, a good deal here that served before,
including such commonplaces as "air, water . . . earth" (vii,
502; 2, 124), "even and morn" (vii, 252, 338, 550; 2, 268), "solid
rock" (ii, 878; 4, 18), "surging waves" (vii, 214; 4, 18), "green
meadow"—"meadows green" (2, 185; vii, 460), "tallest pine(s)"
(i, 292; 4, 416), "branching arms"—"arms branching" (4, 405;
ix, 1104), "sunny hill" (iii, 28; 4, 447), "high mountain" (xi, 851;
3, 265; 4, 26; "mountain high," 3, 252), "and the neighbouring
plain(s)" (xii, 136; 3, 319), "a spacious plain" (xi, 556; 3, 254).
Above, it is the "thin air" (xii, 76; 1, 499), "the air sublime" (ii,
528; iii, 72; vii, 421; 4, 542), and there are adverbial expressions
like "in mid air" (ii, 718; iv, 940; vi, 536; 1, 39), "o'er (all) the
earth" (i, 365; 1, 218), and "nearer view" (vi, 81; 4, 514), which
also occurs in *Samson Agonistes* (723). The second Adam, like
the first, mounts a hill from "whose high top" (viii, 303; 2, 286)
the prospect is pleasant because natural, and a "grassy couch"
(iv, 601; 2, 282) suffices him, as it did the beasts of Eden. At the
end of his abiding, like the Israelites', "in the wide wilderness"
(xii, 224; 2, 232), the angels "set him down On a green bank" (4,
586). The newly created Eve "laid me down On the green bank"
(iv, 457) for the different purpose of scanning herself in a lake.

Jesus is on this occasion refreshed "from the fount of life ambrosial" (4, 590), the same "water from th' ambrosial fount" (xi, 279) to which Eve bade a touching farewell (cf. iii, 357). "Sweet return" once referred to Eve (ix, 250); now it refers to the morning (4, 438). "Sweet recess," on the other hand, which once meant a natural bower (ix, 456) or paradise itself (xi, 304), now means Athens (4, 242), hospitable "to famous wits." The River of Bliss was the "amber stream" (iii, 359); now Choaspes, fit only for kings, is so designated (3, 288). But this, after the fall, remains the world where, in winter, the "winds blow . . . keen" (x, 1066; 1, 317). "Waste . . . wild" (i, 60; iii, 424; 4, 523) fits more than one part of the now defective creation. The movement is from trees "loaden with fairest fruit" (iv, 147; viii, 307) to trees "loaden with stormy blasts" (4, 418). "Sleepless night(s)" (xi, 173; 2, 460), beginning as the lot of the fallen pair, are now the lot of kings.

It is logical for "meats and drinks" (v, 451; 2, 265) to be prominent, what were once pointed to to teach temperance. In the ornate banquet scene "ample space(s)" (i, 725; 2, 339) indicates how much room the food occupied instead of the extent of Pandaemonium, and "fragrant smell(s)" (v, 379; 2, 351) comes not from flowers but from wine.

A case of revision is of particular interest. In his grand portrayal of Rome the poet included "Turrets, and terraces, and glittering spires" (4, 54). In the former poem Satan's first view of the earth is compared to a scout's coming suddenly upon "some renowned metropolis" (was Milton thinking of Rome here, too?), "With glistering spires and pinnacles adorned" (iii, 550). "Glistering" as compared to "glittering" melts the sound, if it does not soften the sheen. One supposes Milton later had "glittering" to go alliteratively with "Turrets and terraces." It has been objected that the line does not fit the architecture of Tiberius's Rome, but the poet surely has a right to transcend strict chronology in dealing with the "urbs aeterna," a complex of visual and bookish impressions. Either adjective is typical as indicating (what much else that he wrote indicates) an eye very ready to be dazzled. Milton's obsession with light is peculiar and probably pathological.

Unsurprisingly, the formulae for speeches persist.[1] Another epic formula is "many more too long," used to cut short a catalogue (iii, 473; 2, 188). There are too many fools in the paradise of fools to specify, though Milton at this point by no means stops naming types. But when Satan in the later poem is rebuking Belial's folly, a list of seven ravished damsels from mythology is thought to be enough. This is comparable to "were long to tell" —"Long were to tell" in *Paradise Lost* (i, 507; x, 469).

Speaking of Belial's folly, we may note that though *Paradise Regained* has no misogynistic speeches like those in *Paradise Lost* and *Samson Agonistes,* the suspicion of the feminine fair continues and Milton does get in the dry remark, comparing Satan's failure now with his success before: "But Eve was Eve" (4, 6). The terseness of this is eloquent. We must note how three phrases from *Paradise Lost* return pejoratively. "Virgin majesty" had served as an honest compliment to Eve (ix, 270), even if she is already faltering at that moment. In Belial's mouth (2, 159) it is simply part of the "amorous nets," "amorous arts" temptation. He uses "passing fair" (2, 155) the same way, and for this there was precedent (xi, 717). Finally "attractive grace," which we have already found to link Eve with Sin (ii, 762; iv, 298) (wittingly or unwittingly), is used a third time (2, 176) as part of the picture of woman as a snare.

Wherein lies true glory had been a preoccupation with Milton since "Lycidas." [2] In that poem "all-judging Jove" had been the "perfect witness" (82) of the individual's achievement. This is reasserted in *Paradise Regained:*

> This is true glory and renown, when God,
> Looking on the Earth, with approbation marks
> The just man. (3, 60)

In the two epics Milton proceeds to ask what God's own glory is. The Creator's glory comes from the gratitude of the created, he says in two passages of identical import linked by the phrase "easiest recompense." Satan, in sight of Eden, is made to admit:

> nor was his service hard.
> What could be less than to afford him praise,
> The easiest recompense, and pay him thanks,
> How due! ...
> I . . . thought one step higher
> Would set me highest, and in a moment quit
> The debt immense of endless gratitude,
> So burdensome, still paying, still to owe.   (iv, 45)

Satan goes on to correct himself in a way that may be out of character but serves admirably to point the moral. The later Satan, trying to seduce Jesus by accusing His Father of an endless seeking of glory, is answered:

> And reason; since his word all things produced,
> Though chiefly not for glory as prime end,
> But to show forth his goodness, and impart
> His good communicable to every soul
> Freely; of whom what could he less expect
> Than glory and benediction—that is, thanks—
> The slightest, easiest, readiest recompense
> From them who could return him nothing else. (3, 122)

This supplies the orthodox *raison d'être* for man: he is brought into being to enhance his creator's glory. But God moves in a mysterious way and can decline "to show forth his goodness," as the famous "retraction" speech suggests: "Though I, uncircumscribed, myself retire, And put not forth my goodness . . ." (vii, 170). "Fame . . . glory" (3, 100; cf. 4, 371; iii, 449), "glory and renown" (vi, 422; 3, 60), "best fulfill" (ix, 230; 3, 177) have behind them, then, similar questions in both poems about how the great purpose is to be carried out. What are "highest deeds" (v, 865; vi, 112; 2, 438)? What have "patience, temperance" (xii, 583; 3, 92) to do with them? How are "high passions" (ix, 1123; 4, 266) to be controlled? Why is Mammon loathsome as "the least erected spirit that fell From heaven" (i, 679)? He cared nothing for

> fame and glory—glory, the reward
> That sole excites to high attempts the flame
> Of most erected spirits, most tempered pure
> Ethereal. (3, 25)

There are those who have only the false glitter: Satan's "royal seat" (v, 756) as contrasted with David's "royal seat" (3, 373), the one "far-blazing," full of show, diamonds and gold, the other conected with the word "true": which, as Satan uses it, has no meaning apart from "much ostentation" (3, 387). It is a paradox with which we shall be further concerned, toward the end of this study.

The destiny of "the race of Israel" (i, 432; 2, 311) is a major concern joining the last two books of *Paradise Lost* with all of *Paradise Regained.* Adam had received the burden—and the hope—of "many ages" (xi, 767; 2, 441). We hear about it in such familiar or inevitable phrases as "the promised land" (iii, 531; 3, 157, 439; cf. xii, 172), "regain . . . seat" (i, 5; 2, 442), "without end" (see below, p. 170; 2, 442; 4, 391), "To . . . worship God aright" (xi, 578; 2, 475). There is the usual quota of expressions having to do with war and domination, e.g., "of battle ranged" (xi, 644; 3, 322), "led captive" (x, 188; 2, 222; 3, 283).[3]

We may conclude the present subject with the quotations that join the two epics most obviously:

> at his birth a star,
> Unseen before in heaven, proclaims him come,
> And guides the eastern sages, who inquire
> His place, to offer incense, myrrh, and gold: (xii, 360)

> A star, not seen before, in heaven appearing,
> Guided the wise men thither from the East,
> To honor thee with incense, myrrh, and gold;
> By whose bright course led on they found the place. (1, 249)

This is far, in its studied and reiterated simplicity, from "the star-led wizards" of the baroque and exotic (and in that phrase Spenserian) Nativity Ode (23). Milton is no more ashamed of the same phrases than of the same key words, such as "place" and "guides-guided."

So much for the kinship between sequels. Let us cross periods and see how Milton's early poetry anticipates, in detail, his later. Approximately thirty years before he wrote the words "Sing, Heavenly Muse" at the start of *Paradise Lost,* he had inaugu-

rated his Hymn on the Nativity with "Say, Heavenly Muse"
(15). The difference in the verbs may be taken as an indication
of his growth in skill and self-assurance. When he alluded, in
Comus, to "the sage poets, taught by th' heavenly Muse" (515)
he was perhaps looking forward to the time when he could allude
to himself as "Taught by the Heavenly Muse" (iii, 19). For, as
everyone knows, his experiments in the "sacred vein" began
early. In the "Vacation Exercise," where he hailed his "native
language" (1) (which Jesus was to do in *Paradise Regained,* 4,
333; cf. xii, 54), he said,

> Yet I had rather, if I were to choose,
> Thy service in some graver subject use,
> Such as may make thee search thy coffers round,
> Before thou clothe my fancy in fit sound:
> Such where the deep transported mind may soar
> Above the wheeling poles, and at Heav'n's door
> Look in, and see each blissful Deity. (29)

What is characteristic in the last three lines needs no pointing
out, except for noting that "Heaven's door" actually turns up in
Paradise Lost (x, 389). We have observed in that poem, indeed,
a certain emphasis on the gates of heaven and hell opening and
shutting. That began with the Nativity Hymn: "Heaven, as at
some festival, Will open wide the gates of her high palace-hall"
(147). Sometimes Milton has merely changed the position of an
adjective. He has "the(ir) great Creator" five times in his epic
(see above, p. 34), "the Creator great" once in the Hymn (120).
It is "the (his) throne supreme" (x, 28; xi, 82); it was "the supreme throne" in "On Time" (17). In "The Passion," which he
did not finish because he found it "to be above the years he had
when he wrote it," Milton remarked:

> These latest scenes confine my roving verse,
> To this horizon is my Phoebus bound,
> His godlike acts, and His temptations fierce,
> And former sufferings otherwhere are found. (22)

In 1630 "otherwhere" does not mean, of course, *Paradise Lost*
and *Paradise Regained.* The allusion is to "Cremona's trump," to

Vida's Latin *Christiad*. But the sacrifice is called "This godlike act" by Michael in *Paradise Lost* (xii, 427). The world was "Forfeit to death" (x, 304). The Hymn celebrates the coming of Him who "our deadly forfeit should release" (6). "The Passion" tries to feel what that entering of the "fleshly tabernacle" (17) must have entailed. The angelic choirs in *Paradise Regained* sing anthems over the deity enshrined in "fleshly tabernacle" (4, 599). Where "The Passion" has, "For now to sorrow must I tune my song, And set my harp to notes of saddest woe" (8), *Paradise Lost* has, "I now must change Those notes to tragic" (ix, 5)— several of the same words, with two others to be added shortly, "woe" (11) and "sad" (13).

To resume a subject begun in the first chapter, the correspondences between the longest poem of Milton's first period and the longest poem of his third period are especially numerous and interesting. There is, for example, "rash hand." It originally referred to "the rash hand of bold Incontinence" (*Comus*, 397) reaching out to "Beauty, like the fair Hesperian tree Laden with blooming gold." Some thirty years later it is Eve's "rash hand" (ix, 780) plucking the forbidden fruit. We thus have one of our opportunities to ask ourselves if we are not in the presence of one or more equations, of Eve with bold incontinence, of the Hesperian tree with the tree of Genesis, of the forbidden fruit with carnality. The first and third of these certainly form part of the moral of *Paradise Lost*, and as for the second, Milton did not fail to have the association when he first wrote of Paradise: "Hesperian fables true, If true, here only" (iv, 250). "Laden with blooming gold" (*Comus*, 394) becomes "laden with fair fruit, like that Which grew in Paradise, the bait of Eve" (x, 550) at precisely that juncture where the fallen angels are metamorphosed into serpents. This need not surprise us, because the fair Hesperian tree "had need the guard Of dragon-watch" (*Comus*, 394). The other tree is guarded by angels—and by a serpent. Indeed, the fallen angel is "the dragon, that old serpent" (Rev. xx, 2) and was often so referred to by Milton (iv, 3; Nativity Hymn, 168; III, 5), apart from the Ovidian transformation scene (x,

529). By following such associations we are helped to explicate another passage in *Comus,* one which has puzzled the commentators: "the dragon womb Of Stygian darkness" (131). "Dragon" is equivalent to "hellish" here. "Dragon womb" and "Stygian darkness" are, in fact, synonymous expressions. Milton associates the dragon with darkness: as when, in the above cited passage from *Of Reformation* (III, 5), he speaks of the martyrs "shaking the powers of darkness and scorning the fiery rage of the old red dragon," an association that comes, of course, from the Dragon's being far removed from light: "Th' old Dragon underground" (Nativity Hymn, 168). Darkness is hell. Light is heaven. Blindness makes one (Milton, Samson) feel deserted by God. All of this can be documented and discussed at length. Milton, as if he were Satan, rejoices in having "Escaped the Stygian pool" (iii, 14). This phrase, "the Stygian pool," was used in a cancelled passage of *Comus* that also brings in the Hesperian garden, so like Paradise, and the dragon guard:

> Amidst th' Hesperian gardens, on whose banks,
> Bedewed with nectar and celestial songs,
> Eternal roses grow, and hyacinth,
> And fruits of golden rind, on whose fair tree
> The scaly-harnessed dragon ever keeps
> His unenchanted eye, and round the verge
> And sacred limits of this blissful isle
> The jealous ocean, that old river, winds
> His far-extended arms, till with steep fall
> Half his waste flood the wide Atlantic fills
> And half the slow unfathomed Stygian pool. (I, 479)

Milton was not one to waste such good material. The dragon's "unenchanted eye" got into *Comus* after all (395), as did roses and hyacinth (998). "Celestial song(s)" got into *Paradise Lost* (vii, 12). But it is, of course, the return, in new contexts, of "the Stygian pool," the dragon, and "fruit burnished with golden rind" (iv, 249), particularly the forbidden "fruit of this fair tree, amidst The garden" (ix, 661) that strikes us most.

To declare that Milton began with the Hesperian tree and

ended with the tree of the forbidden fruit, to declare that he
started with the dragon of Greek mythology and ended with the
dragon of Revelation and Genesis is a way of describing what has
often been described: his evolution as a poet. The principal
weight of theme shifts from classical to Biblical, but the poet
never ceases to be remarkably mobile, so that, whether in youth
or in maturity, in *Comus* and "Lycidas" or in *Paradise Lost,* he
gets the best of both worlds: has his forbidden fruit and eats the
apples of the Hesperides, too. This was in the spirit of the Renaissance: Raleigh in his *History of the World* specifically and sol-
emnly connected these fables.[4]

Comus has "dire chimaeras" (517); *Paradise Lost* has "chimaeras dire" (ii, 628). "Pan or Sylvan(us)" (*Comus,* 268; iv,
707) may be caught hovering near. "Amidst the garden(s)" (connected with "fair," ix, 661; *Comus,* 981), so to speak, of either
poem, one may find the same natural features: "tender grass"
(624; vii, 315), "grassy turf" (280; v, 391; xi, 324), "mantling
vine" (294; iv, 258), "purple grape" (46; iv, 259), "silver
lake(s)" (865; vii, 437), "this wild wood"—"these wild woods"
(312; ix, 910); "huge forests"—"forest huge" (423; i, 547), "per-
plexed . . . path(s)" (37; iv, 176), "readiest way" (305; xii,
216), "torrent flood(s)" (930; vi, 830). "Innumerous boughs"
have become "innumerable boughs" (349; ix, 1089). "Nard and
cassia's balmy smells" return as "flowering odours, cassia, nard,
and balm" (991; v, 293). Obviously the "new delight(s)" (967;
v, 19, 431) are old.

Besides the flowers which "reared high" in *Paradise Lost* (iv,
699), there was Dagon's "temple high reared" (i, 464). That is
sufficiently like Comus's "magic structures, reared so high" (798).
"Starry" dance and "months and years" are still joined:

> the starry quire,
> Who, in their nightly watchful spheres,
> Lead in swift round the months and years.
> > (*Comus,* 112)

> They, as they move
> Their starry dance in numbers that compute
> Days, months, and years . . . . (iii, 579)

This is part of Milton's unrivaled sensitivity to music, of which
"vocal air" (247; ix, 530) and "pastoral reed" (345; xi, 132) and
"soft pipe(s)" (86; i, 561) (heard even in hell) are further signs.
"Barbarous dissonance" is connected with sinful creatures, Comus
(Charles I?)[5] and his revelers (550), "Bacchus" (Charles II?)
and his (vii, 32), whom the true poet (Thyrsis, Milton) has reason to fear (the Orpheus myth again, "the rout that made the
hideous roar," "Lycidas," 61, "the race Of that wild rout that tore
the Thracian bard," vii, 34,—an unforgettable equation of noise
and sin, of women and incontinence).

"Horrid shade(s)" give an ominous air to both poems
(*Comus*, 429; ix, 185), and to *Paradise Regained* as well (1, 296).
Night sat "monarch yet in the mid sky" (*Comus*, 957). Later it is
(or is like) planets clashing "in mid sky" (vi, 314), or birds tow-
ering "The mid aerial sky" (vii, 442). Satan floats through space
"As in a cloudy chair" (ii, 930). This connects him momentarily
with the sinister Thracian goddess Cotytto, whom Comus bids
"Stay thy cloudy ebon chair" (134).

The "gentle pair" were the lost brothers (236); now they are
the lost Adam and Eve (iv, 366). Comus's question about the
brothers is, "Were they of manly prime, or youthful bloom?"
(289) Michael is seen as "prime In manhood where youth ended"
(xi, 245). It was Comus's "cursed crew" (653); now it is Satan's
(vi, 806). The one obtruded "false rules pranked in reason's garb"
(759). The other's ally, Belial, used "words clothed in reason's
garb" (ii, 226). But the circumstance of defeat for which the
words "back recoils" and "back recoiled" are repeatedly used in
Paradise Lost (iv, 17; ix, 172; vi, 194; ii, 759) had been prophesied in *Comus:* "But evil on itself shall back recoil" (593).
The context of the *Comus* passage deals with the cosmogony of
hell, but, just looking at the line, perhaps we think most of all of
Abdiel's "noble stroke" on the proud crest of Satan: "Ten paces
huge He back recoiled" (vi, 194). At any rate, it is interesting to
see the abstract turning into the concrete, evil back recoiling becoming the reeling Satan, while Abdiel is in the position of the
Elder Brother or the Lady, the moral being the same: innocence
and virtue may seem weak but divine assistance renders them

unexpectedly strong: "Or, if Virtue feeble were, / Heaven itself would stoop to her" (*Comus,* 1022). Abdiel puts it more discursively:

> Wherefore should not strength and might
> There fail where virtue fails, or weakest prove
> Where boldest, though to sight unconquerable?
> His puissance, trusting in th' Almighty's aid,
> I mean to try. (vi, 116)

The Elder Brother can speak confidently of the contest as a "happy trial" (592). But fallen Eve uses the words speciously to an Adam about to fall (ix, 975). That guilty pair do not turn instantly into "brutish form(s)" (70; i, 481) like the followers of *Comus,* but Milton manages to get this aspect of his earlier poem into his later also, in speaking of the disguises of the heathen deities (to say nothing of the hissing metamorphosis in Book x, a Circean scene without a Circe). In short, "brutish vice(s)" (xi, 518; *P.R.,* 3, 86) are brutish vices.

E. M. W. Tillyard, on the basis of some resemblance between the First Prolusion, "Utrum Dies an Nox praestantior sit?", and "L'Allegro" and "Il Penseroso," has argued that the pair of lyrics belong to Milton's Cambridge period, instead of his Horton period, where they are usually placed.[6] In view of the general and detailed affinities between *Comus* and *Paradise Lost,* such a method of dating Milton's poetry may now be seen as the specious thing it is. There is no span of years within his productive lifetime across which Milton will not and does not reach to borrow from himself. One could argue as well, probably better, that "L'Allegro" and "Il Penseroso" were written in the Horton period, because of the phrases connecting them with *Comus.* One would cite the following:

> Come, and trip it, as you go
> On the light fantastic toe.

> (" L'Allegro," 33)

> Come, knit hands, and beat the ground
> In a light fantastic round.

> (*Comus,* 143)

And young and old come forth to play
On a sunshine holiday.

("L'Allegro," 97)

Back, shepherds, back! Enough your play,
Till next sunshine holiday.

(*Comus*, 958)

Married to immortal verse.

(" L'Allegro," 137)

Storied of old in high immortal verse.

(*Comus*, 516)

moon ... Stooping through a fleecy cloud.

(" Il Penseroso," 72)

moon ... Stoop thy pale visage through an amber cloud.

(*Comus*, 333)

Here is specific resemblance, in the same language, in the same words, even in the same meter and rhyme, in contrast to the elusive analogies on which Tillyard tries to rest his case. But the point is that neither argument deserves credence. Milton is perfectly capable of inserting, as far as blank verse permits, a bit of "L'Allegro" suddenly into *Paradise Lost:*

fairy elves,
Whose midnight revels, by a forest side
Or fountain, some belated peasant sees. (i, 781)

Actually, "Midnight shout and revelry" is from *Comus* (103), that part of *Comus* which is in the meter of "L'Allegro." Everything is in flux, for we are reckoning with the conscious and the unconscious processes of creation, whose laws have yet to be found. Things we know so well in *Paradise Lost* as "the eastern gate" (iv, 542; xi, 190; xii, 638) and "Elysian flowers" (iii, 359) were already in "L'Allegro" (59; 147). The latter enter in connection with setting Orpheus in paradise, where Milton was to go. Mirth was given "honour due" ("L'Allegro," 37) long before Uriel (iii, 738) and Jesus Christ (v, 817).

In like manner, "hallowed ground," which was to be used of "the Paradise of God" (xi, 106), referred originally to ground hallowed by the Countess Dowager of Derby (*Arcades*, 55). The Arcadians "justly . . . accuse" Fame of not having done her justice (10). This is a far cry from the argument that free creatures cannot "justly accuse Their Maker" (iii, 112). The Countess got "low reverence" (*Arcades*, 37). Now it is one of the oddest of returns that "low reverence" is what Eve, much erring, idolatrous Eve, gave the forbidden tree before hastening with its poisoned fruit to Adam (ix, 835; cf. iii, 349). Is this without significance? It may be as meaningful—or as accidental—as the fact noted by Masson [7] that the poet, between his first period and his third period, gave up the word "lady" and used "woman" and "female" instead (words which do not occur in Milton's poetry in any form before *Paradise Lost*). (On the other hand, "reverend sire" continues: "Lycidas," 103; xi, 719; *Samson Agonistes*, 326, 1456.) "Bad woman"—"bad women" is one of the links between *Paradise Lost* (x, 837) and *Samson Agonistes* (211). While on this subject, we may observe that "furious rage," applied to the devils in hell in the one poem (viii, 244), is applied to Dalila's lust in the other (836). Samson has the "fond wish" (228) that he had never taken her to wife. Adam in his gloomy soliloquy has the "fond wish" (x, 834) that the wrath of God be confined to him and "that bad woman" rather than spread to their posterity. Eve blames herself: "sole cause" (x, 935). Samson blames himself, "Sole author I, sole cause" (376), for having "betrayed . . . to a woman" "The Mystery of God."

The warning from Chapter Two must be repeated, however, that many of the recurring expressions are without tendency, give no opportunity for conjecture, sly or otherwise. If "a trivial toy" refers to female beauty in *Paradise Regained* (2, 223), it refers to "a strayed ewe" in *Comus* (502), and who would undertake to make anything of that, female though a ewe is? [8] "With languished head" was used of a withered rose in *Comus* (744), and had been tried out in Latin, "flores . . . rore languidula erigentes capita" (XII, 138). It would be a curiosity to discover it used of Samson: "With languished head unpropped" (119), if there did not flash into mind a simile of Homer's (*Iliad*, VIII, 306-308) equating a drooping warrior and a bent poppy. [9]

Progression from figurative to literal is illustrated in two cases. "Sudden blaze," which we have found thrice in *Paradise Lost* (i, 665; iv, 818; x, 453), referred earlier to that much complimented Countess: "What sudden blaze of majesty" (*Arcades*, 2) and to ambitious hopes of fame in "Lycidas": "think to burst out into sudden blaze" (74). Philomel in "Il Penseroso" is described as capable of "Smoothing the rugged brow of Night" with her song (58).[10] Belial's temptresses in *Paradise Regained* have power to "smooth the rugged'st brow" (2, 164). The charms of women and of music thus mix, for women have "enchanting tongues" (*ibid.*, 158), which is enough to explain the metamorphosis of Philomel "In her sweetest, saddest plight" ("Il Penseroso," 57).

Does "sweetest, saddest" give the ambivalence of forbidden pleasure ("Néscio cur, miser est suaviter omnis amans," El. VII, 100)? Ostensibly "sweetest" refers to music-making power, "saddest" to the circumstances whereby Philomela became a nightingale. One remembers that the very young poet had ended his sonnet "To the Nightingale" with the claim (not, however, very characteristic): "Whether the Muse or Love call thee his mate, Both them I serve, and of their train am I." Music and poetry had a connection for Milton and the men of his time far more intimate than now. And "sweet," as remarked before, but now some documentation is in order, is his favorite word for music, "sweet music" ("Il Penseroso," 151; XVIII, 338), "music sweet" (Nativity Hymn, 93).

> Such sweet compulsion doth in music lie,
> To lull the daughters of Necessity.
> *(Arcades, 68)*

When does "sweet compulsion" come back? It comes when Satan is so charmed at the sight of Eve that he well-nigh forgets *he* is there to tempt *her:*

> Thoughts, whither have ye led me? with what sweet
> Compulsion thus transported to forget
> What hither brought us? hate, not love. (ix, 473)

The charm of music and of women thus, across the years, meet. But marriage can be pure, and the best music is: no "gross . . . ear" "can hear" (*Arcades*, 72-73; *Comus*, 458) it. Other testimonials to one of Milton's fixed loves are "smooth air" (Son. xiii, 8; viii, 166), "soft lay(s)" (Son. i, 8; "Lyc.," 44; vii, 436), "let . . . organ blow" (Nativity Hymn, 130; "Il Penseroso," 161), "warbled . . . string" ("Il Penseroso," 106; *Arcades,* 87) (which rhymes, of course, with "sing"). We noticed that the angels in heaven had "their golden harps" (iii, 365; vii, 258). It follows that these were of "golden wire" (vii, 597), a link with "their immortal harps of golden wires" of "At a Solemn Music" (13) and Apollo's "touch of golden wires" in "At a Vacation Exercise" (38). "Such pleasure" means music (Nativity Hymn, 99), or the sensual complex (viii, 50; ix, 455, 596, 1024) we have already traced with "sweet."

"Here below" ("Fair Infant," 49, 64; iii, 600) the scene does not necessarily change. There are "rustling leaves" ("Il Penseroso," 129; ix, 519), "branching palm" (iv, 139; vi, 885; *S.A.,* 1735), "dry ground" (xi, 861; *S.A.,* 582), "flowery lap" ("Vacation Exercise," 84; iv, 254) (Peace's or a valley's), "fresh(est) . . . lap" ("Lyc.," 138; ix, 1041), "breath of morn" (*Arc.,* 56; iv, 641, 650) (odorous), "gentle air(s)" (Nat. Hymn, 38; viii, 515; x, 93), "vernal air(s)" (iv, 264; *S.A.,* 628). Night or the Moon throws a mantle: "Over the pole thy thickest mantle throw" in the one case ("The Passion," 30), "o'er the dark her silver mantle threw" in the other (iv, 609). Todd carries an elaborate note of comparison on *P.R.,* 1, 500, "Night . . . to double-shade" with "In double night of darkness and of shades" (*Comus,* 335). The "watchful spheres" we have found in *Comus* (113) are "the spheres of watchful fire" of the "Vacation Exercise" (40). The "hours . . . le(a)d on" (Son. i, 4; iv, 268) "propitious May" or "th' eternal Spring."

"The arched roof" (i, 726; *S.A.,* 1634; Nat. Hymn, 175) consistently refers to a heathen temple, which Pandaemonium may be said to be, which the seat of the oracles and the place that Samson brought down definitely are. The Nativity Hymn anticipates also by mentioning "profoundest hell" (218; i, 251). In this poem of Milton's twenty-first year, he wrote, alluding to Job xxxviii, 6, that "the Creator great . . . cast the dark foundations deep" (120). This is not exactly hell, but it becomes hell in Book vi of *Paradise Lost:* "Fate had cast too deep / Her dark foundations" (869). At the trump of doom it is prophesied that the "Earth . . . Shall from the surface to the center shake" (Nat. Hymn, 162). Under the impact of war in heaven, "had Earth been then, all Earth Had to her center shook" (vi, 219). Both poems distinguish the "middle air" (164; i, 516), as does *Paradise Regained:* "the middle region of thick air" (2, 117).

"Gentle swain(s)" indicates the pastoral guise of the early poems (*Arc.*, 26; *Comus*, 900; "Lyc.," 92). But the parable of the Good Shepherd influences the famous "digression" in "Lycidas," and the "shepherd lad" of *Comus* (619), taken by one interpreter to be St. Paul,[11] readily becomes David in *Paradise Regained* (2, 439). "More than human" makes a traditional compliment to the brothers in *Comus:* "Their port was more than human, as they stood" (297). Satan in *Paradise Regained* suspects Jesus to be adorned "With more than human gifts from heaven" (2, 137). So goes the change from profane to holy. The Lady before Comus (688), like Jesus before the Tempter (2, 250), knows how to be strong "without repast." We must never forget, however, the amount of holy reference before the third period, how, for instance, there are divine "joy and love" ("Lyc.," 177; iii, 67, 338; cf. iv, 509), "joy and bliss" (Son. xiv, 8; xi, 43; cf. xii, 551) before *Paradise Lost*. One can cite a case, too, of movement from holy to profane: whereby the "exceeding love" of Christ's suffering for mankind ("Upon the Circumcision," 15, 16) becomes Adam's "exceeding love" for Eve (ix, 961), as she terms it when he is about to eat the forbidden fruit for her sake.

Such (scarcely intended) parody or irony is not unique. The thought of subjection to God's service wrings "O indignity!" from Satan (ix, 154). Samson breaks out, "But foul effeminacy held me yoked Her bond slave; O indignity!" (411) On the other hand, though Milton may well have become disillusioned with Cromwell,[12] there is probably nothing to be made of his having given him "praises loud" in a sonnet (xvi, 8) and afterward used that combination to describe the tribute to Dagon (*S.A.*, 436). The combination is undistinctive.[13] "Loss / Irreparable" is what the defeated angels have suffered (ii, 330), while "irreparable loss" designates Samson's blindness (644). The hungry sheep in "Lycidas" "Rot inwardly, and foul contagion spread" (127). So Lucifer may be said to have rotted inwardly and certainly "contagion spread" is part of Abdiel's denunciation of him (v, 880). There is pretended anxiety lest Comus contrive some "new device" (941). But we are told that Satan has none (*P.R.*, 4, 443). Two favorite conceptions of Milton's for which the same words are used across a long stretch of years are "free consent" (*Comus*, 1007; *P.R.*, 3, 358) and the self as a dungeon: "Himself is his own dungeon" (*Comus*, 385) and "The dungeon of thyself" (*S.A.*, 156), associated with "dark" (and cf. iv, 20-23).[14]

A category we should expect to be large embraces heroes and great deeds: "heroes old" ("Vac. Ex.," 47; i, 552; xi, 243), "far renowned" (i, 507; *P.R.*, 4, 46; *S.A.*, 341), "eternal fame" (vi, 240; *S.A.*, 1717),[15] "matchless . . . might" (x, 404; *S.A.*, 178), "Favoured of Heaven" (i, 30; *S.A.*, 1046), "wondrous gifts" (xii, 500; *S.A.*, 589), "high attempts" (*P.R.*, 3, 26; *S.A.*, 1221), and on into the realm of war.[16] "Tyrannic power" gathers a host of other words unto it:

> heroic acts, one while
> To rescue Israel from the Roman yoke;
> Thence to subdue and quell, o'er all the earth,
> Brute violence and proud tyrranic power
> Till truth were freed . . .   (*P. R.*, 1, 216)

> To quell the mighty of the earth, th' oppressor,
> The brute and boist'rous force of violent men,
> Hardy and industrious to support
> Tyrannic power, but raging to pursue
> The righteous, and all such as honor Truth!
> He all their ammunition
> And feats of war defeats
> With plain heroic magnitude of mind ... (*S. A.*, 1272)

—"heroic," "quell," "the earth," "brute," "truth." ("Potentiae tyrannicae" did not have this train in *Defensio Prima*, VII, 222.) For Milton "virtue, valor, wisdom," (*P.R.*, 2, 431), "virtue, wisdom, valour" (*S.A.*, 1010)—are bound together.

The transition is to "some great matter" (ix, 669; *S.A.*, 1638).

The "fickle . . . state" (ix, 948; *S.A.*, 164) of "mortal men" (i, 51; iii, 268; xii, 248; *S.A.*, 168, 1682), "living or dying" (x, 974; *S.A.*, 1661), is the preoccupation of the third period. "Future days" was not used seriously in the "Vacation Exercise" (72; vi, 502; xi, 114, 357, 764); now it speaks of the prophets, of "Israel's sons" (*P.R.*, 3, 406; *S.A.*, 1177) and "the . . . ways of men" (iii, 46; *S.A.*, 1407) in relation to "the living God" (xii, 118; *S.A.*, 1140). If there is search for the "just man" (*Comus*, 768; xi, 681, 818, 890; *P.R.*, 3, 62; plural, vii, 570; xi, 577; *S.A.*, 1269) and "purest spirits" (v, 406; *S.A.*, 613), there is the quest for the just God too, as is indicated by all the references to justifying the "ways" of God (i, 26; viii, 226; *S.A.*, 293, 300). "Long debate" (ii, 390; ix, 87; *P.R.*, 1, 95; *S.A.*, 863) characterizes this new and deeper thoughtfulness. Do externals help—"religious rites" (xii, 231; *S.A.*, 1320)? The just man is often found "among the heathen (round)" (x, 579; *P.R.*, 2, 443; *S.A.*, 451, 1430) who rely on the shadowy expiation of "pomp and sacrifice" (*P.R.*, 1, 457; *S.A.*, 436) "of bulls and goats" (xii, 292; *S.A.*, 1671). The hero may be temporarily suffering "dishonour, obloquy" (*P.R.*, 3, 131; *S.A.*, 452). He may face "a living death" (x, 788; *S.A.*, 100) in blindness or the grave. But God is, after all, found to be equated with a father in his "timely care" (x, 1057; *S.A.*, 602).

We may end with a curious speculation. Is there any connection between the "sullen Mole" (the name of a river in Surrey) of the "Vacation Exercise" (95) and "sullen Moloch" of the Nativity Hymn (205)? They join in darkness, the one "runneth underneath" and the other "Hath left in shadows dread / His burning idol all of blackest hue." They are close in time, the two poems being only a year and a half apart. But the important question is one that has been an issue with Milton's modern critics. How often is sound this poet's principal guide? He always had what the first, anonymous biographer called "an excellent ear," [17] and blindness would naturally have enhanced this special sensitivity of his.[18] In *Paradise Lost* he never uses the noun "joint" without following it with "limb," "joint or limb" (cf. *S. A.*, 614). The interesting feature is that, the first time, he writes, "manacled with joint or limb" (i, 426); the second time, "member, joint, or limb" (ii, 668); the third time, "membrane, joint, or limb" (viii, 625). Did one nasal continuant lead to another? Did, in particular, "member" the one time suggest "membrane" the next, an almost shockingly clinical term? How largely aural are Milton's repetitions—and his small variations? On how many occasions does sound beget sense? [19] Rhyme in prose is suspect, especially when it occurs between works, *Tetrachordon* and *Colasterion,* so near in time that, according to Thomason, they were published on the same day. "Marriage, which is the nearest resemblance of our union with Christ" (IV, 98), pairs with "marriage, which is the dearest league of love, and the dearest resemblance of that love which in Christ is dearest to his Church" (IV, 253).

CHAPTER IV

PROSE TO PROSE

Milton's characteristic attitudes are presented in the same words again and again in his prose works. We learn in no uncertain terms what he is for and, especially, what he is against.[1] There is, first, his antiprelatical stand. Here, as elsewhere, he does not waste his darts. He makes them serve more than once.

Laud was wont to speak of "the beauty of holiness" and, such is the "tyranny of prelates" (III, 62, 69), vigorously implement his conviction that outward forms increased it. The Puritan opponent replied to this with a series of paradoxes. The Anglican Church looks well, but is sick. It has exterior ornamentation, but is foul inside. It is rich, but it is poor. We recall the headnote to "Lycidas" about "our corrupted clergy, then in their height." Looking back in 1649, the author of *Eikonoklastes* wrote that "imparity and church revenue" "corrupted and belepered all the clergy with a worse infection than Gehazi's" (V, 213). Milton has nothing but scorn for "outward formality" (III, 416; IV, 126; VI, 114; compare 261, "outward rigor and formality"), "outward conformity" (III, 3; IV, 348; VI, 167; X, 82). "The inward beauty and splendor of the Christian Church" (III, 191), "all corporeal resemblances of inward holiness and beauty are now past" (III, 246). Prelaty "nests itself in worldly honors" (III, 199), the clergy "admire and dote upon worldly riches and honors" (III, 273). The universal ambition is "fat" or "fattest bishopric(s)" (III, 162, 275, 342; V, 205). Here is the start of the trouble: "great riches and promotions to bishops" (III, 24), "great riches in the church" (III, 359). "Christ refused great riches" (III, 362). The Pope has "magnas opes" (VII, 202). The "slothful, the covetous and ambitious hopes of church promotions" (III, 275) connects with the nefarious motives of those who slander the commonwealth: "though done by some to covet-

ous and ambitious ends" (VI, 117), "ambitious ends" (VI, 134).
Similarly "the multitude of hungry and ravenous harpies that
swarm about their offices" (III, 55) connects with the barbarous
invaders of England from the north, the Scots and Picts, "those
ravenous multitudes that minded only spoil" (X, 105). Just as in
"Lycidas" the hungry sheep look up and are not fed, so the country is "nigh famished for want of that which should feed their
souls" (III, 338), since the clergy "bring in a dearth of spiritual
food" (III, 365), "will not serve or feed your souls with spiritual
food" (III, 270). So much for the "haughty prelates" (III, 218),
"the haughty distance of prelaty" (III, 244), and "false doctors"
(III, 288, 313, 355; VI, 155), who have never known what a "high
calling" (III, 41, 165, 187, 261; VI, 250), "the higher calling"
(III, 414), "an extraordinary calling" (III, 82, 155), is. The contrast is with "the . . . purity of the gospel" (III, 199, 262), with
"the heavenly brightness and inward splendor of their more
glorious evangelic ministry" (III, 57), "the inward beauty and
splendor of the Christian Church thus governed" (III, 191).

The bishops are charged with "fleshly . . . pride" (III, 4,
245). "God . . . (Christ hath) made choice" (III, 243, 249) of
humble instruments to "labor in the word and doctrine" (III,
198), "brethren that labor in the word" (III, 274), "the teaching
labor of the word" (III, 362) (adaptations of 1 Tim. v, 17). The
Scriptures "set(ting) out to us 'a perfect man of God' . . . or
bishop" (III, 81, 140).

By Masson's inference [2] Milton was obliged to get better acquainted with the church fathers and councils in order to be able
to meet Bishop Hall and his party on their own ground. These
writings he found to be comparable to "the blind mazes of this
tangled wood" in which virtuous persons got lost in *Comus* (181).
"To pursue them further through the obscure and entangled
wood of antiquity, fathers and councils fighting one against another, is needless" (VI, 95). "I will not now enter into the laby-
rinth of councils and fathers, an entangled wood which the papist
loves to fight in, not with hope of victory, but to obscure the
shame of an open overthrow" (VI, 165). (He switches to
"tangled forest" at III, 35.) The objection to their style puts

them in the same class with "those grammatic flats and shallows"
(IV, 279) of the scholastics and "the flats and shallows of liturgy" (V, 261). The humanist prefers "the elegantest authors
among the Greeks, Romans, and at this day the Italians" (III,
111), "the best and elegantest authors of the learned tongues"
(III, 328).³ He likes "smooth . . . poet(s)" (III, 302; X, 12).
He will appeal to "the rules of best rhetoricians" (III, 312),
"those rules which best rhetoricians have given" (III, 362). Barbarous Latin is perhaps not the least of the charges to be leveled
at the prelates:

Must we learn from canons and quaint sermonings interlined with
barbarous Latin to illumine a period, to wreathe an enthymema with
mastrous dexterity? (III, 287)

How few among them that know to write, or speak, in a pure style,
much less to distinguish the ideas and various kinds of style: in Latin
barbarous, and oft not without solecisms. (III, 347)

Plain and solid men . . . will soon look through and through . . . the
lofty nakedness of your Latinizing barbarian. (III, 348)⁴

The "ignorance and sloth of our clergy" (VI, 264) recall the dark
ages of nations, "degenerating into sloth and ignorance" (X, 1).
    The resolution "of this great controversy" (III, 123, 479) is
to go back to the beginning—which may well mean Genesis: "to
enquire, as our Saviour's direction is, how it was in the beginning"
(IV, 73), "Thus having enquired the institution how it was in
the beginning" (IV, 100), "the institution itself from the first beginning" (IV, 171). Whether the question be church discipline or
divorce, there must be discovered what was and what was "not
. . . divine command" (III, 106, 126). The opposition has had
too much taste for "the sour leaven of human traditions" (III,
54), has "blamefully permitted the old leaven to remain and sour
our whole lump" (III, 356). Let us get back to the "evangelic
ministry" (III, 57, 243). What is "the breath of this divine utterance" (IV, 77), "that divine spirit of utterance" (V, 221)?
What has Scripture to say, for instance "a grave and prudent
law" (III, 454, 484) of Moses? Too long the Bible was thrown
aside. "Then was the sacred Bible sought out of the dusty corners

where prophane falsehood and neglect had thrown it" (III, 5),
"most injured statute of Moses . . . thrown aside with much in-
considerate neglect, under the rubbish of canonical ignorance"
(III, 369).

The truth is plain in "these (those) reforming times" (III,
166; IV, 7) to those with eyes. "A plain solution of this great
controversy, if men would but use their eyes" (III, 479),
"whereby it may be plain enough to men of eyes" (IV, 162):
these words accord with the stand that "The very essence of
Truth is plainness and brightness; the darkness and crookedness
is our own" (III, 33). A little guidance "might open his eyes to a
higher consideration of good and evil" (III, 255), "this and nothing sooner will open his eyes to a wise and true valuation of himself" (III, 262). It is from this period that the decay of Milton's
eyesight and "his perpetual tampering with physic to preserve
it" [5] date, as the following—if not the preceding—may bear witness: "If our understanding have a film of ignorance over it, or
be blear with gazing on other false glisterings, what is that to
Truth? If we will but purge with sovereign eye salve that intellectual ray which God hath planted in us . . ." (III, 33). Banks,[6]
indeed, has statistics indicating an "unusually large number of
medical images" in the prose.

Reformation is a light: "the light of reformation" (IV, 337;
VI, 70), "more than one famous light of the first reformation"
(IV, 16).[7] Truth gives out sparks. Milton in his Commonplace
Book quoted Bacon on "a certain spark of truth" (XVIII, 180)
and used the quotation in *Areopagitica* (IV, 333). The figure he
used in *Of Prelatical Episcopacy:* "to gather up wherever we find
the remaining sparks of original truth" (III, 101).

He calls "truth, the daughter not of time, but of Heaven, only
bred up here below in Christian hearts, between two grave and
holy nurses, the doctrine and discipline of the Gospel" (III, 91).
This, of course, anticipates the title of a pamphlet he was soon
to write.[8] After having found the Parliament ready for "speedy
redress" (III, 227, 339) of the troubles of the English Protes-
tants, Milton rather abruptly discovered that there was that in
domestic life which called for "speediest redress" (IV, 71). It

was part of his long fight for liberty, this struggle against the "forced yoke" (III, 581; IV, 73) of matrimony. He calls it "a servile yoke" (IV, 88), "an abject and servile yoke" (IV, 117), even as he would speak of "a servile yoke of liturgy" (V, 221) and "a far worse yoke of servitude" (VI, 32) and "jugum illud servile" (VII, 216), "servitutis . . . jugum" (VII, 64, 356; XIII, 468, all associated with "cervicibus"; cf. XV, 164) in ecclesiastical and political connections (a transition as easy and natural as from noun, "willing and speedy redress," III, 339, to infinitive, "to redress willingly and speedily," IV, 354). Yet he is at the same time a defender of "the sanctity of marriage" (III, 508; IV, 127). "For marriage must not be called a defilement" (III, 306). "It was for many ages that marriage lay in disgrace with most of the ancient doctors, as a work of the flesh, almost a defilement" (III, 383). This writer holds "bodily benevolence" (IV, 102, 222-223) secondary, and argues vigorously against those who make it primary. Marriage is "the apt and cheerful conversation of man with woman" (III, 382), "when the minds are fitly disposed and enabled to maintain a cheerful conversation" (III, 479), "a cheerful and agreeable conversation" (III, 393). Again and again he makes his Biblical point that it is "the remedy of our loneliness" (III, 374), "a remedy of loneliness" (IV, 87), "a remedy against loneliness" (III, 382), "to remedy man's loneliness" (III, 457), "that remedy of loneliness" (III, 478). It is the "most peaceable estate of household society" (III, 387), "household comfort and society" (IV, 125). When there is "unfitness . . . of . . . mind" (III, 388, 389 — twice, 422, 423) or "contrariety . . . of mind" (III, 388, 416; IV, 244, 245, 246, 254; " contrarieties of mind," 251) "above their strength to endure" (III, 399), "above strength to bear" (III, 414), "above our strength" (III, 482) ("above human strength," X, 322), the couple should by "mutual consent" (III, 388; IV, 104, 175) be allowed a divorce. "Daily experience . . . acknowledges" (III, 418), "experience daily teaches" (III, 461) how easy it is to make a mistaken choice in marriage. "The law never enjoined the fallen estate of man" (III, 477), "the fallen condition of man" (III, 461), to a lifetime of misery for such an error, since "indulgently God provided against man's loneliness . . . doubtless proportionably to our fallen estate he gives it" (IV, 86).

That "adulterous and injurious divorces . . . for hardness of heart" (III, 372, 439) were allowed, but that divorce for incompatibility is not allowed is a shocking fact to this reformer. He knows his argument must be learned, even laborious. "(The) common expositors" (III, 406, 480; IV, 87, 126, 173) embarrass him more often than they help him. He must line up authorities on his side, "Zellius, Hedio, Capito . . . Farrerus and Sturmius" (IV, 10, 224). He must wrestle with passages of Scripture that flatly contradict each other. He must take the words in Malachi, ii, 16, as spoken not against divorce but against "keeping strange concubines, to the . . . vexation of their Hebrew wives" (III, 509; IV, 109). He has consciously to repeat himself.[9] He must qualify, "though [idolatrous] seducement were not to be feared" (III, 407), "although there be no seducement feared" (III, 411), "if therefore seducement be feared" (III, 413), "the moral and evangelic charge we have from God to fear seducement" (III, 414), "fear . . . of an irreligious seducement" (IV, 191), "for fear of seducement" (IV, 201). And, to pass from proselytizing to adultery, he must speak of "the neighbor's bed less attempted" (III, 376) "or stepping to his neighbor's bed" (III, 392) as one of the happy consequences of his own proposal.

Incidentally, he shows his contempt for the woman or man who has the need and art to "hide . . . sloth" (III, 394, 494). This is what we should expect from the creator and special loather of Belial (ii, 226-227). In both the Commonplace Book and the *History of Britain* it is noted against Ethelred that he was "a slothful king" (XVIII, 242; X, 252; cf. 254). It is typical, too—typical of his patriarchal bias—that Milton speaks so often of "that power which Christ never took from the master of family" (III, 468), "to pluck the power of arbitrament of divorce from the master of family" (III, 497), "Shall then the disposal of that power return again to the master of family" (III, 508).

Passing from these matters "of . . . high consequence" (III, 51; IV, 84) to the "civil broils" (V, 95, 217; X, 22, 103) is to reassert "the dignity of reasonable creatures" (IV, 253), "a reason-

able creature, God's image" (IV, 298), the inherent rights of
"freeborn men" (V, 12, 14; singular, IV, 121, 205) against the
maxim that "the King of England can do no wrong" (V, 176; X,
305), "rex non potest facere injuriam" (VII, 418). Once it had
been Milton's purpose "to free ingenuous minds from that over-
awful esteem of those more ancient than trusty fathers" (III,
139). Afterwards his goal was "to . . . set free the minds of ingenuous and apprehensive men from this needless thraldom" of
an unfit marriage (III, 531). But he learns that "an ingenuous
mind" is "far above the presbyters of our age" (X, 94). Finally,
the *Defensio Prima* of liberty is welcomed by "Quicquid uspiam
liberorum pectorum, quicquid ingenui, quicquid magnanimi"
(VIII, 14). This appeal to "free spirits" (III, 60, 112; IV, 18; cf.
III, 272), "the ingenuous reader" (III, 108, 134), "prudent foresight" (III, 339; V, 83), "worthy" or "worthiest men" (III, 55,
63, 96), "far . . . wiser" (V, 215, 242), the "wise" who are also
the "learned" [10] (III, 48, 51, 88, 186; cf. IV, 229; VII, 88; XVI,
254), is the basis of Milton's fame in his own view. Judicious
ears can be counted on to recognize truth—and a good style.
"There is just cause therefore that when the prelates cry out,
Let the church be reformed according to Constantine, it should
sound to a judicious ear no otherwise than if they should say,
Make us rich, make us lofty, make us lawless" (III, 28). The
Remonstrant is answered: "Mince the matter while you will, it
showed but green practice in the laws of discreet rhetoric to blurt
upon the ears of a judicious Parliament with such a presumptu-
ous and overweening Proem" (III, 111). (So in other ways Milton showed how little he thought of Hall as an author.) The
transition to style is completed in the Note on the Verse of *Paradise Lost*: rhyme is "to all judicious ears, trivial and of no true
musical delight." "Fleshly wisdom" (III, 211, 245) is to be dis-
trusted, but "high wisdom" (III, 487; IV, 115; "high point of
wisdom," X, 103) not.

The early position of a majority of the King's critics was that
it was not he but his "evil counselors" who were at fault. This
position had to be modified as Charles became better known. By
the time of *Eikonoklastes* we find Milton using the phrase

against both principal and subordinates.[11] This writer had spoken
of the need for "careful education" (III, 375), had called his own
that (III, 328). It is important "to mend our corrupt and faulty
education" (VI, 132). Charles is himself a product of "corrupt
education" (V, 277). It is no wonder that he was so often caught
perfidiously "breaking . . . pacification(s)" (III, 175; V, 165).
The King "in (the) time of (his) . . . affliction" (V, 86, 308) is
compared to King Ahaz, in his profane behavior.

In negotiating this change from assailing the "jurisdictive
power" (III, 250, 253, 500) of the bishops, "force . . . in (matters) of religion" (VI, 20, 40, 46), "compel . . . in religion" (V,
42; VI, 27), to criticizing the "arbitrary power" (V, 135, 204,
245, 267, 9) of the King, Milton has to show that, far from
being in favor of "lawless . . . anarchy" (VI, 122, 247), "lawless
government" (III, 216; V, 108), he is upholding ancient law
(witness the number of his references to "ancient lawbooks," a
half dozen being listed in the Patterson Index) and precedent.
He recorded in his Commonplace Book, citing "Girard. Hist.
France," that "Dukes, counts, marquises, etc., were not hereditary at first, but only places of government and office in the time
of Charles the Great" (XVIII, 195). This observation was useful
as part of the argument that Charles I was judged by a jury of
his peers: "And so much I find both in our own and foreign story,
that dukes, earls, and marquises were at first not hereditary, not
empty and vain titles, but names of trust and office" (V, 25).

The pamphleteer lashed out against "court parasites" (V,
12), "court parasitism" (VI, 270). He argued against being
"slaves of one man's will" (V, 242), "then is the will of one man
our law, and . . . the Parliament and nation . . . slaves" (V,
180), "slaves and vassals of his will" (V, 255), "unius libidini
omnia permittere" (VII, 166), "a slavish and tyrannous life"
(III, 275), "a slavish life" (III, 299), scorned those who put on
the "badge of their ancient (eternal) slavery" (V, 3; X, 65),
spoke out for "our laws and native liberties" (V, 73), "(their)
native liberty" (III, 336, 372; V, 125; X, 70), "proque gentilitia
Anglorum libertate" (XIII, 18), "In libertate sunt nati" (VII,
546), "jus nostrum natale et libertatem" (XVIII, 10) ("the

birthright of our liberties," V, 122, connects with his also
calling "Christian liberty" "the . . . birthright . . . of" every
true believer, VI, 28, 32: this is "liberty" which is "sacred," VI,
32, 35), even as he had pleaded for the "liberty of . . . printing"
(IV, 293, 332, 354), "de typographia liberanda" (VIII, 132),
"libertate scribendi" (VII, 398), "dicendi libertatem" (IX, 162),
"loquendi . . . libertas" (VIII, 128; XVII, 316; rev. 324). To
the last, even as General Monk tergiversated in London, one
voice was heard on "the danger and confusion of readmitting
kingship in this land" (VI, 107), "the inconveniences and dangers
of readmitting kingship in this nation" (VI, 110).

Grievances merge when the King is charged with upholding
"an antichristian hierarchy" (V, 209, 250). Milton told Salmasius
that the latter was writing in behalf of a "popish king," "pro
rege pontificio" (VII, 192). This term of opprobrium, which runs
through other writings (V, 160, 211, 247, 248; VI, 67), knots the
issue of tyranny—regal and episcopal—with that peculiar horror
of the Puritans: the Roman Church. Charles's chaplains gave
him "easy confession, easy absolution" (V, 261; VI, 179), which
is Romish practice and an attempted "bribe to God" (VI, 82),
"to bribe God" (VI, 179), "to think God appeased by their seeking to bribe Him" (X, 280). If return of the king "will undoubtedly pull down the heavy judgment of God among us, Who cannot but avenge these hypocrisies, violations of truth and holiness" (VI, 103)—God visited "heavy judgments" on the perverse
Britons (X, 112)—so it is clear what is "the worst of superstitions,
and the heaviest of all God's judgments—popery" (VI, 180). In
such ways as these did Milton, one among "worthy" or "worthiest patriots" (III, 370; V, 106) though not "their chosen patriots" (VI, 132, 115), speak out for "our dear mother England"
(III, 50), "your good mother of England" (III, 154), "your glorious mother of England" (III, 354), and do something towards
making it "a nation of prophets" (IV, 341; V, 227). The historian recounts each "new and fatal revolution of calamity on this
land" (X, 187). The prophet, at the end of the *History of Britain*, tells his countrymen "to fear from like vices without amend-
ment the revolution of like calamities" (X, 316). "God turn the

omen from us" or "these days" (III, 50; XVIII, 168). "Deus modo avertat omen" (XII, 96), "which God avert" (VI, 106), "quod Deus avertat" (XIII, 286; XVIII, 52). Milton's vehemence was all the greater for his being a millenarian, one who was awaiting "the eternal and shortly expected King" (III, 78), "the coming of our true and rightful and only to be expected King" (VI, 133), "expectatus ille Dei filius" (VII, 278; cf. 126). "High providence" (III, 238; IV, 320; V, 272) is at work. The "ill success" of the King's party was encouraging to the author of *Eikonoklastes* (V, 124, 307; X, 47, 55, 356, 373).

The opposition in all these controversies is sharply handled ("sharp but saving words," III, 232), as was the manner—or rather the lack of manners—of the time. Among the recurring barbs are "frivolous excuse(s)" (V, 103, 125, 255), "false and frivolous" (V, 125, 200; VI, 154; used by the other side, too, III, 290), "idle fancies" (III, 426; X, 92, 127), "for fashion('s) sake" (V, 5, 180, 239), "affect . . . rigor" (IV, 320; V, 42), "shallow reasonings" (III, 171, 201), "absurd opinion" (V, 12; VI, 268), "fond opinion" (III, 10, 99, 139, 380), "fond conceit" (VI, 134; X, 280), "conceit" which is "low" (III, 386; IV, 172, 329), "trivial cause" (III, 479; IV, 138, 170), "small credit" (III, 10, 285), "shift(ed) . . . off" (infinitive, III, 137, 295, 491), "cunning shift(er)s" (VI, 90; X, 135). "New and dangerous (opinions)" (IV, 14, 63, 352; cf. III, 410; IV, 240), like "sects and schisms" (IV, 343, 344, 346; 350; singular, 341), "schism and sectarism" (V, 73, 206), cause no alarm to the author of *Areopagitica* but are something else again to the historian referring to the Pelagian heresies refuted by Augustine (X, 98). Milton, of course, had his reasons to be tolerant of "heretical opinion(s)" (V, 232; VI, 262). He insists that his views in *Tetrachordon* are "neither new nor licentious" (IV, 218; cf. 232, 113). Besides the aspersions on the "weak and shallow" (IV, 84, 188; V, 147; X, 111) apprehension of the other side, doubt is likewise cast on their integrity: "mental reservation" (V, 31, 229), "politic(al) drift(s)" (IV, 307, 332; VI, 83), "sinister ends" (III, 189, 276), "(other) heinous crimes" (V, 54, 76; VI, 82, 251). Proverbs, xii, 10, is used against them: "As the mercies of wicked men are cruelties" (III,

266), "is the mercy of wicked men; and their mercies, we read, are cruelties" (V, 4). They are accused of the tactics of "odious name(s)" (III, 333; V, 73, 239) and of stirring up "new discord" (V, 3, 38, 39, 270). "Unbounded license" (III, 372, 455) is in contrast to "with(in) due bounds" (III, 373; V, 129) (*Paradise Lost* has, it is to be recalled, "within . . . bounds" twice, vii, 120, 167), and the latter is not unrelated to the "middle way" (III, 372, 487; IV, 174). While Milton has occasion to refer to the "suffrage of the people" (V, 202; VI, 81), he entertains the classical and aristocratic distrust of the "rude multitude" (III, 247, 348; VI, 131; X, 105), "mad multitude(s)" (V, 70, 101; cf. VI, 134), "multitudinis insania" (VII, 246).[12]

Various virtues, skills, and forms of supernatural help are lined up on Milton's side.[13] His "dear (firm) affection to the public good" (III, 335; IV, 63) has something in common with "the dear affection which naturally grows in every not unnatural marriage" (III, 478).

It is the former that led him to give up "other employments" to compose *Eikonoklastes* (V, 65) (he had formerly used the phrase sardonically of the busyness of Prynne, IV, 234). He began his first venture into pamphleteering with the words: "Amidst those deep and retired thoughts" (III, 1). He returned to them in his fourth pamphlet: "Yet ease and leisure was given thee for thy retired thoughts out of the sweat of other men" (III, 232). (But, reverting to the prior adjective, "deep thoughts" is the favorite poetical reference, ii, 421; Son. xxi, 5; *P.R.*, 1, 190; 3, 227.) He had shown this consciousness of responsibilities in his youthful "Letter to a Friend," when he alluded apologetically to "my life as yet obscure and unserviceable to mankind" (XII, 320). The most prominent word here comes back interestingly in *The Doctrine and Discipline of Divorce:* "For if nature's resistless sway in love or hate be once compelled, it grows careless of itself, vicious, useless to friend, unserviceable and spiritless to the commonwealth" (III, 501). This has as autobiographical a sound as anything in the divorce tracts. In the course of some twenty years, "mankind" has become specifically "the commonwealth," which is less a narrowing than a deepening of ambition, like the decision to write the great poem in English instead of Latin. One does not forget his promise that when the present troubles are settled, "someone may perhaps be heard offering at high strains in new and lofty measures" (III, 78). His later version of "at high strains" is "in a higher strain" (III, 433; IV, 150, 300) or "of a higher strain" (IV, 80), which is also his earliest version, for it recalls "Lycidas," 87, "That strain I heard was of a higher mood." [14]

Milton was, happily for posterity, drawn by slander out of "silence and sufferance" (III, 283, 284—twice) to autobiography. "None hath by more studious ways endeavoured, and with more unwearied spirit" (III, 240). This combination of "studious" and "unwearied" in the *Reason of Church Government* turns into "studious" and "wearisome" in the next pamphlet, *An Apology for Smectymnuus,* separated very slightly in time from its predecessor: "if lastly it be but justice not to defraud of due esteem the wearisome labours and studious watchings, wherein I have spent and tired out almost a whole youth" (III, 282). Milton is ready for marriage, goes in *Tetrachordon* from "wearisomeness" of "continual plodding" to the need for relaxation in female company (partly quoted above, p. 6), has, indeed, to defend himself in the present tract against the libel he is looking out for "a rich widow" instead of his real preference, "a virgin of mean fortunes, honestly bred" (III, 342). The third time, "studious" is not used, but "unwearied" is taken from the first quotation and "watching" from the second, to give "unwearied pains and watching for our sakes," applied to the reformer Bucer (IV, 19). "Studious" returns autobiographically in *Areopagitica:* "studious labours" (IV, 296). All in all, it is clear that Milton does not put much stock in the "heat of youth" (III, 241; X, 79).

To study Milton's repetitions is also to become aware of his variations. The trick of altering the position of a modifier, which we found widely used in the poetry, is easily adapted to the freer rhythms of prose. What is "garnished and trimly faced" the first time (IV, 238) becomes "trimly garnished over" the second (V, 64). "In the execution of spiritual discipline over those within their charge" (VI, 250) becomes, a few pages later, "in the spirit-

ual execution of church discipline within their own congregations" (VI, 262-263), then reverts to "in the execution of a spiritual discipline" (VI, 264). The classicist knows all there is to
know about transferred epithets, as well as postpositives.

Certain reiterated expressions in the prose are synonymous
with those in the verse, leaving room for speculation as to why
Milton made the changes he did when he resumed writing with
his right hand. We get, for instance, "in . . . mother dialect" in
the prose (III, 236; IV, 277), of which the equivalent in the
verse (and once also in the prose, III, 379) is "native language"
("Vac. Ex.," 1; xii, 54; *P.R.*, 4, 333). Adam is "our forefather"
(III, 196), "our great forefather" (IV, 95), of which the synonym
in *Paradise Lost* is "(our) great progenitor" (v, 544; xi, 346).
Some might contend that "dialect" and "forefather" are unsuited
to verse, the latter being almost impossible in blank verse, but
this poet's answer is to use each of these words once: "That
structure, in the dialect of men" (v, 761), "The God of their fore-
fathers; but so died" (*P.R.*, 3, 422). It is easy to make, however,
the *ex post facto* assertion that the prose combinations sound less
like Milton's verse than what he changed them to and to point
out that in each case there is a typical move toward words of
Latin origin. The third case is "in an ill hour" (III, 294, 386),
which compares with "in evil hour" in *Paradise Lost* (ix, 780,
1067), an alteration that may be laid to Eve, if not to meter.

In any case, there are times when Milton's prose and poetry
draw nearer to each other than this.

CHAPTER V

THE MEETING OF PROSE AND POETRY

THE PLACE WHERE, if anywhere, we should expect Milton's prose to come verbally close to his poetry is in the Arguments to *Paradise Lost* and *Samson Agonistes*. Actually, the Argument to the drama exhibits no connections of this sort (unless we count "captive . . . blind," *S.A.*, 366, 1474) and the Arguments to the twelve books of the epic very little—extraordinarily little—as if Milton were on his guard against repetition. Where the Argument has "celestial motions" (viii) the poem has "planetary motions" (x, 658); where the Argument has "meditated guile" (ix) the poem has "meditated fraud' (ix, 55). "Future things" in prose (xi) is "future days" in verse (vi, 502; xi, 114, 357), "the fiery sword" (xii) "that flaming brand" (xii, 643). Naturally the subject, "Man's . . . disobedience," is stated the same way (Arg. i; i, 1). It is, in fact, the Argument to the first book that has the most connections, but some of these are matter for detection rather than common observation, since the correspondences lie outside the first book. One recognizes "utter darkness" (Arg. i; i, 72; v, 614) readily enough, and also "Satan, with his angels lying on the burning lake" (Arg. i):

> the Arch-fiend lay,
> Chained on the burning lake (i, 209)

> we lay
> Chained on the burning lake. (ii, 169; cf. 576)

But "array of battle" (i) does not exactly come in until xi, 644. "Driven out of Heaven, with all his crew, into the great deep" (i) is not narratively dealt with until Book vi, when God bids the Son,

> drive them out
> From all Heaven's bounds into the utter deep. (715)

Similarly, everyone notices that the first words of the Argument
to Book ii, "The consultation begun," refer to the last words of
Book i, "the great consult began." But how many notice that
"devoted to death" of the Argument to Book iii becomes, with
the usual increase in Latinity, "to death devote" ("devota
morti," Horace, *Carmina* IV, xiv, 18) in Book ix, 901 (cf. "to
destruction sacred and devote," iii, 208)? The verbal correspondences in the Argument to Book x, the only other Argument
which has any, look not only to Book x but back to Book ii.
The prose is: "they pave a broad highway or bridge over Chaos,
according to the track that Satan first made." The two pieces
of verse are:

> Sin and Death amain,
> Following his track (such was the will of Heaven),
> Paved after him a broad and beaten way
> Over the dark abyss. (ii, 1024)

> Over the vexed abyss, following the track
> Of Satan. (x, 314)

Indeed, so little do the Arguments to *Paradise Lost* and *Samson
Agonistes* echo the poems, that there is room, though not much,
for the recent allegations of Professor Allan H. Gilbert [1] that
there are actual discrepancies between Milton's summaries of
his poems and the poems themselves. This leads to a theory that
the summaries date back to an early period, years before the
poems were written, are somewhat like the "Outlines for
Tragedies" in the Cambridge Manuscript. Certainly there are
"a few similarities of wording" [2] between "Adam Unparadised"
and the Arguments to *Paradise Lost*. In the projected tragedy,
the chorus of angels "prepare resistance at his [Lucifer's] first
approach " (XVIII, 231). In the Argument to Book iv, it is
Satan who "prepares resistance" against the angel guard. Professor Gilbert also lists, "Adam . . . and Eve . . . accuse one
another," of the draft (XVIII, 231), as comparable to "they . . .
fall to variance and accusation of one another" of the Argument
to Book ix.[3] One may add a parallel between the draft and the
poem. In the former we find allusion to Gabriel's "desire to

see and know more concerning this excellent new creature, Man"
(XVIII, 231). In the poem it is Satan who affects this

> Unspeakable desire to see and know
> All these his wondrous works, but chiefly Man. (iii, 662)

The same glozer is to make much of his overpowering "desire To
see . . . and . . . know" Jesus (*P.R.*, 1, 383).

At the beginning of the 1640's Milton put down the title
"Paradise Lost" as the heading of his third draft (XVIII, 229).
Moreover, at the end of a chapter of the *Doctrine and Discipline
of Divorce* he said it would be more realistic "to follow rather
what moral Sinai prescribes equal to our strength, than fondly
to think within our strength all that lost paradise relates" (III,
466). (It is "lost paradise" in *Paradise Regained*, 4, 608.) *The
Reason of Church Government* and *Areopagitica* draw on the
Samson story for elaborate and important figures. The former
we shall have occasion to quote later (see below, p. 137). The
other introduces the "mewing her mighty youth" passage: "Me-
thinks I see in my mind a noble and puissant nation rousing
herself like a strong man after sleep, and shaking her invincible
locks" (IV, 344). If the nation is like Samson, so the Samson
of the poem has the strength of a nation:

> And on his shoulders waving down those locks
> That of a nation armed the strength contained. (1493)

Ten years before "Lycidas" was published, the Cambridge undergraduate assaulted the English clergy. Indeed the worn
patches, "tritis . . . pannis" with which their sermons are said to
be somehow stitched together, "consuendae," (XII, 12) is as
good a source as Virgil for "their scrannel pipes of wretched
straw" ("Lyc.," 124). Jesus in *Paradise Regained*, Samson in
Samson Agonistes, Milton the crusader in prose—all religiously
keep the "public good" (*P.R.*, 1, 204; *S.A.*, 867; IV, 63; V, 129,
237: VI, 106, 265) in mind. Is it not Milton whom we think of
when Dalila alludes to "that grounded maxim," "to the public
good Private respects must yield"—the Milton who laid aside
his plans for the great poem to duel with Hall and Salmasius?

"Civil broils" enters the poetry (xi, 718; V, 95, 217; X, 22, 103),
as does the problem of interpreting divine law, "imposition of
strict laws" (xii, 304), "the strict imposition of this command"
(III, 461). And there are familiar turns of style. "Who would
not sing for Lycidas?" (10) becomes "for who sings not Hylas?"
(IV, 104).

Let us see how his prose meets his verse in the setting forth
of certain doctrines central to Milton's position as a moral
teacher. Take first the subject of Providence, "the ways of God"
(IV, 164; VI, 39; i, 26; viii, 226; *S.A.*, 293). "But this it is to
embroil ourselves against the righteous and all-wise judgments
and statutes of God; which are not variable and contrarious, as
we would make them" (III, 471). Here the goal was to avoid
rhyme. Next time the goal was to achieve it:

> God of our fathers, what is Man!
> That thou towards him with hand so various,
> Or might I say contrarious,
> Temper'st thy providence through his short course.
>   (*S. A.*, 667)

This is in a less confident mood, to say the least. But the reliance
on "high disposal" is rooted deeply:

> Or th'execution leave to high disposal,
> And let another hand, not thine, exact.
>   (*S. A.*, 506)

"When God out of His providence and high disposal hath delivered him [the King] into the hand . . ." (V, 3).

The line, "Sufficient to have stood, though free to fall" (iii,
99), was anticipated by part of a sentence in the *Doctrine and
Discipline of Divorce*, "Yet considering the perfection wherein
man was created, and might have stood, no decree necessitating
his free will" (III, 441). Readers who stumble over the brevity
of the verse, asking dourly, "Who wants to be 'free to fall'? What
a curious thing to say!" get their explication in this prose and
the prose of *Areopagitica*: "Many there be that complain of
divine providence for suffering Adam to transgress. Foolish

tongues! when God gave him reason, he gave him freedom to choose, for reason is but choosing" (IV, 319). The last four words lead to a parenthesis in *Paradise Lost*, iii, 108: "(Reason also is choice)." So much for "divine justice" (III, 445; V, 30, 103, 273, 275; X, 112), "justice divine" (x, 857, 858).

Belial is connected with a number of things, besides the expression "son(s) of Belial" (III, 307; VI, 68; i, 502). He is the prime example of misapplied skill. One remembers first that

> his tongue
> Dropped manna, and could make the worse appear
> The better reason, to perplex and dash
> Maturest counsels. (ii, 112)

This is what "was objected to Socrates by them who could not resist his efficacy, that he ever made the worst cause seem the better" (IV, 70). The good side of this doctrine is seen in Milton's prose statement, also admittedly derived from Plato, that "persuasion certainly is a more winning and more manlike way to keep men in obedience than fear" (III, 181). The metrical version of this is:

> Yet held it more humane, more heavenly, first
> By winning words to conquer willing hearts,
> And make persuasion do the work of fear.
> (*P. R.*, 1, 221)

It is Belial who speaks sublimely of never being willing to forfeit "this intellectual being, Those thoughts that wander through eternity" (ii, 147). The speech is Milton's variation on "To be or not to be." The particular line recalls *Areopagitica*: "gives us minds that can wander beyond all limit and satiety" (IV, 320). It is a sentiment highly characteristic of its author. He gave vent to it at Cambridge, too, in the Third Prolusion: "Sed nec iisdem, quibus orbis, limitibus contineri et circumscribi se patiatur vestra mens, sed . . . divagetur" (XII, 170). Yet this is the Belial whom Milton despises as having "Counseled ignoble ease and peaceful sloth, Not peace" (ii, 227). "Ease" and "sloth" are a habitual combination: empires will decline when they "Shall change their course to pleasure, ease, and sloth" (xi,

794). But still closer to Belial's false position is Petronius Turpilianus, the Roman governor in the *History of Britain,* who "was thought to have pretended the love of peace to what indeed was his love of ease and sloth" (X, 70).

The verse, "He for God only, she for God in him" (iv, 299), has a fame all its own. Its prose original is: "He not for her, but she for him" (IV, 76). This is less refined, and still less refined is the earlier (set down under provocation to correct an excess on the other side), "Who can be ignorant that woman was created for man, and not man for woman?" (III, 475). Whatever we may think of it, it is straight out of Saint Paul, "Neither was the man created for the woman, but the woman for the man" (I Cor. xi, 9). The overtly Pauline basis for this and for the "he not for her, but she for him" passage is worth recalling, since too many readers forgetfully regard the line in the poem as a peculiarly, indeed an outrageously, Miltonic sentiment. In *Tetrachordon* Milton has just quoted two other verses from the same chapter of Corinthians, 3 and 7: "The head of the woman is the man: he the image and glory of God, she the glory of the man." Presumably the authority for the line in *Paradise Lost* is not different.

Procreation, "the genial bed" (IV, 85; viii, 598), is not to be put first in marriage. "Conjugal love" (III, 395; IV, 190, 254; ix, 263), "conjugal affection" (XVIII, 151; *S.A.,* 739) links two souls, and is not to be found so often as one might wish or even, in inexperience, expect. There is much on the sad plight of those who "haste too eagerly to light the nuptial torch" (III, 395).

> then, all in heat,
> They light the nuptial torch.
> (xi, 590)

This is the "in nuptiis taeda" (XII, 272) of the ancients. Wisdom and virtue are no safeguard against a mistaken choice.

it being an error above wisdom to prevent, as examples of wisest men so mistaken manifest. (III, 461-462)

especially knowing that the best and wisest men amidst the sincere and most cordial designs of their heart do daily err in choosing. (IV, 87)

And yet in these matters wherein the wisest are apt to err, all the wariness that can be ofttimes nothing avails. (IV, 120)

But let them know again that, for all the wariness can be used, it may yet befall a discreet man to be mistaken in his choice. (III, 394)

and experience confirms by daily example that wisest, soberest, justest men are sometimes miserably mistaken in their choice. (IV, 256)

All this prepares for *Samson Agonistes*:

> Wisest men
> Have erred, and by bad women been deceived. (211)

> ... wisest and best men, full oft beguiled, (759)

> Whate'er it be, to wisest men and best,
> Seeming at first all heavenly under virgin veil,
> Soft, modest, meek, demure,
> Once joined, the contrary she proves— (1034)

"Wisest men" (see further the Patterson Index), "soberest, wisest, and most Christian people" (III, 78), "best and wisest commonwealths" (IV, 306), "wisest and best words" (III, 311) —these and Scripture form Milton's appeal, whatever he is arguing for, the high standards ever at hand by which to measure himself, just as the poet afflicted with blindness readily summons to his side other bards who were great and blind.

The plaintive strain is rare in this author, a "clear spirit" (III, 162; "Lyc.," 70; cf. *Othello*, III, iv, 143) who was born to be the maker of "heroic song" (III, 61; ix, 25) in either medium, to sing "noble (nobler, noblest) deeds" (III, 260, 335; X, 33; singular, V, 4; *P.R.*, 4, 99; ii, 116) performed by men "of noblest temper" (V, 2; i, 552). "Matchless valor," like the previously mentioned "matchless deeds" (see above, p. 18), runs through his work:

> Him our old patron Saint George by his matchless valor slew.
> (III, 275)

> I say not by whose matchless valor, next under God. (V, 37)

> To matchless valor and adventures high. (*S. A.*, 1740)

> macte tua egregia virtute. (XIII, 348)

> For what avails
> Valor or strength, though matchless, quelled with pain? (vi, 457)

Valor is correlated with "heroic virtue," another favorite phrase:

And valor and heroic virtue called (xi, 690; cf. "heroic valor" VI, 279).

Royal dignity . . . rests . . . upon . . . heroic virtue. (III, 47)

his heart in all virtues heroic (III, 186)

heroically virtuous (III, 399)

yet when others for the deliverance of their country endued with fortitude and heroic virtue to fear nothing but the curse . . . (V, 2)

heroicae . . . virtutis (VII, 64)

This is principally the Latin, the Roman, "virtus." Milton, according to the choice he early made, is "praeclare dicendo" about those who "fortiter agendo" (XII, 168; cf. VII, 8). Or he is the promulgator of a "high (higher, highest) design" (III, 268; ii, 630; *P.R.*, 2, 203) for a further "high enterprise, Lords and Commons, a high enterprise and a hard" (III, 369)—"judging hence what kind of men the Britons generally are in matters of so high enterprise" (X, 103)—"the enterprise so hazardous and high" (*P.R.*, 3, 228). "High (highest) pitch" (IV, 71; viii, 198; xi, 693) is an expression that critics might well borrow to describe his favorite style and subjects.

His pen was ever sharp against the corrupt clergy:

> Enow of such as, for their bellies' sake,
> Creep, and intrude, and climb into the fold!
> ("Lyc.," 114)

On the capacious clerical "bellies" Milton had not a little to say,[4] but we shall pause rather over the second line, especially as "creep" into the fold is Milton's verb, not that of the parable (John, x). He was impressed by the insidious hypocritical approach: how "they for lucre use to creep into the church undiscernibly" (III, 360). "What they are for ministers, or how they crept into the fold . . . we know not." This is like a signature to the otherwise anonymous *Observations on the Articles of*

Peace (VI, 270). It is the same voice ten years later, only a little further from "Lycidas":

Thus we see, that not only the excess of hire in wealthiest times, but also the undue and vicious taking or giving it, though but small or mean, as in the primitive times, gave to hirelings occasion, though not intended, yet sufficient to creep at first into the church. (VI, 50)

Thus he alternates between the "fold" of the parable and the "church" of the parable's reference. (As for "climb into the fold," that is remembered—but it is, of course, the parable which is the common source—when Satan leaps over the barriers of Paradise: "So clomb this first grand thief into God's fold: So since into his church lewd hirelings climb," iv, 192.) A stern judgment hangs over those who "buy and sell the awful and majestic wrinkles of her brow" (III, 72) (which is like taking lightly "the sad and awful majesty" of Old Testament law, III, 507). " Thy awful brow" is next Eve's, in the cozening words of the Serpent (ix, 537). The "majestic brow" is next Jesus'—"one look from his majestic brow" would foil women and devils both (*P.R.*, 2, 216).

"Carnal desire(s)" (III, 110; ix, 1013) are the common weakness of prelates and Adam and Eve. The imperial craving, "high titles" (III, 95; xi, 793), fits bishops. "Orders and degrees" (VI, 53; v, 591, 792) are proper in Heaven, but not within the Church. Here below, Truth, like "the person . . . of many a great man [is] slight and contemptible to see to" (IV, 350). This idiom was used of "a certain shepherd lad" in *Comus*, "Of small regard to see to" (620), but the bestower of a saving plant, also most unprepossessing in appearance ("a small unsightly root"). But certain it is that the "stiff necks" will be bowed.

with these the invincible warrior, Zeal, shaking loosely the slack reins, drives over the heads of scarlet prelates, and such as are insolent to maintain traditions, bruising their stiff necks under his flaming wheels. (III, 314)

> and sturdiest oaks
> Bowed their stiff necks, loaden with stormy blasts.
> (*P. R.*, 4, 418)

The prose reminds us of the two places in *Paradise Lost* where Christ's terrific chariot charge over the rebellious angels is depicted:

> O'er shields, and helms, and helmed heads he rode
> Of Thrones and mighty Seraphim prostrate. (vi, 840)

The other passage even gives us "necks" instead of "heads," and "flaming . . . wheels":

> thou that day
> Thy Father's dreadful thunder didst not spare,
> Nor stop thy flaming chariot wheels, that shook
> Heaven's everlasting frame, while o'er the necks
> Thou drov'st of warring Angels disarrayed. (iii, 392)

The prelates, seeking to stir up civil war, are compared to a bloodthirsty dragon, satisfied with nothing less than to "fill her dark and infamous den with the bones of the saints" (III, 275). Thus, by way of the dark den, these objects of Milton's wrath are again allied with the old dragon, who was driven to "this dark opprobious den of shame" (ii, 58). Is it any wonder, then, that Milton, having said of Hall, "leaving this Remonstrant and his adherents to their own designs" (III, 145), says of the Arch-fiend that "Heaven Left him at large to his own dark designs" (i, 213). If Satan was a master of "ambiguous words" (v, 703; vi, 568), so was the Remonstrant (III, 135). Either faction is consigned to "the bottomless pit" (vi, 866; III, 76; IV, 304), and the letting of either loose upon mankind is a reflection of "God's just anger" (III, 281), "anger and just rebuke" (ix, 10). The author of *Of Reformation* prays the Trinity:

O let them not bring about their damned designs that stand now at the entrance of the bottomless pit, expecting the watchword to open and let out those dreadful locusts and scorpions, to re-involve us in that pitchy cloud of infernal darkness. (III, 76)

The Jesuits had been locusts before Milton wrote, as in Phineas Fletcher's *The Locusts*, and bad priests were again to be so labeled at the end of *The Tenure of Kings and Magistrates* (V, 59). More specifically, the "pitchy cloud" of locusts is back in the first book of *Paradise Lost*, in a simile illustrating how "up they sprung Upon the wing," the devils on the burning lake, at their leader's call:

> As when the potent rod
> Of Amram's son, in Egypt's evil day,
> Waved round the coast, up-called a pitchy cloud
> Of locusts, warping on the eastern wind,
> That o'er the realm of impious Pharaoh hung
> Like Night, and darkened all the land of Nile. (i, 338)

"Pitchy clouds" had gone with "darkness" and hell, though not with locusts, in lines added to *Comus*, 356, in the Cambridge Manuscript:

> So fares as did forsaken Proserpine,
> When the big rolling flakes of pitchy clouds
> And darkness wound her in. (I, 513)

"Wicked deed(s)" registered Milton's indignation at ecclesiastical and political opponents (III, 324; VI, 139), and at the degenerate Britons (X, 111), before it was hurled by Samson at Dalila (826). On the other hand, Milton urged the two nations of England and Scotland to "join your invincible might to do worthy and godlike deeds" (III, 61), in words that were published thirty years before those of the Tempter's explanation to Jesus that he came to "behold thy godlike deeds" (1, 386). If the martyrdom of Polycarp was attended by such a miraculous shining as to constitute a "glorious sight" (III, 95), so, without sarcasm, the stars are a "glorious sight" to Eve (iv, 658). Similarly, the sun is literally "the great luminary" in *Paradise Lost* (iii, 576), while, in *Tetrachordon*, Melanchthon (*a luco lux!*) is "the third great luminary of reformation" (IV, 223). (It is scandalous to the author of *Pro Se Defensio* that Alexander More should have been received "quasi ecclesiae lumen unicum," IX, 218.) A "foul . . . dishonor" (V, 257-58; VI, 82) was cast upon the Scots by the author of *Eikon Basilike*, was laid upon Christ by the supporters of a mercenary church, and soils anyone, according to Adam, who seeks temptation:

For he who tempts, though in vain, at least asperses
The tempted with dishonour foul. (ix, 297)

One must beware not only of smirching but of "false glitter"—
Satan's (x, 452), or that of the "deceitful wares" of "the great
merchants of this world" (III, 230). "A pure elixir" (III, 276),
"elixir pure" (iii, 607), as associated with alchemy and the
"precious bane," is looked on askance by the moralist, even as
the cultivated poet-musician would shun "barbarous noise(s)"
(Son. xii, 3; X, 65) while feeling the appeal, which may also be
deceitful, of "charming pipe(s)" (III, 387; *P.R.*, 2, 363).

He is constantly warning against the "inordinate desires"
(IV, 152; VI, 130; iv, 808; xii, 87) which only reason can keep
down. If reason loses control, the result is best presented by
metaphor: "in a troubled sea of passion tossed" (x, 718), "tossed
and tempested in a most unquiet sea of afflictions and tempta-
tions" (IV, 256; cf. 279). How strong is the mind in its "mansion in this fleshly nook" ("Il Penseroso," 92), "this frail mansion
of flesh" (III, 323)? There is a side of Milton, best seen in
Comus and *Areopagitica*, which welcomes temptation as a glorious trial. Another side, exposed in *Paradise Lost* and *Samson
Agonistes*, feels it had better be avoided, if possible. "Were it
not better done, as others use?" he asks in "Lycidas" (67). "It
would be better done to learn that the law must needs be frivolous which goes to restrain things, uncertainly and yet equally
working to good and to evil," he asserts in *Areopagitica* (IV,
320). The Puritan in him associates "feast" with "riot": "while
they feast and riot" (III, 365), "To luxury and riot, feast and
dance" (xi, 715). "Jollity" is a weakness of "youth": "jest and
youthful jollity" ("L'Allegro," 26), "excusable in a youth,
through jollity of mind" (X, 221). "Jollity" goes with "feast"
as well, but hardly with this writer's blessing:

Meanwhile, welcome joy and feast,
Midnight shout and revelry,
Tipsy dance and jollity.
(*Comus*, 102)

It is Comus who says this; Milton, who says the following:

Others, lastly, of a more delicious and airy spirit, retire themselves (knowing no better) to the enjoyments of ease and luxury, living out their days in feast and jollity. (IV, 279)

Yet there is justice—and another cluster—in Helen Darbishire's observation: [5] "His feeling for the fresh, balmy air of spring was akin to his feeling for the youthful ardour and vivacity of sensuous natures. It is not by accident that he described such natures, 'those of soft and delicious temper,' [III, 239]—'others of a more delicious and airy spirit,' [IV, 279] with the same epithets that bring to life the 'soft, delicious air' breathing its balm in *Paradise Lost* [ii, 400]." The pleasures must be "unreproved," one must "live unreproved": "To live with her, and live with thee, In unreprovèd pleasures free" ("L'Allegro," 39), "His holiest people might . . . live unreproved" (III, 440).

The trouble is, it is not only virtue that presents a charmed cup. We hear of "chastity and love, I mean that which is truly so, whose charming cup is only virtue" (III, 305). But we hear also of

> The daughter of the Sun, whose charmed cup,
> Whoever tasted, lost his upright shape.
> *(Comus,* 51)

We hear of "the lovely shapes of virtues and graces" (III, 191). And this is repeated apropos of Satan's humiliation before Zephon and Ithuriel:

> Abashed the Devil stood,
> And felt how awful goodness is, and saw
> Virtue in her shape how lovely. (iv, 846)

But the possessed serpent manages to display a lovely shape also: "Pleasing was his shape And lovely" (ix, 503). (By contrast, "perfect shape"—*P.R.,* 3, 11; IV, 337—joins "Truth . . . with her divine Master." [6])

Ultimately it is the elect whom Milton is addressing. "To such my errand is," says the Attendant Spirit *(Comus,* 15). "My errand is to find out the choicest and the learnedest," says the reformer in prose (III, 378). A rigid education does help, then, though "instinct of nature" (III, 237, 500; *S.A.*, 1545), "instinct and presage of nature" (III, 302), "natural instinct" (V, 24), is well spoken of. The Lady was not "unprincipled in virtue's book" (*Comus*, 367). But many a statesman comes forth from Oxford or Cambridge "unprincipled in virtue" (IV, 279).

Of the means by which "pure(st) . . . spirits" (IV, 20; v, 406) soar to "great . . . renown" (III, 383; *P.R.*, 1, 136), learning is one. The thirst after knowledge may be a sign of grace, in an individual:

> divine
> Historian, who thus largely hast allayed
> The thirst I had of knowledge, (viii, 8)

or in a people: "the earnest and zealous thirst after knowledge and understanding which God hath stirred up in this city" (IV, 341). But it can be carried too far, as the same divine historian warns. His learning did not keep Salmasius virtuous, for instance. The younger Milton was patient to "find out the precious gem of truth as amongst the numberless pebbles of the shore" (III, 113). But revulsion set in, not unassociated with efforts and disillusions that would have crushed a lesser spirit. For the older Milton, much study is an uncalled for weariness of the flesh:

> many books,
> Wise men have said, are wearisome; who reads
> Incessantly, and to his reading brings not
> A spirit and judgment equal or superior
> (And what he brings what needs he elsewhere seek?),
> Uncertain and unsettled still remains,
> Deep-versed in books and shallow in himself,
> Crude or intoxicate, collecting toys
> And trifles for choice matters, worth a sponge,
> As children gathering pebbles on the shore.
> (*P. R.*, 4, 321)

Thus the simile returns to serve a very different purpose.

How may all be kept "in . . . even balance" (IV, 130; V, 72; i, 349)? Law is "public reason" (V, 83), but "public reason" (iv,

389) may become "the tyrant's plea." Here enters the revolutionary, the fighter for liberty. "Confined and pestered in this pinfold here" is the complaint in *Comus* (7) about life "here below" ("Fair Infant," 49, 64; iii, 600; III, 401; IV, 14). The two key words come back to form Milton's objection to the liturgy, "confine by force into a pinfold of set words" (V, 221). Even the prayer book is a tyranny (and certainly it was associated with tyranny in this period of English history, was the very start of the trouble in Scotland in the year of "Lycidas"): Adam and Eve are as happily and pointedly free from it as they are from clothes. "Sighs . . . unutterable" (xi, 5; V, 224) can suffice. Milton is not constitutionally set against change in the "face of things" (which sometimes means "naturae facies," "Naturam Non Pati Senium," 9): it all depends:

Although, since the writing of this treatise, the face of things hath had some change, (VI, 111)

> now reigns
> Full-orbed the moon, and, with more pleasing light,
> Shadowy sets off the face of things—(v, 43)

How first this World and face of things began, (vii, 636)

He looked, and saw the face of things quite changed. (xi, 712)

But kings are afraid of all change. The one part of *Paradise Lost* that caused the censor to hesitate before licensing the poem was the lines in Book i:

> In dim eclipse, disastrous twilight sheds
> On half the nations, and with fear of change
> Perplexes monarchs. (i, 598)

The Archbishop's deputy, Tomkyns, might have hesitated still longer, had he connected this with the allusion in *Eikonoklastes* to "those who, being exalted in high place above their merit, fear all change" (V, 220). "The fear of change" figures in *The Tenure of Kings and Magistrates* too (V, 4).

The wily Charles was more like the Pope than Moloch in veering from "open war" (V, 256; X, 118; ii, 51) ("aperto Marte," "In Q.N.," 113) to disguised. His "glozing words"

(V, 290) look back to the "well-placed words of glozing courtesy" of Comus (161), and forward to Satan's "glozing lies"
(iii, 93). Such "subtle shifts" (V, 70)—the Stoics are accused
of them by Jesus (*P.R.*, 4, 308)—will all too easily fool the multitude, unless better instructed. Interestingly, Puritanically,
Milton associates "base" with "besotted." That dates back to
Comus, too: " But with besotted base ingratitude" (778) (compare "Quis tantae ingratitudinis foeditatem," VIII, 210). The
multitude, "with a besotted and degenerate baseness of spirit"
(V, 69), are ready to fall flat before a king or his memory.
Milton spoke more truly than he knew, here in *Eikonoklastes*.
Eleven years later he cannot stem the tide, however vigorously
he warns the English people against the incredible ignominy of
being ready "basely and besottedly to run their necks again into
the yoke which they have broken" (VI, 123). He is like an Old
Testament prophet fulminating against idolatry: "let them who
now mourn for him as for Thammuz" (V, 88), "In vain the
Tyrian maids their wounded Thammuz mourn" (Nativity Hymn,
204). It was again in *Comus* that this author began slighting the
"courts of princes" (325; IV, 312).

He has a complex association of "gale(s)" which are "gentle"
with "wings" and fanning:

God ... sent out a gentle gale and message of peace from the wings
of those his cherubins that fan his mercy seat. (III, 60)

Now gentle gales,
Fanning their odoriferous wings, (iv, 156)

fresh gales and gentle airs
Whispered it to the woods, and from their wings
Flung rose, flung odors from the spicy shrub; (viii, 515)

and winds
Of gentlest gale Arabian odors fanned
From their soft wings, and Flora's earliest smells.
(*P.R.*, 2, 363)

It is a regular cluster, with "odours" added to the poetry.[7]

Figuratively or literally there is a good deal of mounting of
hills for a better view. The result on two occasions is the con-

nection of "hill" with "goodly prospect": "straight conduct ye
to a hillside . . . so full of goodly prospect" (IV, 280).

> Obtains the brow of some high-climbing hill,
> Which to his eye discovers unaware
> The goodly prospect of some foreign land. (iii, 546)

Failing a hill there is a watchtower—the lark's in "L'Allegro"
(43): "From his watchtower in the skies"; God's in *Of Reformation*: "From his high watchtower in the heavens" (III, 60).
Another phrase involving the wider view is "(to) all posterity"
(III, 61, 278, 465; X, 33; *S.A.*, 977), a frequent reference for
fame, good or ill, for which Milton's Latin is "posthac per omnes
gentes" (VII, 64), or "omnes eorum posteri" (XV, 180, 182).

Hills and valleys also serve to redouble sound:

The enemy passes on securely, and German thrice aloud cries
" Halleluia," which answered by the soldiers with a sudden burst of
clamor, is from the hills and valleys redoubled. (X, 109; cf. 365)

> Their moans
> The vales redoubled to the hills.
> (Son. xviii, 9)

So "hill and valley rings" at the end of one of the most surprising similes in *Paradise Lost* (ii, 495).

One veritable obsession of this writer who, as G. Wilson
Knight has noted, is predominantly fond of military language
and imagery, is the "(en)compassed round"—"environed round"
—"beset round" complex. It seems to have grown on him in his
blindness, for reasons that may easily be imagined, but it started
in the prose written when he had his eyesight. He retorts to the
Remonstrant, "This is but to fling and struggle under the inevitable net of God, that now begins to environ you round" (III,
170). Next he animadverts on "the vulgar expositor, beset with
contradictions and absurdities round, and resolving at any peril
to make an exposition of it" (IV, 169). In the *History of Britain*
"beset round" is literal: "In this confused fight Scaeva, a Roman
soldier, having pessed too far among the Britons, and beset

round, after incredible valour shown, single against a multitude, swum back safe to his general" (X, 38). This takes us immediately to Satan's heroic struggle through chaos in *Paradise Lost*:

> and through the shock
> Of fighting elements, on all sides round
> Environed, wins his way. (ii, 1016)

But it is Abdiel, too (commended by *his* General for what he did, "single . . . Against revolted multitudes," vi, 31):

> The flaming Seraph, fearless, though alone,
> Encompassed round with foes, thus answered bold. (v, 876)

And of course it is Milton: "In darkness, and with dangers compassed round" [8] (vii, 27) (compare "encompassed and in great danger," X, 56; Sin has her application: " 'With terrors and with clamours compassed round Of mine own brood, that on my bowels feed,' " ii, 862). The Satan-Abdiel-Milton equation is, certainly, not new. We remember also that this poet complained of a too northerly climate, a fact that makes "and the cold environs round" (ix, 636) seem more appropriate (the construction here is as dubious as "Angel[']?]s ken," i, 59,— "Angel" stands near the noun "ken" at iii, 622—but "environs" is probably, as usual, a verb, not a noun; the other appearance of the form is in the second *Tetrachordon* sonnet: "When straight a barbarous noise environs me," Son. xii, 3). The pattern continues in *Paradise Regained*, with Jesus as the heroic figure:

> And, with dark shades and rocks environed round, (1, 194)

> Infernal ghosts and hellish furies round
> Environed thee. (4, 422)

It can be found in the Latin: "hostibus vel occultis vel jam prope imminentibus cincta undique et pene obsessa sit" (XIII, 326). (Cf. "ab infestis undique hostibus petitum atque obsessum, XII, 106.) Only once, in all Milton's writings, is the combination used to signify comfort, when Michael assures the Adam who must leave Paradise:

> Yet doubt not but in valley and in plain
> God is as here, and will be found alike
> Present, and of his presence many a sign
> Still following thee, still compassing thee round
> With goodness and paternal love, his face
> Express, and of his steps the track divine. (xi, 349)

Such is the poet's resolution from despair, his answer to the encirclement by unseen enemies who have pursued him out of the lost paradise. "How many evils have enclosed me round!" exclaims Samson (194), and a little further on falls completely into the pattern when he speaks of "the men of Judah" who "beset me round" (257). But this hero, like all the others, broke free.

In "good hour" (IV, 269; ii, 848) we come to a few parallels involving the "more than human" (III, 423, 424; *Comus*, 297; *P.R.*, 2, 137) subject, "our eternal King" (VI, 58; cf. III, 78; see above, p. 15) and the creation and "joy and bliss" (III, 79; Son. xiv, 8; xi, 43; cf. xii, 551), the "beatific vision" (III, 79; IV, 337), "vision beatific" (i, 684). Milton was "at heaven-gate" in prose (IV, 187; x, 22), and before he lined up the "angelic squadron bright" in *Paradise Lost* (iv, 977) knew "angelic brightness" as an impassioned pamphleteer (III, 246). In *The Reason of Church Government* he spoke of

a work ... to be raised ... by devout prayer to that eternal Spirit who can enrich with all utterance and knowledge, and sends out His seraphim, with the hallowed fire of His altar, to touch and purify the lips of whom He pleases. (III, 241; cf. 260)

This "altar" of "hallowed fire" was never far from his inner sight. He spoke of it in the Nativity Hymn:

> And join thy voice unto the angel quire,
> From out His secret altar touched with hallowed fire. (28)

He said in the *Doctrine and Discipline of Divorce*, "The vigor of his law could no more remit, than the hallowed fire on his altar could be let go out" (III, 440). To put it less concretely, the "diminution" of God's "glory" (IV, 294; *S.A.*, 303) is zealously guarded against. That is what the "gift of God" (III, 126,

238, 511; IV, 106; *S.A.*, 201; "Dei munus," XII, 258; VII, 10; "donum Dei," XIV, 138; XV, 378; XVI, 74, 118; also in plural) is for.

"The . . . great Author" (IV, 133; v, 188; cf. x, 236) was the author of the Bible and the craftsman who "formed and fashioned" (III, 353; viii, 469) the visible creation, not out of nothing, but out of pre-existing material. This is the first heresy in *Paradise Lost*:

> That shepherd who first taught the chosen seed
> In the beginning how the heavens and earth
> Rose out of Chaos. (i, 10)

Milton started to write his opening lines in the *Doctrine and Discipline*: "the first and last of all his visible works, when by his divorcing command the world first rose out of Chaos . . ." (III, 420). For good, and as it were Lucretian, measure, he said it in his First Prolusion at Cambridge: "mundum recens emersum e Chao" (XII, 134). The *Doctrine and Discipline* passage goes on: "nor can be renewed again out of confusion,"—an association of Chaos and confusion to be found in ii, 894-897, 951-960; vi, 871-872. (Incidentally, battle is attended by confusion and "heap": "horrid confusion heaped Upon confusion," vi, 668; "The battle was a confused heap," X, 78.)

"Loud hosannas" ring through Heaven when Jesus offers Himself for man (iii, 348). A humble and therefore great church receives them in *The Reason of Church Government* (III, 252). The "universal lord of all mankind" is Christ in *The Ready and Easy Way* (VI, 133); with this "universal lord" (v, 205; viii, 376) Adam and Eve were, as we know, in direct communication. Adam had his chance, but the time comes for God to say to the Son: " 'be thou in Adam's room The head of all mankind, though Adam's son' " (iii, 286). Adam, by the way, while he was lord, had "all creatures . . . to make him sport" (IV, 83). This is carried through in the elephant's "lithe proboscis" passage, which some critics persist in being solemn about, though it contains the words "Sporting" (iv, 343) and "To make them mirth" (346).

Finally, we can catch Milton saying of the composition of *Eikonoklastes* what he said of the composition of *Paradise Lost*: "beginning it so late, and finishing it so leisurely" (V, 64), "long choosing and beginning late" (ix, 26), though the all-important difference is between "a work assigned" him and one he always wanted to write,

> If answerable style I can obtain
> Of my celestial patroness. (ix, 20)

In his capacity as editor of Sir Walter Raleigh's *Cabinet Council* in 1658, he said, "I thought it a kind of injury to withhold longer the work of so eminent an author from the public; it being . . . answerable in style to other works of his already extant, as far as the subject would permit" (XVIII, 273).

We could not hope for a better summary than this last parallel affords us. Milton's style in prose and his style in verse are indeed answerable, as far as the subject (sometimes identical) would permit. The evidence gathered here, with more to come in the next three chapters, may serve to enliven the cliché that he wrote a poet's prose.

CHAPTER VI

LATIN BORROWINGS

A s HAS already been partly shown, Milton's borrowings
from himself are not confined to one language. Indeed,
if he had written more in Greek and Italian, there is
every reason to suppose that his habit of echoing himself would
have continued in those languages as it does in Latin. But, not
counting his metrical translation of the 114th Psalm, all the
Greek he has left us consists of two epigrams, one of five lines,
the other of four. The first of these yields the tag, "σοφώτατον . . .
κάρηνον" ("Philosophus ad regem," 2), which can be found in the
plural in *Tetrachordon*, "wisest heads" (IV, 207). The second
Milton came sufficiently close to starting to put into Latin. That
is to say, the opening words, "'Αμαθεῖ γεγράφθαι χειρὶ" ("In Effigiei
Ejus Sculptorem"), are verified in *Pro Se Defensio*: "me im-
perito scalptori . . . infabre scalpendum permisi" (IX, 124). We
have a little more in Italian, five sonnets and a canzone, and
(accordingly) a little more autoplagiarism. "Suoi lacci" has
already been cited (above, p. 7). *Paradise Lost*, ii, 665, "the
labouring moon," has classical precedent, but also that of Sonnet
iv, 12: "la faticosa luna." The "gentle spirit" of two evidently
autobiographical passages in the prose (III, 304, 399) likewise
has an Italian original, "spirto gentil," Sonnet ii, 4 (Petrarch
thus commences one of his poems, *Rime*, liii).

In Latin, there is every possible combination of borrowings:
within the Latin verse, within the Latin prose, between the two,
and between the Latin prose and verse and the English prose
and verse—seven possibilities, seven actualities, in all. Two of
these combinations, however, are rare. The beginning of a famous
statement in *Areopagitica* is: "Many a man lives a burden to the
earth;" (IV, 298). This harks back to Elegia II, in which the
young poet, mourning the university beadle, complains (as he
would in "Lycidas") of death's lack of discrimination: why does

it not carry off, instead, the numerous tribe "qui pondus inutile terrae" (19)? So much for the disdainful contrast with "the precious life blood" of a good beadle, or a good book. Nothing else is to be instanced between the Latin verse and the English prose except the rather common figure (in more barbarous times a reality) of the treading of feet on necks: "Sacraque calcabit pedibus tua colla profanis" ("In Q.N.," 111), "the length of that foot that is to tread on their necks" (III, 37).[1] Between the Latin verse and the Latin prose there is also something traditional, Cimmerian darkness: "Cimmeriis nati in tenebris" ("In Q.N.," 60), "Cimmeriis occlusus tenebris" (XII, 146) (equally metrical, by the way). Compare the "dark Cimmerian desert" of "L'Allegro," 10. More individually, there is the rose or other flower that breathes odors: "Iam rosa fragrantes spirat silvestris odores" ("Carmina Elegiaca," 9) (compare "fragrant smell(s)," v, 379; *P.R.*, 2, 351), "Caltha quoque et rosa . . . odores suos . . . profuse spirant" (XII, 136). This, like so much of Milton's Latin, runs over into his English, partly in

> his altar breathes
> Ambrosial odors and ambrosial flowers, (ii, 244)

partly in

> the bright consummate flower
> Spirits odorous breathes. (v, 481)

The more mechanical repetitions between the Latin poems have already been put on record (Ch. I, note 45). Sometimes the same words will have different meanings. "Diva secunda" means "second goddess" in Elegia III, 16, but "divos divasque secundas" means "favorable gods and goddesses" in "In Quintum Novembris," 129. "Obscuras umbras" alludes to the shades of night in "Mansus," 31, "obscuris umbris" to departed spirits in "Epitaphium Damonis," 22, a typical reference, however different each is, like "Fugit ad . . . Lethen," referring to the devil in "In Quintum Novembris" (132), and "Fugere Lethen," referring to an author's hope of fame in the Ode to Rous (45). Nothing could be more characteristic of this poet than his

"a (nostro) ... carmine laudes" ("In Q.N.," 194; "Ad Patrem,"
55) attitude. He combined ivy with laurel before "Lycidas"
("Ad Patrem," 102; El. VI, 16; cf. "Mansus," 6). Incidentally,
the next line of the Ode to Rous begins, "In Iovis aulam," which
is of course the "Jove's court" of the first line of *Comus*. Milton's
future as the poet of great distances is anticipated by the "in
extremis . . . oris" (El. III, 49), "extremis . . . ab oris" ("In
Q.N.," 116) and the "uterque polus" (El. I, 56; "Naturam Non
Pati Senium," 21) ("from pole to pole," iii, 560; ix, 66) recurrences. He put "This pendent world" (ii, 1052), "The pendulous
round earth" (iv, 1000) into Latin verse twice, too, "pendulus
orbis" (El. I, 76), "pendulum telluris orbem" ("In Obitum
Procancellarii Medici," 3). Likewise he tried the trick "Fallor?
an et" to begin lines in three different poems (El. V, 5; El. VII,
56; "In Prodit. Bomb.," 3) before he carried it over into English
in *Comus*, "Was I deceived? or" (221). There were "Tartareos
ignes et luridum olentia sulphur" ("In Q.N.," 35), "Tartareo
sublime rotatus ab igne" ("In Prodit. Bomb." III, 11), before
there were "Tartarean sulphur and strange fire" (ii, 69), "fire,
Sublimed with mineral fury" (i, 235). The "proles Iunonia,"
Vulcan or Mulciber, fell before Adam. Indeed, the two lines
must be quoted, for "Qualis in Aegaeam proles Iunonia Lemnon"
("Naturam," 23) gives us "On Lemnos, th'Aegean isle" (i, 746),
and "Sic dolet amissum proles Iunonia caelum" (El. VII, 81)
gives us nothing less than a "paradise lost" situation.

The Latin poems were, again and again, a proving ground for
expressions and images that are famous in English. For example,
the air is made to seem exceptionally solid in *Paradise Lost*,
even when it is not called "marble":

> winds with ease
> Through the pure marble air his oblique way
> Amongst innumerable stars, (iii, 563)

a word that editors, from Hume on, hasten to explain means
" glistering." Nevertheless, the impression here and elsewhere
is that Satan or other winged creature must steer carefully in

order to avoid bumping into something. The medium itself is dense, like water, calls for swimming or oarage:

> piceis liquido natat aere pennis; (" In Q. N.," 45)

(we get "with black wings" with reference to the south wind in *Paradise Lost,* xi, 738)

> pennis cedentes remigat auras ("In Q. N.," 208)

> In Iovis aulam remige penna ("Ad Rous.," 46)

> then with quick fan
> Winnows the buxom air (v, 269)

> Wing silently the buxom air. (ii, 842)

"Buxom" means yielding ("cedentes auras"), but it is odd, and corroborates the present point, that this has to be said: we see the effort that these superhuman creatures have to make to get somewhere. Of course it can be, and has been, remarked that Milton inherited some of this from Virgil's description of Mercury: "Volat ille per aëra magnum Remigio alarum" (*Aen.* I, 300). Still, his palpable air goes with the rest of his "materialism" in *Paradise Lost,* a materialism that can never be totally avoided by a poet who sets out to make the abstract concrete, but was particularly congenial to this poet and his early tendency. It is all part of the same picture that he prefers to believe in "chaos" rather than in "nothing," and gives his angels a good, detailed digestive system.

The scorner of "our late fantastics" came closest to imitating them when he wrote, in the Nativity Hymn:

> So when the Sun in bed,
> Curtain'd with cloudy red,
> Pillows his chin upon an orient wave, (229)

an image he was well on the way to in the "Carmina Elegiaca": "Flammiger Eois Titan caput exerit undis" (5). A line that Professor Stoll is fond of quoting as symptomatic of Milton's romanticism,[2] "Where the bowed welkin slow doth bend" (*Comus,* 1015), is a happy development from "longo flectens cur-

vamine caelos" ("In Q.N.," 166). This has been noticed often
enough, as has the descent of "unexpressive nuptial song"
("Lycidas," 176) from "inenarrabile carmen" ("Ad Patrem,"
37). In all these cases the English version is more daring. So it
is with "Unhoused thy virgin soul from her fair biding place"
("Fair Infant," 21), "unhoused" representing a conceit not
present in "Semideamque animam sede fugasse sua" (El. III,
30). But it is good, Milton concludes, to be rid of "this earthy
load" (Son. xiv, 3), "mole carnea" ("In Obitum Praesulis
Eliensis," 37).

In the last named elegy the poet has heard a voice bidding
him cease his outbursts against death: "Caecos furores pone"
(27). This comprises a pun, the meaning shifting if one letter is
capitalized: "Set aside the blind Furies," an interpretation encouraged by the following lines: "Quid temere violas non nocenda
numina, Subitoque ad iras percita?" And in line 33 the Fury
(singular) is present, "Erinnye." So we may well say that, with
marked steps, "Comes the blind Fury with th' abhorred shears"
of "Lycidas" (75)—a frenzy also to be quieted with a voice,
Phoebus's. Likewise the last lines of "In Proditionem Bombardi-
cam" II prepare for the Paradise of Fools, "in caelum pelle cu-
cullos" (7) curiously foreshadowing "Blows them . . . Into the
devious air . . . Cowls" (iii, 488).

In other cases the translation is straightforward. "Pater
omnipotens" ("Naturam," 33) is "the Almighty Father" (iii, 56,
386; vi, 671; vii, 11), "Aethereus Pater" ("In Q.N.," 221)
"Celestial Father" (v, 403), "sempiterni . . . patris" ("In Obitum
Praesulis Eliensis," 41), "the Eternal Father" (above, p. 34).
"Muta silentia" ("In Q.N.," 149) is associated with darkness by
way of Ovid (*Met.*, VII, 184), and so too "the mute silence" in
"Il Penseroso" (55). "L'Allegro" says, "And ever against eating
cares, Lap me in soft Lydian airs" (136). What song is asked to
do here Damon's friendship had done, but alas can no longer do,
athwart "Mordaces curas" ("Epit. Dam.," 46). "The dragon
womb Of Stygian darkness" (*Comus*, 131) has its original in
"Stygiis quae vivas clausa tenebris" (El. IV, 95), except for
the dragon, which has been otherwise accounted for (above, p.

57). Other dragons, some commentators opine they are the same,
are those of the line in "Il Penseroso," "While Cynthia checks
her dragon yoke" (59), which goes back to this reference to the
moon goddess in "In Obitum Praesulis Eliensis" (57), "dum
coercebat suos Fraenis dracones aureis." After having written,
"The folded flocks penned in their wattled cotes" (*Comus*, 344),
Milton turned, *mutatis mutandis*, the line of blank verse into
a Latin hexameter: "Dum solus teneros claudebam cratibus
haedos" ("Epit. Dam.," 141). If *Comus* has,

> We, that are of purer fire,
> Imitate the starry choir,
> Who, in their nightly watchful spheres,
> Lead in swift round the months and years, (111)

"Ad Patrem," close in time to it, has

> Spiritus et rapidos qui circinat igneus orbes
> Nunc quoque sidereis intercinit ipse choreis, (35)

the same conglomeration: starry choir, fire, spheres, swift round.
There were "Volatiles . . . milites", "winged warrior(s)", early
and late ("In Obit. P.E.," 47; "Circumcision," 1; iv, 576).
"Sedesque beatas" referred to an academic retreat ("Rousium,"
76) before the poet began to write of "the blissful seat" of
Paradise (i, 5; iii, 527). Due allowance made for the difference
in mothers, "Whom lovely Venus, at a birth . . . bore" ("L'Allegro," 14) is "Effera quos uno peperit Discordia partu" ("In
Q.N.," 142). A still more productive mother is Nature or Earth,
the "rerum publica mater" with the "Omniparum . . . uterum"
("Naturam," 10). She gives Eve her wide choice in the preparation of a meal: "Whatever Earth, all-bearing mother, yields"
(v, 338). And, to complete the listing in this category, a multiple
birth of this mother is flies, which, having served Homer as a
simile, serve Milton in two epics, "Qualiter . . . Agmina mus-
carum" ("In Q.N.," 179), "Or as a swarm of flies" (*P.R.*, 4, 15).

A relatively unfruitful category is the borrowings within the
Latin prose. They are numerous, but may prudently be consigned
to the notes.[3] We reap a more interesting harvest by going back
and forth between the Latin prose and the English prose. Here

we find the old appeals, to "wisest men" (see above, p. 88), "sapientissimorum virorum judicio" (VII, 168), "Virorum . . . sapientissimorum" (VII, 190), to authorities, "Lutherum nempe, Zuinglium, Calvinum, Bucerum, Paraeum" (VII, 64), "Lutheris, Zwingliis, Calvinis, Buceris, Martyribus, Paraeis" (VII, 202), "Luthero, Zuinglio, Calvino, Bucero, Martyre, Paraeo" (VIII, 202), "Lutherus, Calvinus, Zuinglius, Bucerus" (VII, 346) (cf. IV, 10, 224). It was the "tyranny of prelates" (III, 62, 69) which could not be borne; now it is "tyrannidem pontificiam" (VII, 34). If the opposition used "false and frivolous" words (above, p. 78), it still does: "Multa falsa, multa frivola" (VII, 496). "Ambition and avarice" (III, 98) "avarice and ambition" (III, 163) still put on a pious front: "avaritiam et ambitionem" (VII, 132), "avaritia(m) . . . ambitione(m)" (VII, 60; VIII, 240). (Milton anticipates "precious bane," i, 692, by calling "pecunia, ecclesiae toxicum," VIII, 234.) We know what weapons Milton brought to bear against "tyranny and superstition" (IV, 294). He desperately reminds the readers of *The Ready and Easy Way* of "our victory at once against two the most prevailing usurpers over mankind, superstition and tyranny" (VI, 116). This was, whether Milton expected it to be recognized or not, an echo from the exhortation closing the *Defensio Prima*: "Quae duo in vita hominum mala sane maxima sunt, et virtuti damnosissima, tyrannis et superstitio" (VII, 552). But the Good Old Cause is lost. It is the old story of the Circean cup: "dabitur sane Circaeum poculum" (XII, 280); "like men enchanted with the Circean cup of servitude" (V, 204). He once argued, against Old Testament citation, "A servitute regum Aegyptiorum ideo liberatus, ut uni ex fratribus suis duriore si libuisset servitute opprimendus traderetur?" (VII, 98). But these words are but too applicable to the majority of the English people in 1659-1660, "qui servitutis olim Aegyptiacae desiderio capti" (VII, 544), "when so great a part of the nation were desperately conspired to call back again their Egyptian bondage" (VI, 102). However much stock this idealist may have put in "the persuasive power in man" (III, 165), "eloquentiam . . . vimque ejus demonstrativam" (IX, 222), however much truth can be grasped even "by meanest capacities" (VI, 76), "whereof the meanest understanding may be apprehensive" (III, 346), "nihil vel ad infimi cuiusque captum accommodatius" (XV, 264), "base minds" (VI, 270), "viles et imbelles animos" (VII, 20), prevail. The state was not ready for his kind of stability: "at least the foundation firmly laid of a free commonwealth" (VI, 125) (compare "laying everywhere the firm foundation of a long peace," X, 96), "for what can be expected firm or steadfast from a floating foundation" (VI, 128), "jacta strenue fundamenta fuisse" (VIII, 254), "stabilivisse se regnum, multoque majus ac diuturnius . . ." (VII, 214). He had often appealed to the Parliament in vain; the present effort, which would have had to convince a still wider audience, was even more foredoomed, "the last words of our expiring liberty" (VI, 148), "vindicata libertas quam prope extincta apud vos" (VII, 18). Liberty becomes something to recover: "ancient liberty recovered to heroic poem from the troublesome and modern bondage of rhyming" (II, 6), "libertas pristina impetrari" (XIII, 442), "ad libertatem pristinam restitutio" (XV, 370), "summo denique recuperandae libertatis pristinae studio" (XII, 58).[4]

What is the use of abundance of argument—"hac ego argumenti faecunditate nimia laboro" (XII, 252), "the abundance of argument that presses to be uttered" (IV, 108)—against those who will not listen? Luxury (which means dissipation, "lewdly pampered luxury," Comus, 770) and sloth go together, and both with slavery: "broken with luxury and sloth" (X, 198), "luxus et segnities" (VII, 256), "ignavia atque luxuria" (VII, 510). "With what unbounded license" (III, 372), "effraenatam licentiam" (VIII, 8), refers to moral corruption; "effraenata quadam licentia" (XI, 2) to mental confusion. The connection between doing right and knowing right is obvious. So a barbarous style, such as that of the monkish chroniclers, "in expression barbarous" (X, 101), or a student orator's fear of "quicquid est barbarae, incultae et obsoletae locutionis" (XII, 214) in his own prolusion, can generate something resembling moral indignation. But Milton was never one to be overawed by "huge tomes" (III, 358), "great books" (VI, 41), "immania . . . volumina" (XII,

158), "ingentia . . . volumina" (XII, 174). (In Elegy IV he pictured his former teacher, Young, leafing through the "veterum praelarga volumina Patrum," 43, and there is faint distaste even here.)

It is "majestate plenius" (VIII, 158) to try a king than to put him to death without trial. This recalls another kingly reference, to an emperor of Russia: "no less was his countenance full of majesty" (X, 368). But this is standard.[5] It contrasts with the grim reference to the King in *Eikonoklastes,* he "knew not that the like fate [Hotham's] attended him" (V, 149), which next forms a threat to Salmasius, as part of a comparison between him and Judas, "quin te etiam idem exitus maneat" (VII, 550).

Sumner (XVII, 482) noted "a remarkable similarity" between the remark in *De Doctrina Christiana,* "Partes doctrinae Christianae duae sunt: Fides seu cognitio Dei, et Charitas seu Dei cultus" (XIV, 22), and that in *A Treatise of Civil Power in Ecclesiastical Causes*: "What evangelic religion is, is told in two words, Faith and Charity, or Belief and Practice" (VI, 21). This is the first in a series of verbal parallels involving *De Doctrina Christiana* that Sumner gathered. Nearly all of those now to be pointed to were first cited by him, and it must be admitted that, as regards both the English prose and the English verse, they make an impressive sum. They range from small phrases like "limbus patrum" (III, 353; abl. XVII, 310) and "implicit faith" (VI, 170), "fidem implicitam" (XVI, 266); through proverbs or traditional observations like "where else are all our grave and faithful sayings, that he whose office is to forbid and forbids not, bids, exhorts, encourages?" (IV, 156), "Sed vulgo dictum est, Qui non prohibet cum potest, Iubet" (XV, 76), and "the form, by which the thing is what it is" (IV, 101), "Forma est causa per quam res est id quod est" (XI, 58), "sic enim forma definitur, per quam res est id quod est " (XVII, 8), " essentiam suam, per quam est id quod est" (XIV, 220); on to more typically controversial or more individual doctrines and literary devices. To take the last first, a device we have come to associate with Milton (though it is more than a manner of

speaking, and is by no means confined to him) is invocation of
divine aid in commencing a work. This comes prefatory to
Milton's wrestling with the difficult question, "De Filio Dei":
"Nunc divina ope subnixi rem ipsam aggrediamur" (XIV, 178).
It initiates his longest work in English prose: "imploring divine
assistance . . . I now begin" (X, 3) and his grand *Defensio Prima*:
"Ad divinam opem recurro" (VII, 8). Indeed, God himself is
found to speak like one deliberating on the verge of creation.
"God here presents himself like to a man deliberating . . . to
show us that the matter is of high consequence" (IV, 84).
"Facturus autem hominem Deus tanquam maius adhuc opus,
consultanti similis praefatur" (XV, 36).

We can pass in bilingual review various doctrines that Milton
stood for. "It will not be denied that in the Gospel there be but
two ministerial degrees, presbyters and deacons" (VI, 53).
"Ecclesiae particularis ministri ordinarii sunt presbyteri et dia-
coni" (XVI, 286). "But the gospel is our manhood" (III, 363).
"Sub evangelio et baptismo nascimur viri" (XVI, 178). "We
[are] now under Christ, a royal priesthood" (VI, 57); "cum in
Christo aeque omnes sacerdotes simus" (XVI, 208). "Every true
Christian . . . hath . . . the mind of Christ within" (VI, 7), "habet
mentem Christi" (XVI, 264). "He hath revealed and taught . . .
us in the Holy Scriptures . . . with strictest command to reject
all other traditions" (VI, 166). "Humanae autem traditiones
sive scriptae sive non scriptae palam prohibentur" (XVI, 280).

I Corinthians v, 5 means expulsion "from the fold of Christ
and kingdom of grace to the world again, which is the kingdom
of Satan" (VI, 38), "id est rursus mundo, qui extra ecclesiam
cum sit, Satanae regnum est" (XVI, 332). Those who seek
emoluments within the Church have strayed into the wrong
kingdom. "For if it must be thus, how can any Christian object
it to a Turk, that his religion stands by force only; and not justly
fear from him this reply, yours both by force and money, in
the judgment of your own preachers?" (VI, 97). "Immo vero si
vi et pecunia stat Christiana religio atque fulcitur, quid est
quamobrem non aeque ac Turcarum religio suspecta esse videatur" (XVI, 298)? They should be ashamed, those "who cry

out with the distinct voice of notorious hirelings, that if ye settle
not our maintenance by law, farewell the Gospel" (VI, 97),
"si ecclesiasticos tollis reditus, actum est de evangelio" (XVI,
298). These are the wolves, or at least greedy sheep rather than
shepherds. "They have fed themselves, and not their flocks"
(III, 170): "Pascuntur magis quam pascunt" (VIII, 180). "Non
gregi suo, sed ipsi sibi laetiora subinde pascua sectantur" (XVI,
302). It is small wonder that the Church split up. "The Christian Church is universal, not tied to nation," but "consisting
of many particular churches complete in themselves" (VI, 64),
"seeing the Christian Church is not national, but consisting of
many particular congregations" (VI, 83), "nunc nationalis nulla
est, particulares vero sunt multae" (XVI, 308).

Of more immediate interest is the parallel between a passage
in the *Areopagitica*:

It was from out of the rind of one apple tasted . . . the knowledge
of good and evil . . .   And perhaps this is that doom which Adam fell
into of knowing good and evil, that is to say, of knowing good by
evil; (IV, 310-11)

and this in *De Doctrina Christiana*:

Dicta est autem scientiae boni et mali ab eventu: post eam enim
degustatam, non malum tantummodo scimus, sed ne bonum quidem
nisi per malum; (XV, 114)

which elucidates a point that many miss in *Paradise Lost*. Incidentally, what Milton says in the Argument to Book I of that
poem, "that Angels were long before this visible creation was
the opinion of many ancient Fathers," he elsewhere confirms:
"Multi certe ex Patribus Graecis, et nonnulli ex Latinis, angelos,
utpote spiritus corporeo hoc mundo longe prius extitisse cen-
suerunt" (XV, 32). For a like reason the hell which received the
fallen angels is "not in the Centre (for heaven and earth may be
supposed as yet not made, certainly not yet accursed)," "veri-
simile non est, ut infernus intra mundum, et visceribus terrae
nondum maledictae pararetur" (XVI, 374).[6]

The seventh and last category—Latin prose-English verse
—one would not expect to be fruitful, but actually it yields some

of the outstanding specimens of cross-fertilization. Four or five
of these were seen in the first chapter. Others come, again, from
De Doctrina Christiana. Austere though that treatise is, it turns
out to have an impressive number of coincidences of phrasing
with *Paradise Lost*. If it was the poet's purpose to "assert Eternal
Providence,/And justify the ways of God" (i, 25), so it is the
theologian's, "ad asserendam iustitiam Dei" (XV, 212). Neither
will allow "least . . . shadow of fate" (iii, 120), "minimam neces-
sitatis umbram" (XIV, 76) on man's free will.

> But God left free the Will; for what obeys
> Reason is free; (ix, 351)

Decrevit Deus . . . angelos atque homines rationis, adeoque liberae
voluntatis compotes creare. (XIV, 82)

Creatures cannot justly accuse their Maker,

> As if Predestination overruled
> Their will, disposed by absolute decree
> Or high foreknowledge. (iii, 114)

non ex praescientia Dei tandem producitur . . . sic novit Adamum sua
sponte lapsurum . . . non necessario, quia sponte sua. (XIV, 84-86)

Not seldom the treatise explicates the poem, as when the wide
meaning of death is given: "Mala autem omnia et quicquid
ducere ad interitum videtur, sub mortis nomine summatim Scrip-
tura complectitur" (XV, 202), a convenient gloss on "Brought
death into the World, and all our woe" (i, 3).[7]

Lessons in close translation are to be had from examining
the designation of subjects, such as "the whole race of mankind"
(iii, 161), "hominumque genus universum" (XVI, 354; cf. "uni-
verso generi humano," VII, 74).

> Why should not Man,
> Retaining still divine similitude
> In part (xi, 511)

is "Quaedam enim in homine reliquiae sunt imaginis divinae"
(XIV, 128), "restare adhuc aliquas imaginis divinae in nobis
reliquias" (XV, 208), which appears as English prose in *Tetra-*

chordon: "For there are left some remains of God's image in man" (IV, 80). As for the Savior,

> his obedience
> Imputed becomes theirs by faith—his merits
> To save them (xii, 408)

which is "sic iustitia sive merita Christi per fidem imputantur nobis" (XVI, 26). Before, there had been law:

> And therefore was law given them, to evince
> Their natural pravity, by stirring up
> Sin against Law to fight, (xii, 287)

Quae causae totius legis ferendae afferuntur praecipue, ad pravitatem videlicet nostram irritandam. (XVI, 130)

Christ was "of all creation first" (iii, 383), "rerum creatarum primum" (XIV, 180). The angels sing of God's Son, "on thee/ Impressed the effulgence of his glory abides" (iii, 388), which, more than the other "effulgence of . . . glory" passage (vi, 680), translates "filio qui effulgentia gloriae illius et character substantiae est" (XIV, 340). Another sort of impressing is wrought by the Holy Spirit: "His Spirit within them, and the law of faith/Working through love upon their hearts shall write" (xii, 488), "what the Spirit within/Shall on the heart engrave" (xii, 523), "inde fidelium cordibus per Sanctum Spiritum inscripta" (XVI, 112), "Christus internam Dei legem per spiritum suum fidelium cordibus inscribit" (XVI, 150), "the law was then written on tables of stone . . . the gospel, our new covenant, upon the heart of every believer" (VI, 25). "In likeness of a dove/The Spirit descended" (*P.R.*, 1, 30). "Descensio igitur, et columbina species illa spiritus sancti" (XIV, 366). But there is no faith without works, the call being for "Deeds . . . answerable" (xii, 582), "facta . . . respondeant" (XVI, 356). As it is understood, however, of God: " 'No need that thou/Should'st propagate' " (viii, 419), "qui propagatione prorsus non indiget" (XIV, 186), so it follows, " 'God doth not need . . . man's work' " (Son. xix, 9), "iis operibus . . . quibus omnino non indiget Deus" (XVII, 22). This is oddly like Jesus' logic against reading, " 'And what he brings what needs he elsewhere seek?' " (*P.R.*, 4, 325). So Milton reasons on the Son, "Si homo et summus ipse Deus, cur omino petiit quod penes se erat?" (XIV, 230).

The angels are the "sons of God" (v, 447; cf. xi, 622; *P.R.*, 1, 368; 4, 197; cf. 2, 179; 4, 520), "filii Dei" (XV, 34). They "circle his throne" (v, 163), "circa thronum Dei stant" (XV, 100). Michael is "the Prince of Angels" (vi, 281), "angelorum princeps . . . Michael" (XV, 104), even as Satan is "the author of all ill" (ii, 381), "Author of Evil" (vi, 262), "omnis auctor maleficii" (XV, 110), and Eve "Mother of all things living" (xi, 160), "matrem viventium" (XV, 44). "Amor . . . coniugalis" (XV, 176; abl. XVI, 64), "conjugal love" (ix, 263) continues to figure largely. A wife can be "a thorn/Intestine" (*S.A.*, 1037), a noun implicit in "Malum . . . intestinum . . . amoliri" (XV, 156).

"With sincere intent" (iii, 192) is "sincero animo" (XVI, 164), "With grateful memory" (viii, 650), "grata recordatione" (XVI, 164). Milton's English in some cases makes better Latin. "Let us with a gladsome mind/Praise the Lord, for He is kind" does not seem to be very close as a translation ("Psalm CXXXVI"), and does ring quaintly, like the boyish production it is supposed to be. We can contrast Milton's Latin in maturity: "Gratiarum actio est qua pro divinis beneficiis laeto animo gratias agimus" (XVII, 118). Sumner pauses over "in profluentem aquam" (XVI, 168) as illuminating "in the profluent stream" (xii, 442). The same commentator accounts for "through all numbers absolute, though One" (viii, 421) as "a Ciceronian expression" imitated elsewhere: "suis in se numeris omnes absolutae" (XVI, 310), "per se ipse Parlamentum omnibus numeris absolutum et legitimum . . . constituebat" (VII, 488), "hypocritam numeris omnibus absolutum" (IX, 142).

Other coincidences derive from the letters and prolusions. In the seventh of the latter, that eloquent defense of knowledge, Milton has a lofty reference to the "magnum mundi opificem" (XII, 252)—"the great Architect" of the passage where Raphael parries Adam's inquiries "concerning celestial motions":

the great Architect
Did wisely to conceal, and not divulge
His secrets, to be scanned by them who ought
Rather admire." (viii, **72**)

The change in attitude does not necessitate a complete change
in phrasing. The young Milton strained for the "summa . . .
sapientia" (XII, 26), which "highest wisdom" (vii, 83) the
mature Milton knew belonged to Heaven alone.

If "the songs of Sirens" (*Comus*, 878), "Sirenum cantus"
(XII, 98), represents no rare allusion, the same cannot be said
of the formation of the great simile,

—which cost Ceres all that pain
To seek her through the world—(iv, **271**)

which is foreshadowed with remarkable closeness in an early
letter: "Nec tanto Ceres labore, ut in fabulis est, Liberam fertur
quaesivisse filiam" (XII, 26). "That" in the poem is *ille*—"the
famous," which compresses "ut in fabulis est" and "fertur."
The rest (like "that," for that matter) is simply inspired translation. All that is wanting is "through the world"—and that is
supplied in another early Ceres simile, "per universum terrarum
orbem . . . quaerat" (XII, 166)!

Nor is the famous prayer,

So much the rather thou, Celestial Light,
Shine inward, (iii, **51**)

unprecedented. The blind author was conscious of this inward
illumination at the time of the *Defensio Secunda*: "illustrare
rursus interiore ac longe praestabiliore lumine haud raro solet"
(VIII, 72). Here is another instructive case of a poet's translation, in the course of which "ac longe praestabiliore"—with a
happy transition from the adjectival to the adverbial—becomes
"so much the rather," and "interiore" "inward." The continu-
ation of the invocation,

and the mind through all her powers
Irradiate;

has the essential verb also to be found in this part of the *Defensio Secunda*: "possim in hac obscuritate sic ego irradiari." Indeed the respective passages warrant very careful comparison, their relations being intimate and complicated. It is here, in the poem, that Milton misses the "human face divine" (iii, 44). But in the prose he says, "in meis tenebris divini vultus lumen eo clarius eluceat." This, which also could have influenced "So much the rather," may, the "divini vultus," have prepared for "human face divine" (anthropomorphism in reverse—theomorphism). But perhaps the foundations for that were rather laid in the *Defensio Prima*: "divinum, ut ita dicam, hominum genus" (VII, 114; cf. 72).

Additionally, this fruitful page of the *Defensio Secunda* yields something worth carrying off as a prize by those who like to connect Milton with his dynamic Satan. The particular link is the phrase "immortalis . . . vigor"—"Immortal vigor." The Latin reads:

Est quoddam per imbecillitatem, praeeunte Apostolo, ad maximas vires iter: sim ego debilissimus, dummodo in mea debilitate immortalis ille et melior vigor eo se efficacius exerat. (VIII, 72)

This transports us to, not this time the beginning of the third, but of the second book of *Paradise Lost*, Satan's speech from the throne:

> since no deep within her gulf can hold
> Immortal vigor, though oppressed and fall'n,
> I give not Heaven for lost: from this descent
> Celestial Virtues rising will appear
> More glorious and more dread than from no fall. (12)

There is no difficulty about applying this to Milton's situation, except possibly the words "fall'n" and "fall." If these can be understood as referring to his blindness and his defeat in the cause for which he fought (as if he had been repudiated by God —in any case, he does use "fallen" of himself, "on evil days though fallen"—and can recover from despair only by what

some would call rationalizing), the passage is emotionally as
well as verbally related to the words about his blindness in
Defensio Secunda. The "within her gulf" is "in meis tenebris"
(the familiar darkness-hell equation), and we have seen how he
expected to rise more glorious out of weakness—the world knows
how he did rise—and could still boast of the light of the divine
countenance. He says "maximas vires," but is moving toward—
with "immortalis . . . vigor" very nearly reaches—the adjective
that the blasphemer does not hesitate to use, "Celestial Virtues."
Of course both sides in the still surprisingly lively Milton-Satan
identification controversy differ only in the degree of identification they will allow or claim. Sometimes they appear to differ
only in the phrasing to be used to sum up their identical impressions. The elementary fact persists, however much ignored, that
some degree of self-identification is the *sine qua non* of an
author's projection of a major character. One ought to keep in
mind, too, Keats's observation: "The poetical character itself
. . . has as much delight in conceiving an Iago as an Imogen.
What shocks the virtuous philosopher delights the chameleon
poet." [8] This is still applicable, if less applicable to Milton than
to Shakespeare.

We regularly find Milton using more words in the Latin prose
version of a thought. This is not the difference between two
languages but between the media of prose and verse. In concluding *Defensio Secunda*, he passes from praise of his fellow
citizens' deeds in war to an exhortation to beware of various
tyrants within their own breasts, now that peace has come.
"Hos vincite in primis, haec pacis militia est, hae sunt victoriae, difficiles quidem, at incruentae, illis bellicis et cruentis
longe pulchriores" (VIII, 240-242). These words, published in
1654, recall the words of the Sonnet to Cromwell, May, 1652.
The octet commemorated his military successes. The sestet struck
a different note:

> yet much remains
> To conquer still; Peace hath her victories
> No less renowned than War.

The fifteen words here as opposed to twenty-one above (and the Latin goes on and on in the same vein) does not, of course, mean that Latin requires more words for a thought than English. The reverse is the case. It is easy to prune Milton's Latin sentence to show how, if the economy of verse had been at all his aim, he could have taken advantage of the natural economy of the one language as compared to the other: "Hos vincite . . . pacis . . . hae sunt victoriae . . . illis bellicis . . . pulchriores." As for the difference in the adjective, it would have been ungracious and unbalanced for Milton to lessen praise of Cromwell's feats of generalship by speculating on his possibly still "pulchriores" future peaceful victories. But as a moralist addressing his countrymen at large, he does not hesitate to put the emphasis where he thinks it belongs, even as, in the same work, he addresses Cromwell in an admonitory tone.

The young poet sang that Christ would "with His Father work us a perpetual peace" (Nativity Hymn, 7). The publicist points to a pact of "perpetuam pacem" or "pacem . . . perpetuam" with the United Provinces (XVIII, 94; VIII, 194), or to hopes of the same among all the Protestant peoples (XIII, 258).

Relatively straightforward and unindividual, probably accidental, is a case of correspondence between an illustration in *Accidence Commenced* and a line or two of *Comus*. To show that "quandoquidem" takes the indicative, Milton writes, "Dicite quandoquidem in molli consedimus herba" (VI, 350; cf. "mollior herba," "Epit. Dam.," 130). If we get "tender grass" in *Paradise Lost* (vii, 315), we get "tender grass" in connection with sitting and telling in *Comus*:

> Which when I did [i. e. sing], he on the tender grass
> Would sit . . .
> Telling . . . (624)

a parallel not spoiled by the telling's being three lines removed from the sitting. The situation, the language, is traditional, like the path of virtue–hill of virtue complex:

whereas the paths of honesty and good life appear now rugged and difficult, though they be indeed easy and pleasant, they would then

appear to all men both easy and pleasant, though they were rugged
and difficult indeed. (III, 239)

which way will lead him best to this hilltop of sanctity and goodness
above which there is no higher ascent . . . . (III, 261)

That labor up the hill of heavenly Truth. (Son. ix, 4)

Viam virtutis . . . illam arduam ac difficilem, qui solius virtutis clivus
est, tua sponte libentius, etiam cum labore ac periculo, possis ascen-
dere. (XII, 112)

. . . on the top of Virtue's hill. (*P. R.*, 2, 217)

When the poet wrote "To a Virtuous Young Lady," "Lady, that
. . . Wisely hast shunned the broad way and the green," he may
have been thinking of what he was grateful to his father for:
"Neque enim, pater, ire iubebas Qua via lata patet" ("Ad
Patrem," 69). "Hard are the ways of truth, and rough to walk"
(P.R., 1, 478). The allegory, as old as the Choice of Hercules and
the *Works and Days* of Hesiod (287 ff.), was to be rejuvenated
by Bunyan, with his Hill Difficulty and the many places where
his pilgrims come to a parting of the ways, where the path that
looks hard is the only right one. Milton still has the view of
"certamen virtutis gloriosissimum" (VIII, 6). But, as we have
noted, "glorious trial" is ironic when it appears in *Paradise Lost*
(ix, 961, 1177).

The virtuous and the knowing are in a minority. "Fit audience find, though few" (vii, 31) is but the best-known phrasing
of a proud, lifelong stand. He was already telling his fellow under-
graduates in his First Prolusion, telling an audience who, with
few exceptions, stared at him with hostile bias: "A quibus etiam
quantumvis paucis, equidem probari malo quam ab innumeris
imperitorum centuriis" (XII, 120). In 1645 he presented a
volume of his tracts to Patrick Young, the King's Librarian, with
this inscription: "Ad doctissimum virum, Patricium Junium,
Joannes Miltonius haec sua, unum in fasculum conjecta mittit,
paucis hujusmodi lectoribus contentus" (XVIII, 269). He knew
his *Doctrine and Discipline of Divorce* would be unpopular, but
calmly awaited its reception "among the wise and right under-

standing handful of men" (III, 377). In the Preface to *Eikono-klastes* he declared that the truth he was offering would "find out her own readers: few perhaps, but those few, such of value and substantial worth, as truth and wisdom, not respecting numbers and big names, have been ever wont in all ages to be contented with" (V, 65). "In a graceless age" "they who adhere to wisdom and to truth" are "so few as to seem a sect or faction" (V, 73-74). The attitude governs his politics as well as his poetry: "qui prudentia, qui rerum usu, industria, atque virtute pollent, hi mea quidem sententia, quantumvis paucis, quantovis numero, plures erunt, et suffragiis ubique potiores" (VIII, 154).

CHAPTER VII

WOMEN AND BISHOPS

H ow SIGNIFICANT can a parallel be? One of Milton's principal preoccupations is, as everyone knows, the position
of women. References to Eve and her daughters have
naturally not been infrequent in this review, however specialized, and it cannot have escaped notice, moreover, how often
they are associated with something sinister—snares and devils
in particular. The purpose of the present chapter is to present
several parallels not pointed to before and to show, by delving
into the background, how accurately they sum up Milton's attitude toward women, which turns out, after all, to be not very
different emotionally from his attitude towards episcopacy and
the Roman Church.

The topic, "Milton and Women," has regularly, until recent
years, generated more heat than light. The misconceptions got
off to an early start when Mrs. Sadleir, in the winter of 1652-
53, wrote Roger Williams: "For Milton's book [*Eikonoklastes*],
that you desire I should read, if I be not mistaken, that is he
that has wrote a book of the lawfulness of divorce; and, if
report says true, he had, at that time, two or three wives living.
This, perhaps, were good doctrine in New England; but it is
most abominable in Old England." [1] This, to be sure, illustrates
the general scandal and confusion that will prevail through the
centuries, rather than exaggeration on the particular point with
which we are concerned. That we begin to get with the *Lettres
Critiques sur le Paradis Perdu* by Bernard Routh (1731). The
conversation in Eden, this critic remarks, is no doubt charming;
but its charm is "un peu gâté quelquefois par le soin que prend
Adam de rappeler trop souvent à Ève son autorité sur elle, la
supériorité de ses talents et le besoin qu'elle a de lui, les défauts
qu'il lui trouve, etc. De pareilles leçons ont bien mauvaise grâce
dans la bouche d'un honnête homme et d'un tendre époux." [2]
Here is the typically French impatience with didacticism in a

poem designed for adults. Adam and Eve must not be human beings only: they must also be models. It is idle to resent, and wrong to ignore, the double obligation under which the poet labored in presenting the first man and the first woman. At all events, Routh is temperate compared to Dr. Johnson, who states in his "Life of Milton": "There appears in his books something like a Turkish contempt of females, as subordinate and inferior beings." [3] To borrow a phrase, this comes with "bien mauvaise grâce" from one who is famous for having remarked, "Sir, a woman's preaching is like a dog's walking on his hind legs. It is not done well; but you are surprised to find it done at all," [4] and who sent to Mrs. Thrale from Auchinleck this impression of Boswell's wife: "She is in a proper degree inferior to her husband; she cannot rival him; nor can he ever be ashamed of her." [5] That Johnson had prejudices is well known (was well known even to Johnson!), but it is surprising how often this particular view of Milton gets echoed. To skip to our own century, the author of a short life of Milton that appeared in the reign of Edward VII pauses thus after his account of the poet's first marriage: "This is a convenient place to say that Milton's views concerning the relative position of man and woman were more akin to those that prevail in Oriental countries than to the opinions held in our own day among Western people." [6] No wonder the writer feels obliged to admit, in his Preface, having "had continually by my side . . . Johnson's *Life*"! [7] The unhistorical view died hard. Perhaps it will be enough to call two distinguished witnesses more, these from the liberal age of Victoria. W. E. Gladstone charged Milton with "conceptions as to the character and office of Christian women, and the laws and institutions affecting them, which descend below historic heathenism, and approximate even to brutality." [8] George Saintsbury, in an early book, considered it to be among the "propositions which I cannot conceive to be disputed by any competent critic aware of the facts" that Milton "held in the most peremptory and exaggerated fashion the doctrine of the superiority of man to woman." [9]

Only with modern historical critics has sanity replaced vituperation, and the demonstration come that Milton's view is "of an age" and is moreover fully supported, if not occasioned, by the Bible. (Dowden, before the nineteenth century was out, declared Milton's attitude "Hebraic" [10]: "Pauline" has been much and properly used since.)

Now it happens that the key to Milton's attitude is in two words, two words that he uses in three widely scattered places: the *Doctrine and Discipline of Divorce* (III, 475), *Paradise Regained* (2, 219), and the *History of Britain* (X, 60). The two words are "female pride." And the best, as well as the freshest place, in which to make sure of his attitude is in that important and much neglected work last named.

There is reason to believe that in the *History of Britain* Milton was giving vent to a passing mood, but it was—if ever these words are to be applied to his writing—sharp and arrogant while it lasted. Herein we have a contrast with the evidence usually cited. Just preceding the composition of the early books of the *History* had come the divorce tracts, where the author made an heroic effort at impersonality, and perhaps only his images betray him; it would take a very sensitive critic to analyze them. Years later came *Paradise Lost* and *Samson Agonistes*, where, as Professor Gilbert has warned,[11] the interpreter must tread lightly, for the poet in the angry outbursts of Adam and of Samson was not ostensibly speaking in his own person but rather writing as a dramatist. In fact, Milton had something to say on this subject in correcting the misapprehensions of two of his opponents:

for he who was there personated was only the Remonstrant; the author is ever distinguished from the person he introduces. (III, 294)

scito, inquam, non quid poeta, sed quis apud poetam quidque dicat, spectandum esse: variae enim personae inducuntur, nunc bonae, nunc malae, nunc sapientes, nunc simplices, non semper quid poetae videatur, sed quid cuique personae maxime conveniat loquentes. (VII, 306)

But these quotations can be balanced by two others, the parenthetical remark further on in the *Defensio Prima*: "sensum fere suum poetae personis optimis affingere solent" (VII, 326), and the lecture on "decorum" in the *Defensio Secunda* (VIII, 48-50). The straightforward prose work now to be considered does not present these problems. In the *History of Britain* the voice that speaks out on the inferiority and proper subjection of women is at times unmistakably Milton's own. To heap up discredit on what John Knox called "the monstrous regiment of women" he will go out of his way, whether by parenthetical remark, or by free alteration of his sources, or, in one case, by sheer misinterpretation of the original Latin.

To be sure, the old chronicles had not a little to say themselves against women as rulers. One must take care to distinguish what is Milton's from what was "history" or historical comment before he wrote. For instance, while admitting that Cordelia was "worthy" (is one great poet here under the sway of another?) he has to report that Cordelia's nephews, "not bearing that a kingdom should be governed by a woman" (X, 21), put her down. This phrase used of Cordelia's nephews, and its counterpart found in the story of Sexburga, Kenwalk's wife, who was also "driven out, saith Mat. West., by the nobles, disdaining female government" (X, 170),[12] are fair translations of the Latin authorities. It cannot be augured from these phrases what Milton's own feelings are. He could be merely a neutral transcriber. Only in context with other phrases in the *History*, phrases that are Milton's indubitably, do these become significant, part of a consistent whole.

The consistent whole is that any manifestation of "female ambition" stirs in Milton disdain. It may be Kenelm's "elder sister Quendrid, who with a female ambition aspiring to the crown, hired one who had the charge of his nurture, to murder him, led into a woody place upon pretense of hunting" (X, 194). It may be Vortigern's daughter:

Vortigern, nothing bettered by these calamities, grew at last so obdurate as to commit incest with his daughter, tempted or tempting him out of an ambition to the crown. (X, 119)

"Tempted" is in William of Malmesbury: "filiam suam spe regni sollicitatam." [13] But "tempting" is Milton's own highly characteristic contribution.

He refuses to credit his sources when they tell of a wise or noble queen. The story of Martia he rewrites to suit himself.

Guitheline ... is also remembered, as a just and good prince, and his wife Martia to have excelled so much in wisdom as to venture upon a new Institution of Laws. Which King Alfred translating called *Marchen Leage*, but more truly thereby is meant the Mercian Law; not translated by Alfred, but digested or incorporated with the West Saxon. In the minority of her son she had the rule, and then, as may be supposed, brought forth these laws not herself, for laws are masculine births, but by the advice of her sagest counsellors; and therein she might do virtuously, since it befell her to supply the nonage of her son: else nothing more awry from the law of God and Nature than that a woman should give laws to men. (X, 26)

This is she whom Geoffrey of Monmouth [14] commended for her "proprio ingenio," she whom Holinshed,[15] Milton's immediate source, called "a woman of perfect beauty and wisdom incomparable." Milton has begun to dispose of her with his verb "venture upon." Another woman renowned not only for her beauty but for her independent activity [16] is dismissed more summarily, put in the category of fables: "the rest, as of Hamo the Roman captain, Genuissa the Emperor's daughter, and such like stuff, is too palpably untrue to be worth rehearsing in the midst of truth" (X, 56). Of course, here too enters in the critical historian, who finds a good deal "not worth rehearsal" (X, 182) in his Dark Age sources.

This historian could not forgive the ancient Britons their unmanly ways, a recurrent symptom of which was "the uncomeliness of their subjection to the monarchy of a woman" (X, 62). Resistance to such rule, he is grieved to find, is "a piece of manhood not every day to be found among Britons" (*ibid.*). There was this case of Venutius, "thus debarred [by his wife's adultery] the authority of ruling his own household" (X, 63), an authority for which Milton, like any good Puritan (whose text was Ephesians v, 22-24), always stood firm. Redwald is a later case of a man whose wife ruled him: she "still, it seems, was his chief counselor to good or bad alike" (X, 153).

It is well known how prejudiced is the account of Boadicea. Here Milton goes to greatest length in concluding that " 'all was

but a show Rather than solid virtue'" (Adam to Eve, x, 883).
The national idol[17] is thoroughly shattered. Milton, who ends
by making her a frenzied bungler, begins by stripping her of
her eloquence.

a woman also was their commander-in-chief. For Boadicea and her
daughters ride about in a chariot, telling the tall champions, as a great
encouragement, that with the Britons it was usual for women to be
their leaders. A deal of other fondness they put into her mouth, not
worth recital. (X, 67-68)

Even the classical historians, whom Milton ordinarily prefers,
are not listened to when they make Boadicea a noble orator:

this they do out of a vanity, hoping to embellish and set out their
history with the strangeness of our manners, not caring in the meanwhile to brand us with the rankest note of barbarism, as if in Britain
women were men, and men women. (X, 68)

The old sore rankles again. With a woman as commander-in-
chief the Britons naturally had no chance in the field.

Hitherto what we have heard of Cassibelan, Togodumnus, Venutius,
and Caractacus hath been full of magnanimity, soberness, and martial
skill: but the truth is, that in this battle, and whole business, the
Britons never more plainly manifested themselves to be right bar-
barians; no rule, no foresight, no forecast, experience, or estimation,
either of themselves or of their enemies; such confusion, such im-
potence, as seemed likest not to a war, but to the wild hurry of a dis-
tracted woman, with as mad a crew at her heels. (X, 68-69)

Milton's male disgust could hardly have found more vigorous
expression. This is history with a vengeance.

In contrast to his moral indignation against the barbarous
Britons, Milton criticizes the Roman conquerors relatively
seldom. It is worth noting, moreover, that women are behind
two of these rare outbursts against imperial but civilized Rome.
("Chief sway" means "this great empire of the Romans," X, 101,
or that of the "laws of virtuous education," IV, 318.) The historian acquits Venutius when he

justly turns his anger against the Romans themselves, whose magnanimity, not wont to undertake dishonorable causes, had arrogantly

intermeddled in his domestic affairs, to uphold the rebellion of an adulteress against her husband. (X, 63)

In the second instance Milton embroiders Tacitus in treating of the galling spectacle of a woman on a throne. The occasion is the pardon of Caractacus and his family by Claudius.

They all unbound, submissly thank him, and did like reverence to Agrippina, the Emperor's wife, who sat by in state: a new and disdained sight to the manly eyes of Romans, a woman sitting public in her female pride among ensigns and armed cohorts. (X, 60)

So much for a woman "with all her bravery on, and tackle trim." Using such color words as "disdained" and "manly" and "female pride"—that key recurrence—Milton has been passionate where the Roman historian was reserved.[18]

The last major citation some would seize on as of psychoanalytic interest. It treats of abstinence in marriage:

Another adversity befell Ecfrid in his family, by means of Ethildrith his wife, King Anna's daughter, who having taken him for her husband and professing to love him above all other men, persisted twelve years in the obstinate refusal of his bed, thereby thinking to live the purer life. So perversely then was chastity instructed against the apostle's rule. At length obtaining of him with much importunity her departure, she veiled herself a nun, then made abbess of Ely, died seven years after the pestilence; and might with better warrant have kept faithfully her undertaken wedlock, though now canonized Saint Audrey of Ely. (X, 173-174)

The disproportionate space given the episode shows that Milton has it very much on his mind. This is the only certainty; the rest is sheer conjecture, appertaining to the novelist rather than to the critic. How personal is Milton's vexation? Is there purely religious prejudice here, or is sexual prejudice mixed in with it? The latter complication seems much more likely in the light of other passages, if not in the light of Milton's own marriage. Mary Powell had lately come back to her husband, and we hear nothing of further matrimonial difficulties, though to speak of him, as Professor Hanford [19] does, as under "the pressure of novel and exacting household cares" during the years 1646-49 is certainly no exaggeration of the known facts, which embrace the sheltering under his roof of the whole Powell family, failing health and eyesight, the birth of two daughters, and nonpublication on the part of an author who had proved himself—and was again to prove himself—prolific. Indeed, one has only to read the lines—not *between* the lines—of the tenth of the "Familiarium Epistolarum," that to Dati, April 21, 1647. But the point is that the above quotation brings to mind Mark Pattison's suggestion,[20] —which has been adopted by Raleigh and Saurat, that the original trouble between Mary Milton and her husband lay in a refusal parallel to Ethildrith's (though Mary Milton's refusal was not, in anyone's view, motivated by piety). Pattison, as well as his followers, was apparently unaware of the above passage, which constitutes a better "support" for his theory than the ambiguous one in the *Doctrine and Discipline of Divorce* which is supposed to have given rise to it.[21] It is proper, too, to point out that the phrase, "the obstinate refusal of his bed," has its parallel in *Tetrachordon*, "the obstinate refusal of conjugal due" (IV, 227), but there Milton was only citing in passing "Felix Bidenbachius."

Actually, the bulk of the evidence runs the contrary way —toward Milton's disgust with an animal function [22] that too many authorities had made the prime consideration in marriage. If Milton's pamphlets on divorce reflect a refusal, they reflect a refusal far more likely to have come from the husband. Be it noted that later on, in that part of the *History* written after a lapse of years, he returns to this subject of "mistaken chastity" (X, 306),[23] but not in anger. In the second case it was the man who denied his wife. The oddest illustrative sentence in *Accidence Commenced*, considering it as a grammar designed for children, is: "Commune animantium est conjunctionis appetitus" (VI, 334). The words are Cicero's,[24] but Milton, by leaving out Cicero's next two words, "procreandi causa," has turned a scientific statement into a judgment. The translation (with the same omission)[25] is to be found in *Tetrachordon*: "conjunction hath nothing in it above what is common to us with beasts" (IV, 148). And this is Milton's point, made with varying degrees of revulsion, again and again.

As said before, Milton makes a great and remarkably successful effort in the divorce tracts not to sound as if he were speaking of his own case. ("For what concerns it us to hear a husband
divulge his household privacies?" V, 138. He had, to say the
least, a sense of decorum in regard to "arcanum domesticum,"
IX, 68.) Scarcely three passing allusions to what *was* his case,
desertion, can be found.[26] There are those who see Mary Powell
behind virtually all his references to, his literary treatment of,
womankind after 1642, and it may very well be they are right.
But if any "household privacies" are betrayed, it is simply this:
that Mary Milton had a will of her own. The Ecfrid-Ethildrith
passage, like so many others in and outside the *History*, has less
to do with conjunction than with sovereignty. The question in
the Wife of Bath's tale, "What thyng is it that wommen moost
desiren?" would not have puzzled Milton.

There are other signs of which way the wind of his wrath
was blowing. Granted that it is legitimate to berate a frankly
evil woman like Eadburga (X, 191 ff.), whose deeds no one
could condone, an earlier case is less legitimate. By misconstruing
Gildas, his source, Milton manages to add double murder to the
already sufficient sins of Maglocune's second wife:

Who not refusing the offer, if she were not rather the first that en-
ticed, found means both to despatch her own husband, and the former
wife of Maglocune, to make her marriage with him the more un-
questionable. (X, 137-138)

This shifting of responsibility for the murders comes from taking "dura cervix illa multis jam peccaminum fascibus onerata"
as a reference to a woman, whereas it is reasonably clear from
the context [27] that Gildas is merely continuing his passionate
rehearsal of the crimes of Maglocune himself. The woman was
a partner in the crime, Gildas indicates, but she was not the
main partner, as Milton makes her out to be. It has been con-
jectured that Milton made some use of the translation of 1638,[28]
but here he departs from that translation, which has "that stiffe
necke of thine" [29] (i.e., Maglocune) for "dura cervix illa." In
other words, the above biased reading of Gildas is peculiarly
Milton's own. Lastly, that the polyandry of the Britons should

have been found "more absurd and preposterous" (X, 87; cf. 51
—these adjectives had seen service before, or rather, considering composition dates, were to see it again, VI, 52) than the
polygamy or adultery of other nations is not surprising. In *De
Doctrina Christiana* (XV, 122 ff.) Milton took pains to show
that the law of God, as found in the Bible, sanctions polygamy.
In the *History of Britain* he appeals to the law of nature. It is
"a liberty not unnatural for one man to have many wives"
(X, 87).

These quotations have come from the first four books of the
History. We know, because Milton so informs us in *Defensio
Secunda*,[30] that the *History* was interrupted after the completion
of these books. When Milton resumed work on it his spell of
bitterness against presuming womankind was gone, all passion
spent. He writes detachedly of such wicked women as Elfrida
(X, 246 ff.) and the incestuous wife of Ethelbald (X, 205). The
former, among other misdeeds, shows her "ambitious will" (X,
250) in laboring "to have had her son Ethelred, a child of seven
years, preferred . . . that she under that pretense might have
ruled all" (X, 249). And before her there was Algiva, "who had
such power over" (X, 241) Edwi on the very day of his corona-
tion. Women continue to aspire now without particular remon-
strance from the historian. He joins in the praise of Godiva
(X, 301), and gives the "martial woman" Elfled her due (X,
228).[31] The last two books, in their almost benign objectivity,
stand apart from the first four.

Yet we have his stand, unmistakable, and consistent with all
his other writings. We shall never catch Milton bestowing such
praise on the great Elizabeth as Donne (who has been called a
misogynist) granted her, who proclaimed her such "as scarce
any former king hath equalled." [32] In fact he never praises her
at all in his published works, unless the youthful reference to
her in "In Quintum Novembris" (105), as an Amazon, counts
as praise. He mentions her reign only to remark that reformation
did not make headway in it (see the Patterson Index). It is true
that in his Commonplace Book he observes, via Camden, that
"the wealth of the Crown without oppression of subjects may

be seen in the expenses which Queen Elizabeth was at in maintaining war with her monies in divers places abroad, and at the same time paying her debts at home" (XVIII, 185). But this is obviously jotted down less to Queen Elizabeth's credit than to Charles I's discredit.[33] And the very next entry reads: "Mulieres a publica rerum administratione omni excludi solitas ostendit lib. cui titulo Franco Gallia apud Thuan. hist." His eulogy of the distant Christina is a return of courtesy, she having had the perspicacity to know when Salmasius had met his master. He says as much: "Quod Serenissimae Suecorum Reginae grates potius, quam laudes persolverim," etc. (IX, 84). One must note, too, that his last compliment to her is that he hears she thinks so little of reigning she may abdicate! (VIII, 108) (a subject returned to at the end of the second book of *Paradise Regained*, where some editors find a topical allusion to the abdicating queen).

Any suggestion of uxoriousness invariably makes Milton flare up. After the exclamation "Palpably uxorious! " and immediately after the words "female pride" in the *Doctrine and Discipline of Divorce*, he writes:

" I suffer not," saith Saint Paul, " the woman to usurp authority over the man." If the apostle could not suffer it, into what mold is he mortified that can? (III, 475)

Then Solomon is quoted: "that a bad wife is to her husband as rottenness to his bones," etc.; but the authority so useful here is the weak sinner in *Paradise Lost*: "that uxorious king whose heart, though large,/Beguiled by fair idolatresses, fell/To idols foul" (i, 444). In no less than eight places in the *Defensio Prima* (VII, 160, 280, 348, 390, 400, 420, 510, 548) and once in the *Defensio Secunda* (VIII, 16) Salmasius is taunted as being under the sway of his wife and therefore—it is several times implied—no man at all. One of Charles's troubles came from the fact that his papist wife ruled him. "To sum up all, they [the King's captured letters] showed him governed by a woman" (V, 251), "in . . . potestate . . . uxoris" (VIII, 204) (in fact, he is compared with Solomon in this respect, VII, 142). The general, repeated lesson is not to be "swayed By female usurpation" (*S.A.*, 1059), "overswayed at home under a feminine usurpation":

Examples are not far to seek, how great mischief and dishonor hath befallen to nations under the government of effeminate and uxorious magistrates; who, being themselves governed and overswayed at home under a feminine usurpation, cannot but be far short of spirit and authority without doors, to govern a whole nation. (V, 139-140)

Frustra enim libertatem in comitiis et foro crepat, qui domi servitutem viro indignissimam, inferiori etiam servit. (VIII, 132)

Stopford Brooke was accurate, if brief, when he alluded to "the love of power which Milton held to be inherent in woman." [34] "Despotic power" is political in *The Tenure of Kings and Magistrates* (V, 37), domestic in *Samson Agonistes*:

> Therefore God's universal law
> Gave to the man despotic power
> Over his female in due awe,
> Not from that right to part an hour,
> Smile she or lour. (1053)

This is not Samson. This is the Chorus. It may jar on us, but Milton's original readers were used to such doctrine. To come back to the subject of a woman's preaching, a she-Brownist, Katherine Chidley, went so far in 1641 as to argue in print with a man, in her pamphlet entitled *The Justification of the Independent Churches of Christ: being an Answer to Mr. [Thomas] Edwards his Book, which he hath written against the Government of Christ's Church*. But there were limits to the presumption of even this stalwart pioneer, as shown by her humble, *zeitgeistig* close: "If you overcome me, your conquest will not be great, for I am a poor woman, and unmeet to deal with you." [35]

"The faith and morals . . . which Milton held" were not, let us emphasize, those of a misogynist.[36] At the same time there is even less reason to call him a feminist. He would not thank us for overmodernizing him. The fact of his attitude, when it is related to a seventeenth-century Puritan, or, more broadly, to a man of the Renaissance, calls for no apology. In common with the men of his time and those of preceding periods, and more moderately than many,[37] he did believe that women had their "not equal" (iv, 296) place and should keep it. This conviction happens to have emerged with particular clarity in the first four books of the *History of Britain*. Milton's mood changed, but not his conviction. We can see in crude form here what was later refined and linked to a great principle in the universal history of *Paradise Lost*: the principle of order and degree in the cosmos,[38] successive violation of which by Satan, and by Eve, and by Adam, and by mankind since, accounts for "all our woe."

We must not forget the curious lines in which Milton literally marries Eve to the Serpent. The fallen angels fabled

> how the Serpent, whom they called
> Ophion, with Eurynome, the wide-
> Encroaching Eve perhaps, had first the rule
> Of high Olympus, thence by Saturn driven
> And Ops, ere yet Dictaean Jove was born. (x, 580)

The excuse for this is etymological, the seeming connection between Ophion [39] and ὄφις, a serpent. (It seems pertinent to remember, too, that, according to the Manichaeans, Satan and Eve were the parents of Cain and Abel.) But Milton's associating Eve with the Serpent and calling her "wide-encroaching" are just what we have been taught to expect. As a matter of fact, "Eurynome" does not mean literally "wide-encroaching": it means "wide-ruling." Here exactly is the point. A woman who rules encroaches.

As pride, the deadliest of the seven sins, leads Eve to violate the cosmic order, and as it first led Satan—as Milton loses no time in emphasizing:

> what time his pride
> Had cast him out from Heaven, with all his host
> Of rebel Angels, by whose aid, aspiring
> To set himself in glory above his peers,
> He trusted to have equaled the Most High,
> If he opposed; and, with ambitious aim
> Against the throne and monarchy of God,
> Raised impious war in Heaven and battle proud,
> With vain attempt; (i, 36)

("vain" following upon "proud" is perhaps the most serious pun ever made in an epic poem)—so it motivated bishops, who are thus linked with other miserable sinners. "Lucifer before Adam was the first prelate angel, and both he, as is commonly thought, and our forefather Adam, as we all know, for aspiring above their orders, were miserably degraded" (III, 196). Pride blackens—blackens alike—women and bishops.

But the two are connected in a more curious way, a way that has to do with "smile she" and "tackle trim," the ornamentation that fronts the pride. The key is in a parallel that, duly noted by Todd in his edition of 1801, has never received the attention it deserves, the parallel between the famous approach of Dalila:

> But who is this, what thing of sea or land?
> Female of sex it seems,
> That, so bedecked, ornate, and gay,
> Comes this way sailing,
> Like a stately ship
> Of Tarsus, bound for th'isles
> Of Javan or Gadire,
> With all her bravery on, and tackle trim,
> Sails filled, and streamers waving,
> (S. A., 710)

and the mocking of episcopal dignity in *Of Reformation*:

they would request us to endure still the rustling of their silken cassocks, and that we would burst our midriffs, rather than laugh to see them under sail in all their lawn and sarcenet, their shrouds and tackle, with a geometrical rhomboides upon their heads. (III, 74)

The passages have but two words in common, "sail(s)" and "tackle," but are clearly much more interrelated than that bare fact might suggest. Nor is the comparison with a ship the point of greatest interest. What we have here is a brilliant illustration of Milton's tendency to speak of a skirted bishop as he would of a woman of doubtful virtue. His favorite adjective for the bishops is "carnal," and, however wide the older meaning of that term, it had a modern flavor with this author. He instinctively thought of the state as a Samson betrayed by "the strumpet flatteries of prelates":

I cannot better liken the state and person of a king than to that mighty Nazarite Samson, who, being disciplined from his birth in the precepts and the practice of temperance and sobriety, without the strong drink of injurious and excessive desires, grows up to a noble strength and perfection with those his illustrious and sunny locks, the laws, waving and curling about his godlike shoulders. And while he keeps them about him undiminished and unshorn, he may with the jawbone of an ass, that is, with the word of his meanest officer, suppress and put to confusion thousands of those that rise against his just power. But laying down his head among the strumpet flatteries of prelates, while he sleeps and thinks no harm, they wickedly shaving off all those bright and weighty tresses of his laws, and just prerogatives which were his ornament and strength, deliver him over to indirect and violent councils, which, as those Philistines, put out the fair and far-sighted eyes of his natural discerning, and make him grind in the prison house of their sinister ends and practices upon him. (III, 276)

A few pages earlier he had found the corrupted church "false-whited, a lawny resemblance" to the gospel purity, like the phantom "air-born" Helen; this church "gives up her body to a mercenary whoredom under those fornicated arches which she calls God's house" (III, 268). (One must admit that "fornicated" is a brilliant, if etymological, pun.) Such language was encouraged by the Bible, of course—e.g., the expression "go a whoring after (strange) gods" [40] (Milton's version is, "go a whoring after all the heathen's inventions," III, 355). A Puritan saw, moreover, only too much resemblance between Laudian episcopacy and "the great whore" (III, 78; V, 205; cf. VI, 81) of Rome. "Ah, like a crafty adulteress," the latter "forgot not all her smooth looks and enticing words at her parting" (III, 355). Then there is "the widowed whore Plurality" of the sonnet "On the New Forcers of Conscience under the Long Parliament" (3).

In brief, it is a not wholly unaccountable step, psychologically, from *Comus* to the antiprelatical tracts. Professor Barker makes the point well, without adducing, perhaps without needing to adduce, a great deal of evidence:

In the ecclesiastical dispute between the bishops and the Puritans he dimly perceived the counterpart of his own conflict. Episcopacy assumed in his eyes the lineaments of Comus; it was the public manifestation of the perversions of carnal sensuality against which he had striven in favor of high seriousness. The reformed discipline of the

Puritan church similarly assumed the aspect of the virgin Lady, possessed of transcendent spiritual powers. Its triumph over episcopacy corresponded to the triumph of chastity over lust; and like the triumph of the Lady—and of Lycidas and Damon—it seemed to promise the fulfilment of his spiritual aspirations and their expression in divine song.[41]

To round out the sensual-ecclesiastical-political complex, there is G. Wilson Knight's observation,[42] published in the same year, that in Milton the "domination of woman by man" falls "midway between the rule of lust in the individual and mass-instinct in the community." (It is not to be forgotten, for Milton reminds us, that domination by Circe is domination by a woman: "non enim Eurylochus, sed Elpenor es, id est vile animal Circeum, porcus immundus, turpissima servitute etiam sub femina assuetus"; VII, 510: both Eve and Dalila are definitely linked to Circe: "more duteous at her call/Than at Circean call the herd disguised," ix, 521; "Thy fair enchanted cup, and warbling charms," *S.A.*, 934.) This in turn may recall Saurat's argument (which is difficult to refute) that Eve stands for sensuality, Adam for reason. (In this connection, it being our delight to cross periods, let us not forget, amidst all the gossip over Mary Powell, how "Il Penseroso" begins: "Hence, vain deluding Joys,/ The brood of Folly without father bred!") In any case, the over-all point, reached in our special way, one may also find in Knight: "A great poet rarely modifies his primary impressionisms, but, using them as constants, gears them to the ever-changing world of his experience." [43]

There is a further significance in the *Of Reformation-Samson Agonistes* ship figure. It is typical of Milton's lifelong distrust of the "bedecked." With him "fair" goes with "fallacious" (V, 137; *S.A.*, 533). This is the whore again: to this Puritan, Laud's church, *a fortiori* the Roman Church, is a painted woman, not the beauty of holiness. One could begin by quoting the second marathon sentence of *Of Reformation*, if it were not so long. Part will suffice, the scorn against those who think to put

the very shape of God himself into an exterior and bodily form, urgently pretending a necessity and obligement of joining the body in a formal reverence and worship circumscribed; they hallowed it, they fumed it, they sprinkled it, they bedecked it, not in robes of pure innocency, but of pure linen, with other deformed and fantastic dresses, in palls and mitres, gold, and gewgaws fetched from Aaron's old wardrobe, or the flamens' vestry.

What have the bishops done to the "poor threadbare matron," Christ's Gospel?

Her chaste and modest veil surrounded with celestial beams they overlaid with wanton tresses, and in a flaring tire bespeckled her with all the gaudy allurements of a whore. (III, 25)

What was that which made the Jews figured under the names of Aholah and Aholibah go a whoring after all the heathen's inventions, but that they saw a religion gorgeously attired and desirable to the eye? (III, 355)

When the Remonstrant objects, "Our liturgy symbolizeth not with popish mass, neither as mass nor as popish," he is answered:

A pretty slip-skin conveyance to sift mass into no mass and popish into not popish; yet, saving this passing fine sophistical bolting hutch, so long as she symbolizes in form, and pranks herself in the weeds of popish mass, it may be justly feared she provokes the jealousy of God, no otherwise than a wife affecting whorish attire kindles a disturbance in the eye of her discerning husband. (III, 129)

There is no extravagance Milton will not commit—even to likening God to a jealous husband—in the grip of his obsession. In short, he strongly feels what he says in the Commonplace Book, "Quicquid speciosum est non statim virtus est dicenda" (XVIII, 130).[44] In fact, by the same psychological process—or, should we rather say, by the same process of trial followed by error?— by which "speciosum" becomes "specious," this turns into a positive grudge against the fair and glittering. And this is definitely connected with his ambivalent attitude toward women, with their "venereal trains"—the attraction and yet repulsion of Eve, Dalila, and other embodiments of sensual charm.

> Is it for that such outward ornament
> Was lavished on their sex, that inward gifts
> Were left for haste unfinished? (S. A., 1025)

... this fair defect (x, 891)

No one has been more painfully forceful than he on the subject
of the "innumerable Disturbances on Earth through female
snares" (x, 897). Adam's struggle (not to say Samson's) was
Milton's own, and sometimes—in some parts of some works—
the bitterness of it breaks through.

But again we must not underrate the purely literary influences. Just as his youthful master, Spenser, preceded him in
warning against uxoriousness in the Radigund episode (to say
nothing of the kindred Greek myth of Hercules and Omphale),
so in the Duessas [45] and snowy Florimells the same sage poet
(but Homer was first in the *Odyssey*) instilled another lesson—
to beware of the fair exterior. (Previously there was Ariosto's
Alcina, called by Harington "nothing but a shew of virtue," [46]
which returns us to Adam's discovery about Eve, " 'all was but
a show, Rather than solid virtue,' " x, 883.) What C. S. Lewis
has remarked of Spenser fits Milton perfectly: "he had learned
from Plato to see good and evil as the real and the apparent," [47]
and "distrust of 'the World' and worldly ambition, even to a
fault, is the essence of the man." [48] There loom large, too, the
Old Testament warnings against idols and the paradoxes of the
New Testament, whereby the first shall be last and it is hard
for a rich man to enter into the kingdom of heaven. So Milton's
attitude—like the more modern prejudice that the poor are good,
the rich bad—became a distinct bias against wealth and ornamentation, whether in a church ("gay religions full of pomp and
gold," i, 372) or in a woman. (Nor is Milton's individuality im-
pugned by pointing out that this attitude is what we should
expect in a Puritan, and that the same bias can even be found
in Bishop Hall.[49]) One symptom of the Anglo-Saxons' degener-
ation after the death of Bede is "the spruce and gay apparel of
their priests and nuns" (X, 196). This is of the same cloth as the
lesson the historian derived from the Britons' having the "gal-
lantry" to paint their naked skins: "a vanity which hath not
yet left us, removed only from the skin to the skirt, behung now
with as many colored ribands and gewgaws" (X, 50). Women,

"proud fair, best quitted with disdain" (iv, 770) (these are the two points in his indictment, that they are "proud" and that they are "fair"); bishops; silken, long-haired cavaliers (Adam's hair, be it observed, came "not beneath his shoulders broad," iv, 303)—what is the essential moral difference?

Yet he cannot get away from regal and luxurious imagery, the kings and the gold and the glitter, to which the poet in him was attracted.[50] But he can, and does, take it away from earth and give it to heaven, while not ceasing to insist that it can be found in hell.

CHAPTER VIII

PARALLELS AS CLUES

I T MAY BE GRANTED by now that parallels can be significant. This final chapter, devoted to considering how far they may aid in solving specific problems of text and interpretation, will insist that there is nothing easy or automatic about the clarity toward which parallels are instrumental. One must find out, by a careful appraisal of all the evidence, what key opens what door, or whether what one has seized on as a key opens anything: false parallels seductively abound. For instance, to mention the most mysterious door of all, the "door" of "Lycidas," 130, everyone who has thought himself possessed of the secret of "that two-handed engine" has come forward with at least one quotation, in or outside Milton. Yet a count that is probably not exhaustive reveals no less than thirty different interpretations of this crux, so that, at the least, twenty-nine false parallels have been produced, with, no doubt, since these are published interpretations, the greatest good will to the propagation of truth.

Let us begin by considering two lines from "Lycidas" that most of the editors apparently do not regard as a problem, for they give either one or the other of two possible interpretations without so much as mentioning the rival interpretation. The lines open the second paragraph:

> Begin, then, Sisters of the sacred well
> That from beneath the seat of Jove doth spring.

Let us hear a classical scholar, Sir John Edwin Sandys, on the problem:

This " sacred well " is sometimes identified with the Pierian spring, at the foot of the Thessalian Olympus, the great Homeric seat of the gods, the first home of the Muses, the daughters of Zeus and Mnemosyne, before their worship was transferred to the Boeotian Helicon.[1] I agree, however, with those who hold that Milton is here

referring, not to Olympus, but to Helicon, the "Aonian mount," above
which he "intends to soar," in *Paradise Lost* (i, 15), and that the
source of this invocation is to be found, not in Homer, but in Hesiod.
The *Theogony* begins thus: " From the Muses of Helicon let us begin
to sing." In the context, the Muses are described as " dancing round
the altar of the mighty Zeus." This is certainly the same as " Jove's
altar," " round about " which the Muses sing in " Il Penseroso "
(47 f.); and it is probably the same as " the seat of Jove " in this
passage of " Lycidas." The Muses are next described by Hesiod as
bathing in the fountain of Hippocrene, one of the springs of Helicon,
probably the " sacred spring " of our text.[2]

If all of Milton's references outside "Lycidas" were to Olympus-
Pieria as the locale for the Muses, if it could be shown that
this was the spot that he, again and again, without exception,
liked to think of as their haunt, that would tip the scale (which,
in fact, is evenly balanced) the other way, considering that
Mount Olympus is the obvious place for "the seat of Jove" and
yields one famous name for a spring, in accordance with Milton's
singular, "well," whereas Helicon is associated not only with
Hippocrene but with Aganippe (two editors say the well *is*
Aganippe [3]) and forms a relatively recondite reference for "seat
of Jove." But Milton, who relished the recondite, referred to
Jove's Heliconian altar with its dancing Muses, not only in "Il
Penseroso," but in his Second Prolusion:

> And hears the Muses in a ring
> Aye round about Jove's altar sing.

Hinc quoque Musarum circa Jovis altaria dies noctesque saltantium
ab ultima rerum origine increbuit fabula; (XII, 154)

—an unmistakable allusion to the *Theogony*. What Sandys does
not tell us is that Hesiod in the same poem loses no time in
associating the Muses with Olympus and telling of their birth
in Pieria. Parallels are of no help. Milton refers to Pieria(n) four
times (not to count his Olympian references), and, though he
never names directly Aganippe or Hippocrene, he has the
Helicon-Aonia locale eight times (the "Aonian mount" of
Paradise Lost, i, 15, is the "Aoniis . . . collibus" of Elegy VI, 17).
Once he indulges in an orgy of allusions, getting in the *three*

places known to fame for poetic springs—Aonia, the twin-peaked
Parnassus (with "bifidi . . . iugi" compare "Bifidoque Parnassi
iugo," "Ad Ioannem Rousium," 66), with its Castalian "mero,"
and the "Pieros . . . latices":

> Primus ego Aonios illo praeeunte recessus
> Lustrabam, et bifidi sacra vireta iugi,
> Pierosque hausi latices, Clioque favente
> Castalio sparsi laeta ter ora mero.
>
> (El. IV, 29)

Fortunately, it is Apollo, not Jove, who is associated with
Parnassus. But clearly we are no nearer a decision than we were
as to which of the other two places is the "Lycidas" one. There
seems to be no basis for a preference. The lesson is that a fair
and knowing editor will make his readers cognizant of both
possibilities.

To go from an uncertainty to a certainty, what does Milton
mean when he refers, in *An Apology for Smectymnuus,* "to the
divine volumes of Plato and his equal Xenophon" (III, 305)?
Does he mean that Xenophon is equal in genius to Plato? That
no more agrees with his own recorded estimate of Plato than
with ours. The commentators rightly remark that "equal" here
means "the contemporary of," "one approximately the same age
as." They can point to Milton's use of the word a few paragraphs
earlier, when he is speaking of his student days at Cambridge:
"that more than ordinary favor and respect, which I found
above any of my equals at the hands of those courteous and
learned men, the fellows of that college wherein I spent some
years" (III, 297). If there were still room for doubt, they could
fill the vacancy with a sentence from the Latin Grammar:
"Xenophon et Plato fuere aequales" (VI, 329), for "aequales,"
unlike "aequi" and "equal," can have only the temporal meaning.

The eighteenth-century commentators, from Bentley on,
were troubled over the seeming inaccuracy of Satan's remark:

> But see! the angry Victor hath recalled
> His ministers of vengeance and pursuit
> Back to the gates of Heaven: the sulphurous hail,
> Shot after us in storm, o'erblown hath laid

The fiery surge that from the precipice
Of Heaven received us falling; and the thunder,
Winged with red lightning and impetuous rage,
Perhaps hath spent his shafts, and ceases now
To bellow through the vast and boundless Deep.

(i, 169)

The Richardsons are a convenient early guide here:

This Passage, with v. 326, II, 78, and 996, represent the Angels Press-
ing the Reprobates when they were driven down to Hell, in direct
Contradiction to the Account the Angel Raphael gives to Adam, VI,
880. But does Milton therefore Contradict Himself? No; His Scheme
is Consistent and Exceeding Noble; and This which has been thought
a Blemish is a Vast Beauty in the Poem. Let it be Consider'd only
Who tells These Different Stories: in the two first Passages 'tis Satan;
Moloch speaks in the Third. They Imagin'd they were persu'd by
Millions of victorious Spirits; but were Too much Terryfied to look
Behind them, and Too much Confounded to Judge of what was doing
Above them. Chaos is the Other Relator; is He a Witness Worthy
of Credit? All three of them, or if there were a Million of Such,
should not induce Us to Believe Thus was the Fact; They only say
what their Terrify'd Imaginations Suggested to them. Raphael tells
Adam what he Knew to be the Truth; (which agrees with Another
Passage ... III, 395).[4]

A commentator of 1732, who signed himself "Semicolon," offered
the alternative that Milton in "ministers of vengeance" was
personifying the hail and thunder and lightning referred to immediately afterward.[5] In short, "Semicolon" was inclined to
make much of the ambiguity of the colon. But we shall, with
other commentators, rather stand with the Richardsons, adding
this reason: that Milton in *De Doctrina Christiana* calls the
angels ministers of vengeance sent from heaven: "Sunt et nonnunquam divinae ultionis ministri ad peccata mortalium puni-
enda caelitus missi" (XV, 102).

There has been wider disagreement over Sonnet xx:

Lawrence, of virtuous father virtuous son,
Now that the fields are dank, and ways are mire,
Where shall we sometimes meet, and by the fire
Help waste a sullen day, what may be won

From the hard season gaining? Time will run
On smoother, till Favonius reinspire
The frozen earth, and clothe in fresh attire
The lily and rose, that neither sowed nor spun.
What neat repast shall feast us, light and choice,
Of Attic taste, with wine, whence we may rise
To hear the lute well touched, or artful voice
Warble immortal notes and Tuscan air?
He who of those delights can judge, and spare
To interpose them oft, is not unwise.

What is the import of the last two lines? What does "spare to interpose them oft" mean? Does it mean spare *time* to interpose those delights often, or does it on the contrary convey a warning against interposing them too often? For "spare" can mean "forbear," "refrain from." The latter usage is not only good Latin (*parcere* plus the infinitive), which would be reason enough for Milton; but it is also, as Smart [6] pointed out, "good literary English." Here, then, is a contest between meaning 8c of "spare" in the *Oxford English Dictionary*, "afford," and meaning 6c, "forbear." Most editors have sensed that Milton meant the latter, that he was, characteristically, explaining that he was setting the seal of his approval on discreet indulgence, which was finely to be discriminated from overindulgence. The opposite interpretation, Thomas Keightley's, has lately been renewed by two scholars,[7] who are, however, careful not to look at Milton's use of "spare" elsewhere. The passage to quote is this from a book of *Paradise Lost* that may, in fact (not that such a condition is indispensable), be very close in time to this late sonnet:

> She spake, and at her words the hellish Pest
> Forbore: then these to her Satan returned:
> " So strange thy outcry, and thy words so strange
> Thou interposest, that my sudden hand,
> Prevented, spares to tell thee yet by deeds
> What it intends . . . ." (ii, 735)

As if to help make *this* "spare" unmistakable, a synonym, "forbore," is hovering near. And, for neither rhyme nor syntax but for a similar effect metrically and alliteratively (note how the first two and a half feet of either line are hedged in with "t"), "interpose" has returned—not a case of psychological pattern, for the two passages have nothing else in common, but a mild case of verbal conglomeration that sends us back to the sonnet with a more distinct suspicion than we should otherwise have had that Milton's use of "spare" in both cases is the same.

The first two lines of the sestet emphasize the lightness and Attic refinement of the repast; the next two proclaim that the music is of no common sort. Is it any surprise, then, that the close is also qualified? Professor Neiman declares that it is not logical to have Milton saying, "Come to a frugal meal, but be careful not to come to frugal meals often." But the meal is not frugal; that is not the poet's word or sense. No doubt Lucullus would find it frugal; but Milton is presenting it as something special, a luxury by comparison with his ordinary meal, which lacks the companionship and may well lack the wine and the music. So he says, "sometimes"—and the "sometimes" (line 3) is surely in contradistinction to "oft"—let us (comparatively speaking) indulge. Professor Jackson's objection that the conjunction in line 13, "and," ought then to be "but" or "yet" is to be answered by understanding "judge" as meaning "be judicious about": he who can appraise these delights discreetly and not fall into too frequent indulgence in them "is not unwise."

The litotes is presumably an emphatic answer to those strict Puritans (e.g., Prynne) who would not concede so much as Milton has.[8] But "sometimes" is still not "oft." Oft feasting, "crebro convivantur," is what the author of *Defensio Secunda* publicly charged the clergy with, the year before the assigned date of this sonnet: "atque inter haec tamen et apud discipulos et apud discipulas, tam crebro convivantur, ut quid domicaenium sit, aut domiprandium pene nesciant" (VIII, 182). He would hardly have meant to associate himself with anything resembling this. Indeed, the ambiguity itself may only be plausibly explained as the consequence of his having fallen into a habit of thought and (Latin) expression without realizing that this time he was laying himself open to being misunderstood by readers who take the two lines in isolation.

Let us not, in our enthusiasm at finding the poet (whom we may have a professional self-interest in making as "modern" as possible) in a comparatively relaxed mood, take it as more relaxed than the evidence—the bulk of the evidence, internal and external—indicates it was. We may not like to think that he was always injecting a note of caution. But he always was. Professor Neiman cites Sonnet xxi as parallel, and to be sure it is: "Today deep thoughts resolve with me to drench In mirth *that after no repenting draws.*" There is the qualification again. (And the tone of the closing lines is again that of a man giving "measured" answer to the overrigorous.) *"Spare* temperance" (*Comus*, 767) is his constant message. No doubt W. J. Rolfe was drawing too close to the hated "personal heresy"[9] when he stoutly declared of the disputed passage: "no one who knows Milton as a man ought to misinterpret it." Let us rather say, no one who knows Milton's *works*—the *opera omnia*—ought to misinterpret it.

Then there are the textual problems. In *Areopagitica*, is it "true wayfaring Christian" or "true warfaring Christian" (IV, 311)? The former is what the original edition printed, but the Columbia editor observes:

That Milton intended "warfaring" seems not improbable.   There are extant three copies of the original edition which in all probability passed through his hands (IV, 366).   In each as in several other copies examined by the editor "y" has here been struck out by the pen and "r" inserted above the line.   In none of the three copies mentioned does any similar emendation appear elsewhere in the text. In each case ink and writing appear contemporary, and the emendation is made in the same way.   The form of Milton's "r" in extant autographs is such as might easily have been mistaken by a printer for "y." The inserted "r" in this instance closely resembles his "y."   That the insertion was made by the author's own hand is not unlikely.   Compare *Doctrine and Discipline of Divorce* [III, 373], "what more suttle stratagem against our Christian warfare." (IV, 367)

Two other parallels can be added: "You are not armed, Remonstrant, nor any of your band, you are not dieted, nor your loins girt for spiritual valour and Christian warfare" (III, 110), and "Let him cast from him, as in a Christian warfare, that secular encumbrance which either distracts, or overloads him" (V, 263).[10]

Let us, now, move on to the very next sentence of *Areopagitica*, italicizing to emphasize a parallel:

I cannot praise a fugitive and *cloistered* virtue, unexercised and un-breathed, that never sallies out and *seeks her adversary*, but slinks out of the race, where that immortal garland is to be run for, not without *dust and heat.*

Atqui oportuit aut non in ludicro primam fere aetatem *umbratiles* consumpsisse, aut aliquando cum patriae, cum Reipublicae est opus, relictis rudibus, *in solem ac pulverem* atque aciem audere; aliquando veros lacertos contendere, vera arma vibrare, verum *hostem petere.* (IX, 224)

It is neat, and "hostem petere" for "seeks her adversary" is as accurate as anyone could wish. And "seeks her adversary" is what a long and distinguished line of modern scholars and critics are under the impression that Milton said, as proved by their quotations: those who so quote him include Sir Walter Raleigh,[11] Sir Arthur Quiller-Couch,[12] E. M. W. Tillyard,[13] Basil Willey,[14] G. Wilson Knight,[15] and, not to keep to the other side of the Atlantic, Martin Larson [16] and Kathleen Hartwell.[17] And this is what an edition of *Areopagitica* published by Cambridge University Press, with notes by Sir Richard Jebb and A. W. Verity, has.[18] But the original edition of *Areopagitica,* and all early editions, read "sees her adversary." "Seeks" is a misprint that has crept unnoticed into the Bohn edition,[19] which, since it served for almost a century as the standard edition of Milton's prose (for some still serves, apparently), has thus led astray so many by the margin of one letter. Now the parallel just offered raises the question of whether the reading that has been *textus receptus* for an incalculable number of readers is not, after all, what Milton intended and would have corrected the 1644 edition to, if he had noticed the missing letter. For this, unlike "wayfaring-warfaring," is something the eye can easily miss—*expertis crede.* In favor of the more aggressive "seeks" [20] are two stylistic considerations: that it makes a better correlative, in meaning, with "sallies out," and that it forms a consonance with "slinks." The Bohn misprint may represent the right instincts on the part of all concerned. But this, admittedly, is just a speculation in passing, and no recommendation that the editors make any exception to the sacred rule of following the original text, where it makes sense.

The point that should emerge from all the illustrations in this chapter is that it would be well to have other evidence to put beside that of parallels before drawing a conclusion. This caution is applicable to all questions, including those of authorship. The internal evidence for viewing the Ovid stanzas as a youthful production of Milton's is highly satisfactory, has been worked out, with great thoroughness, by Candy.[21] If only there were some external evidence to go with it! (That Samuel Morland's oration to the Duke of Savoy was composed by Milton Masson [22] decided on the basis of similarities of phrasing with Milton's known works, one phrase, "montesque nivibus coopertos," XIII, 478, being identical with one in the Letter to the Duke of Savoy, XIII, 158, another, "totius nominis Italici studiosissimum," XIII, 476, being reminiscent of that in the second letter to Philaras, "totius Graeci nominis . . . cultor," XII, 64.) On the other hand, it seems safe to say that if they had not been published in the 1673 *Poems,* no one would ever have ascribed the metrical renditions of Psalms I-VIII and LXXX-LXXXVIII to Milton. But with the information that they are Milton's, one goes through them and finds surprisingly many pieces of the as yet unwritten epic: "encompassed round" (LXXXI, 30; see above, pp. 98-100), "holy mount" (III, 12; v, 712; vi, 743; vii, 584), "countenance bright" (IV, 30; ii, 756), "dishonor foul" (VII, 18; ix, 297), "honor due" (LXXXIII, 59; iii, 738; v, 817), "the Cherubs bright" (LXXX, 5; "bright Cherubim," xii, 254), "glory bright" — "gloriously bright" (LXXXIV, 42; iii, 655), "hand in hand" (LXXXV, 44; iv, 321, 689; xii, 648; used in prose, III, 61), "utmost ends" (LXXXVII, 15; sing., x, 1020), "sacred songs" (*ibid.,* 26; iii, 148), "dark oblivion" (LXXXVIII, 52; vi, 380), "peace and righteousness" —"righteousness and peace" (LXXXV, 43; xii, 550), and "incessant prayers"—"prayer Incessant" (LXXXVI, 19; xi, 307), not to mention internal repetition of "fierce wrath" (LXXXV, 11; LXXXVIII, 65) and such prose combinations as "just and equal" (LXXXII, 12; III, 503, 504; V, 203), or "justa et aequa" (XIII, 72; "quod aequum, quod justum," *ibid.,* 214), and "free access" (LXXXVI, 23; IV, 198), or "liberum aditum" (XIII, 302). "Her grapes and tender shoots" (LXXX, 56) looks back fourteen years to the "ripe clusters from the tender shoots" plucked by the lost brothers (*Comus*, 296), just as "safe abode" (*Comus*, 693; LXXXIV, 14) was and remains the object. Something of Milton will come through, even in his worst and seemingly most mechanical productions.

To return, finally, to "Lycidas," with which we began, a few words should be said about the "two-handed engine at the door" for its bearing on Milton's verbal and psychological pattern. My exposition of this, the most famous crux in English literature,[23] has appeared, at length, in an article,[24] and it is not necessary to repeat it here. But four or five points are worth making in the present context. First, the engine gives us Milton in the role of "God's angry man," a role he would frequently assume. Secondly, I concluded that the meaning of the "two-handed" threat was returned to—though in different words—in the thundering last sentence, last paragraph, of Milton's first tract in prose against the bishops, *Of Reformation*. So here is theme and variation. The raw material was a commonplace to which Milton came recognizably back in *Defensio Prima* when, alluding specifically to the removal of the bishops, he wrote: "mirifica Dei manus . . . liberavit" (VII, 462).[25] Thirdly, it may be said that the figurative meaning of "two-handed" was signaled in the reference to St. Peter's keys: "the golden opes, the iron shuts amain," (111) these being "the keys of hell and of death" (Rev. i, 18). What is of particular interest to us now is that one of these keys had been introduced—in the same words—in *Comus*: "that golden key . . . opes the palace of eternity" (13). Moreover, in the light of my conclusion—in itself an old one—that the engine is a sword, a two-handed sword, it is very much worth remembering that the only time Milton used "two-handed" again was in connection with a heavenly sword (vi, 251). This, of course, has been noticed before, but now that this author's impressive habit of recurrence has been brought to light, this fact—though not by itself enough on which to base a conclusion—doubtless carries more weight than before. Finally, since it was my conclusion that the picture in "Lycidas," 130-131, is that of a corrupt church about to be smitten, about to be tumbled to "ruin," by the sword of the Lord, it should be noted that this is a dominant pattern in Milton: the fall of a rotten, idolatrous structure, from *Comus*.[26]

> Till all thy magic structures, reared so high,
> Were shattered into heaps o'er thy false head, (798)

to *Samson Agonistes*:

>   those two massy pillars
> With horrible convulsion to and fro
> He tugged, he shook, till down they came, and drew
> The whole roof after them with burst of thunder
> Upon the heads of all who sat beneath,
> Lords, ladies, captains, counselors, or priests, (1648)

itself reminiscent of a prose warning against the Restoration: "which will undoubtedly pull down the heavy judgment of God among us" (VI, 103). Whether "Lords, ladies, captains, counsellors, or priests," those who "aspire to high dignity, rule, and promotion" (III, 79) he spent a lifetime as a writer hurling to their ruin.

The last poetry Milton wrote was the five lines he prefixed to the twelfth book of *Paradise Lost* in the second, 1674 edition:

> As one who, in his journey, bates at noon,
> Though bent on speed, so here the Archangel paused
> Betwixt the world destroyed and world restored,
> If Adam aught perhaps might interpose;
> Then, with transition sweet, new speech resumes.

The lines are significant, and not only because Milton was, according to his habit of fifty years, echoing himself, "bent on speed" going back to "Bent all on speed" (iv, 568). One can find in them a parable of creation, which of course includes artistic creation: how it comes from rearrangement of the old creation, which presupposes destruction—"the world destroyed," out of which the "world restored" arises. In Milton one can often trace the "transition sweet" from his old speech to his new, because he embeds the old in the new, giving visibility to a process that is usually to be felt rather than seen. He demonstrably is, what he called the Phoenix, "self-begotten" (*S.A.*, 1699).

NOTES

Preface

[1] (London, 1924), p. 36. Grant McColley ("*Paradise Lost*," *An Account of Its Growth and Major Origins,* Chicago, 1940, p. 280) says: "He definitely manifested a tendency to carry phrases, ideas, and patterns of thought from one composition to another"; but in context this does not have the force of Candy's statement. It appears to refer principally to Milton's borrowings from others.

[2] *John Milton* (New York, 1950), p. 29.

[3] But Bradshaw's *Concordance* has the defect of sometimes omitting from record Milton's deliberate, closely recurring repetitions. "Listen and save" can be found under either verb as *Comus*, 866, but its recurrence as line 889 is not indicated at all; there is the same oblivion with respect to the repeated phrases in *Comus*, 221-224, and in some passages of *Paradise Lost* (e. g., iii, 339-340).

Chapter I

[1] It has lately been argued that *Samson Agonistes* was composed before the Restoration (William R. Parker, "The Date of *Samson Agonistes*," *Philological Quarterly*, XXVIII, 1949, pp. 145-166; cf. Allan H. Gilbert in the same issue, p. 106, and in *On the Composition of "Paradise Lost*," Chapel Hill, 1947, p. 24, note), but I give here the conventional, and I think correct, view.

[2] Beginning, perhaps, with Henry Newbolt in *English Review*, XIV (1913), 517-534; reprinted in *Living Age*, CCLXXIX (1913), 73-85.

[3] *Studies in Literature, Second Series* (New York, 1922), p. 120. F. R. Leavis also, but with infinite regret, finds "At a Solemn Music" anticipatory. *Revaluation* (London, 1936), pp. 57-58. Of "On the Morning of Christ's Nativity," written when Milton had just come of age, F. E. Hutchinson says (though with some exaggeration, I think): "This ode foreshadows the poetry of *Paradise Lost*; already we hear the sonorous Miltonic line, especially in the Alexandrine which ends the opening stanzas as well as each verse of the Hymn that follows." *Milton and the English Mind* (London, 1946), p. 17. James Russell Lowell wrote in 1872: "The strain heard in the 'Nativity Ode,' in the 'Solemn Music,' and in 'Lycidas,' is of a higher mood,

as regards metrical construction, than anything that had thrilled the English ear before, giving no uncertain augury of him who was to show what sonorous metal lay silent till he touched the keys in the epical organ-pipes of our various language, that have never since felt the strain of such prevailing breath." *Writings* (Boston, 1890), IV, 97. A year and a half before the Nativity Hymn, in "At a Vacation Exercise," 48-49, Milton had grandly declared his ambition to compose epic poems, "Such as the wise Demodocus once told In solemn songs at King Alcinous' feast." The miniature epic, "In Quintum Novembris," was even then one year behind him. Indeed, there is no limit to which hindsight may not carry us. See John Bailey's observations on the lines Milton wrote when he was fifteen, "Who by His all-commanding might Did fill the new-made world with light" ("Psalm cxxxvi," 25), in which the critic finds "two of Milton's life-long themes." *Milton* (New York, 1915), pp. 95-97.

⁴ See Arnold's "On Translating Homer" (1861) in *Essays* (London, 1914), especially pp. 290-291. Also "A French Critic on Milton" in *Mixed Essays* (New York, 1899), p. 201: "Alone of English poets, alone in English art, Milton ... is our great artist in style, our one first-rate master in the grand style." In his last words on Milton (*Essays in Criticism, Second Series*, London, 1894, pp. 56-68), Arnold spoke rather of "the great style," but "the grand style" was already the phrase that others were using, e.g. Augustine Birrell the year before (*Obiter Dicta, Second Series*, New York, 1887, pp. 36, 49) and Stopford Brooke in his *Primer of English Literature* (1876, as quoted by Arnold, *Mixed Essays*, p. 146) and in *Milton* (New York, 1879), pp. 84, 141, 151. George Saintsbury set the seal on the phrase with his essay, "Milton and the Grand Style," *Milton Memorial Lectures* (London, 1909), pp. 83-107, an essay which, by the way, largely deals with "Lycidas."

⁵ He would be emulating the effect of the Greek language on him: "quae Iovis ora decebant Grandia magniloquis elata vocabula Graiis." "Ad Patrem," 80-81. Cf. "grandius quiddam, quod eloqui possim, quaeram" (VIII, 12).

⁶ *Milton* (London, 1879), p. 142. Thomas Warton took a similar stand as editor of the *Poems upon Several Occasions* (London, 1791), pp. xiii ff.

⁷ *Life of John Milton* (London, 1890), p. 5.

⁸ This is James Holly Hanford's final view, *John Milton, Englishman* (New York, 1949), pp. 171-174, which seems to be shared by

C. M. Bowra, *From Virgil to Milton* (London, 1945), pp. 227-228, and which differs from that in Hanford's *Milton Handbook*, Fourth edition (New York, 1946), p. 190. Ten lines (iv, 32-41) go back to circa 1642, as we learn from Edward Phillips ("Life" in Helen Darbishire, editor, *The Early Lives of Milton*, London, 1932, pp. 72-73). The most elaborate defence of the view comes from McColley, *op. cit.*, pp. 301 ff.

⁹ Hanford, *John Milton, Englishman*, p. 26.

¹⁰ *A Milton Handbook*, p. 85.

¹¹ See the prayer to the Holy Trinity, III, 76.

¹² The word, which gets fifteen columns in the Patterson *Index*, occurs in Milton's first poem (or one of his first two poems)—in the second line of "A Paraphrase on *Psalm 114*" "done by the Author at fifteen years." Line 10 of the cotemporaneous *Psalm 136* is also interesting: "Who doth the wrathful tyrants quell," not being in the original, though it can be found by those who take Todd's advice to look into Buchanan's rendering: "Cui domini rerum submittunt sceptra tyranni."

¹³ See Hanford's interesting analysis, "The Temptation Motive in Milton," *Studies in Philology*, XV (1918), 176-194. See further Margarete Bastian, *Das Problem der Versuchung bei Milton* (Marburg, 1930).

¹⁴ Warton in H. J. Todd, ed., *Poetical Works of John Milton* (London, 1801), VI, 242-243; C. S. Jerram, ed., "*Lycidas*" and "*Epitaphium Damonis*" (New York, 1881), pp. 61-62; A. W. Verity, ed., *Ode on the Morning of Christ's Nativity, L'Allegro, Il Penseroso and Lycidas* (Cambridge, 1891), p. 133; Merritt Y. Hughes, ed., *Paradise Regained, The Minor Poems, and Samson Agonistes* (New York, 1937), p. 288. One editor (F. A. Patterson, *The Student's Milton*, New York, 1933, Notes, p. 59) brings considerable pressure to bear, thus: "Either to engage in the writing of light amatory poetry, such as that of the Cavalier poets, or to occupy oneself with light love-making. Which interpretation fits in better with the text and with Milton's character?" David Masson, ed., *Poetical Works* (London, 1890), III, 259, and W. P. Trent, ed. *L'Allegro, Il Penseroso, Comus, and Lycidas* (New York, 1897), pp. 162-163, are on the other side, as are also, without debating the matter, G. Wilson Knight, *The Burning Oracle* (London, 1939), p. 70, Arthur Barker, *Milton and the Puritan Dilemma* (Toronto, 1942), p. 14, and David Daiches, *A Study of Literature for Readers and Critics* (Ithaca, 1948), p. 182. Warton admitted that

Amaryllis is a "common poetical name." If Milton was thinking
of a particular one, it was Virgil's "lentus in umbra, Formosam re-
sonare doces Amaryllida silvas " (Ecl. I, 4-5). He may have had in
mind Tasso's words:

> Signor, non sotto l'ombra in piaggia molle
> Tra fonti e fior, tra Ninfe et tra Sirene,
> Ma in cima a l'erto e faticoso colle
> De la virtù riposto è il nostro bene.
> Chi non gela, e non suda, e non s'estolle
> De le vie del piacer, là non perviene.

Gerusalemme Liberata, XVII, 61, 1-6. In Fairfax's translation (1600)
" le vie del piacer " becomes " pleasure's lap."

[15] One can get nearer than the " vincla " of the Scotch Buchanan.
There is Thomas Lodge's *Rosalynde* (ed. E. C. Baldwin, Boston, 1910,
p. 13): " The trammels of her hair, folded in a caul of gold, ... the
tresses that folds in the brows of Apollo were not half so rich to the
sight, for in her hairs it seemed love had laid herself in ambush, to
entrap the proudest eye that durst gaze upon their excellence."
Thomas Carew alludes to " nets in your hair " as a poetical commonplace (" To a Lady that Desired I would Love Her," 23), and Richard
Lovelace, after Milton, has

> When I lie tangled in her hair
> And fettered to her eye

" To Althea," 5-6; likewise Andrew Marvell:

> I could have fled from one but singly fair;
> My disentangled soul itself might save,
> Breaking the curlèd trammels of her hair.
> But how should I avoid to be her slave,
> Whose subtle art invisibly can wreathe
> My fetters of the very air I breathe?

" The Fair Singer," second stanza. It goes at least as far back as
three sonnets of Petrarch, *Rime*, CXCVI-CXCVIII. See William
Empson, *Some Versions of Pastoral* (London, 1935), pp. 176-177, on
Eve's hair.

[16] Not even Edwin Greenlaw in "A Better Teacher than Aquinas,"
SP, XIV (1917), 196-217. I paused over it in a review, *Modern
Language Quarterly*, IX (1948), 361.

[17] *The Tempest*, I, ii, 418 ff.

[18] I have dealt with the implications and background of the phrase

as used here in " New Light on the ' Haemony ' Passage in *Comus*,"
PQ, XXI (1942), 283-298.

[19] This is itself (as Warton noted) an imitation of *Iliad*, II, 23,
quoted by Milton in "An Early Prolusion," XII, 288; cf. *Aeneid*, IV,
560.

[20] George C. Taylor, *Milton's Use of Du Bartas* (Cambridge, Mass.,
1934), p. 83; M. Y. Hughes, ed. *Paradise Lost* (New York, 1935),
p. 251.

[21] Noted by Todd a century and a half ago; edition cited, III, 86.
Sylvester's Du Bartas is not what I should point to as the source.
How many times had Milton, from childhood on, seen the famous
Estienne device of the man plucking olives with the motto *Noli altum
sapere?*

[22] George C. Taylor, " Did Milton Read Robert Crofts' *A Paradice
Within Us or The Happie Mind?* " *PQ*, XXVIII (1949), 207-210.

[23] This is one of the instances where I have noted a parallel inde-
pendently and afterward found it remarked on by another, in this case
E. M. W. Tillyard in his Introduction to *Milton's Private Correspondence and Academic Exercises*, translated by Phyllis B. Tillyard,
(Cambridge, 1932), p. xxxviii. Less close in language though not in
thought is the statement in *De Doctrina Christiana*: " Restitutio
hominis est, qua is a Deo patre per Iesum Christum peccato et morte
liberatus, ad statum gratiae et gloriae longe praestantiorem quam
unde exciderat evectus est." XV, 250.

[24] What other major English writer, however, operated under the
conditions that make Milton's case of peculiar interest—a strong
personality, a scholar's retentive memory, and a voluminous production in verse and prose extending over fifty years, and in more than
one language? A curious and thrilling light is thrown on Shakespeare's associative processes by Edward A. Armstrong, *Shakespeare's
Imagination: A Study of the Psychology of Association and Inspiration*
(London, 1946), who deals with image clusters, which are, of course,
often word clusters. Milton was more ratiocinative than " Fancy's
child "; his associations are, accordingly, easier to account for. Paul
Valéry once made a reference to " those recurrences of terms that
reveal the bent, the characteristic frequencies, of a mind." *Southern
Review*, IV (1938), 165. Leo Spitzer, as if taking advantage of this
aperçu, has constructed nothing less than a " psychogram " out of
the repetition of " voir " in the " Récit de Théramène " in *Phèdre*, or
the occurrence of " grand " six times in the first strophe of an ode by

Paul Claudel. *Linguistics and Literary History: Essays in Stylistics* (Princeton, 1948), pp. 106 ff. and 198 ff. What might not then be hoped for from the recurrence of larger units than a single word? It depends, of course, on the author, if not on the audacity of the critic. (Similarity of phrasing is an old test of authorship: used most recently for Shakespeare by J. Dover Wilson in the Introduction to his edition of *Titus Andronicus*, Cambridge, 1948, pp. xx ff.)

[25] It is to be understood that I am not concerned with cases where Milton was openly quoting himself, as when he wrote in an autograph album in 1639 the last two lines of *Comus* (XVIII, 271), or defended in *An Apology for Smectymnuus* expressions he had used in *Animadversions upon the Remonstrant's Defense*, such as " flanks and briskets " (III, 311, 177), " spare your ladle " (III, 311, 114), or the simile of the toothed sleekstone (III, 327-328, 114), or the misfortune of meeting the " night-walking cudgeller " (III, 300, 113). Instances in other works include IV, 265, III, 417; VI, 46, 4; IX, 70 (" obaeratus aufugisti "), VIII, 40 (" obaeratus aufugit "); IX, 178, VIII, 126; IX, 184, VIII, 94. Often enough Milton used quotations from others more than once, e. g. *Eikon Basilike* on suppressing errors and schisms, VI, 143, V, 281; Hall as " this modest confuter " (III, 283, 289) who can make " light froth sink " (III, 114, 155); the proverb on tyrant custom (III, 208, 272, VIII, 238) or of the wise physician (III, 429, IV, 259); various other opponents, such as More (" dii boni," IX, 62, 68, 94), or supporters, such as St. Paul (I Cor. i, 27 is hidden in III, 248, 364; Hebrews i, 14 in III, 69, vi, 167). For overt Biblical quotations that are repeated, see Harris F. Fletcher, *The Use of the Bible in Milton's Prose* (Urbana, 1929).

[26] *The Burning Oracle*, pp. 59-113; *Chariot of Wrath* (London, 1942).

[27] *Milton's Royalism: A Study of the Conflict of Symbol and Idea in the Poems* (Ithaca, 1943).

[28] *Milton's Imagery* (New York, 1950). See also the edition of the 1645 *Poems* by Cleanth Brooks and John Edward Hardy (New York, 1951), *passim*, and especially " The Dominant Images," pp. 255 ff.

[29] Maurice Kelley, *This Great Argument: A Study of Milton's " De Doctrina Christiana " as a Gloss upon " Paradise Lost "* (Princeton, 1941). But see the present work, pp. 114 ff., 145.

[30] See Zera S. Fink, " Milton and the Theory of Climatic Influence," *MLQ*, II (1941), 67-80. B. Rajan, *" Paradise Lost " and the Seventeenth Century Reader* (London, 1947), p. 32, notes: " Yet he him-

self told Phillips (and Phillips subsequently told Aubrey) that ' his
vein never happily flow'd but from the *Autumnal Equinoctial* to the
Vernal.' " (This discrepancy has also been commented on by Verity,
editor of *Areopagitica*, pp. 104-105 as cited below, p. 190, note 18.)

[31] The last development of this, in *Paradise Lost*, is also of interest:
ii, 552-555.

[32] See Hanford, " The Youth of Milton," in *Studies in Shakespeare,
Milton and Donne* by Members of the English Department of the
University of Michigan (New York, 1925), pp. 136 ff.

[33] Emmanuel Des Essarts (*De Veterum Poetarum tum Graeciae,
tum Romae apud Miltonem Imitatione*, Paris, 1871, p. 22) has
pointed out (or rather, meant to point out, but he quoted the wrong
verse) that " unconquered virgin " translates Aeschylus' " ἄγαμον
ἀδάματον," verse 153, *Supplices*.

[34] An example of the borrowing of a word more technical than
individual is the repetition of the word " pigmentum " in reference to
Salmasius' gaudy style: " tritissimum orationis tuae pigmentum "
and "copiosissimi hominis pigmentum " (VII, 224, 342).

[35] Cf. Douglas Bush, " *Paradise Lost* " *in Our Time* (Ithaca, 1945),
pp. 35 ff. It was Calvin who made " Christian liberty " current.

[36] Allan H. Gilbert, *A Geographical Dictionary of Milton* (New
Haven, 1919), p. 82.

[37] There needs to be much more investigation than there has been
as to what were and what were not stock phrases. C. V. Wedgwood
has soundly observed of Spenser: " Even when the influence of his
style had faded, his phrases remained the common property of literature." *Seventeenth-Century English Literature* (London, 1950),
p. 48. J. B. Leishman has given examples to back up the following:
" For both here and elsewhere Milton reveals a very considerable
indebtedness, not merely to the diction of Shakespeare, but to that of
many other sixteenth- and seventeenth-century poets, some of them
very minor ones. Some of his most memorable phrases are often
appropriations, with certain additions and modifications of his own,
of what were almost *clichés.*" " *L'Allegro* and *Il Penseroso* in their
Relation to Seventeenth-Century Poetry," *Essays and Studies 1951*,
English Association (London, 1951), p. 29. I have gone through
Harington's Ariosto and found fifty of Milton's phrases, including a
number of his repeated phrases such as " cursed crew," " shady bank,"
" high attempts," etc.

[38] Ewald Pommrich, *Miltons verhältnis zu Torquato Tasso* (Halle,

1902), does not cite Fairfax as much as he might have, though after comparing *Paradise Lost*, vi, 876 f. and *Godfrey of Bulloigne*, IX, 59, he observes (page 31, note 1): "Es wird sich noch mehrmals zeigen, dass Milton mit Fairfax übereinstimmt. Wir können darin eine Bestätigung des Vermutung erblicken, dass er die englische Übersetzung der 'Gerusalemme Liberata' gelesen und hochgeschätzt hat." One can even find in it three words of the Piedmont Sonnet, "Alpine mountains cold" (XIII, 60, 4).

[39] W. R. Parker has advanced a heresy in "Milton's Last Sonnet: Addressed to First or Second Wife?" *Review of English Studies*, XXI (1945), 235-238, answered by Fitzroy Pyle, "Milton's Sonnet on His 'Late Espoused Saint'," *RES*, XXV (1949), 57-60. The argument continues in *RES*, New Series, II (1951), 147-154.

[40] Armstrong, *op. cit.*

[41] Including the music of poetry: "Or sweetest Shakespeare, Fancy's child, Warble his native wood-notes wild." "L'Allegro," 133-134.

[42] Sylvester's Du Bartas has this argument prefacing the fall of man:

> The World's transform'd from what it was at first:
> For Adam's sin, all creatures else accurst:
> Their Harmony distuned by his jar:
> Yet all again consent, to make him war.

Quoted by Taylor, *Milton's Use of Du Bartas*, p. 105.

[43] The coming of Christ is the coming of music. Nativity Hymn, stanzas ix ff.

[44] See Tillyard, *Milton* (New York, 1930), p. 373.

[45] Twice to begin a line with "Tu modo da" (El. IV, 61; El. VII, 101) is scarcely to arouse comment, and the same is true of two other desiderative formulae, "O utinam" (El. I, 21; El. VII, 87) and "Parce precor" (El. VII, 93; Prodit. Bomb. II, 4). "Crede mihi" begins five lines (El. V, 91; El. VI, 6, 43; El. VII, 91; Prodit. Bomb. II, 10) (twice with "vix" in the immediate neighborhood). "Ah quoties" begins four lines (El. I, 53, 55; El. V, 79; Epit. Dam., 142), "Nec mora" three (El. III, 35; El. VII, 69; In Q. N., 208), "Ast ego" three (El. I, 85; El. IV, 57; El. VII, 77), "Ergo ego" two ("Ad Patrem," 101; "Mansus," 24), "Et vocat ad" two (El. I, 28; El. VI, 50). "Usus ope" ended two (El. I, 88; Prodit. Bomb. II, 6), once in a context anticipatory of the haemony "of divine effect" passage: "divini Molyos usus ope." "Posse sequi" (El. I, 72; El. VI, 4) and "tali ... amictu" (El. 3, 57; In Q. N., 90) are no more striking in Latin than they would be in English, but "dulcia ... carmina" (El. VI, 35; "Ad

Patrem," 33; " dulci ... cantu," "Ad Salsillum," 32) is something else again and has its English equivalent, " songs ... sweet," *Comus*, 878. Having referred to the unavailing " artes medentum " in his poem on the death of Vice-Chancellor Gostlin, a physician (" In Obitum Proc. Med.," 22), the poet sadly recalled Diodati's " artesque medentum " in two consecutive lines of " Epitaphium Damonis " (152). Spring goes both in the indicative—" tempora veris eunt " (El. I, 48)—and in the subjunctive—" tempora veris eant " (El. V, 138)—ending an elegiac line in each instance. Twice twilight is late, " sera crepuscula " (In Q. N., 54; El. V, 119). The Cambridge students are " Palladium ... gregem " (El. II, 2), " Palladio gregi " (" In Obitum Proc. Med.," 33).

[46] In the words of *Of Reformation*, " a poet ... with his garland and singing robes about him." III, 235.

[47] In 1654 he could look back with some satisfaction and say he *had* celebrated: VIII, 252. Hutchinson (*op. cit.*, p. 84) comments: " In some true if incomplete sense he was delivering to the world, in his first and second *Defence of the English People*, that epic ' doctrinal and exemplary to a nation,' to which he had early dedicated his powers." Cf. Tillyard, *Milton*, p. 198, and Sir H. J. C. Grierson, *Milton and Wordsworth* (Cambridge, 1937), pp. 71-72.

CHAPTER II

[1] Milton headed it "Anno aetatis 17," but actually it appears to belong to 1628. W. R. Parker, " Milton's *Fair Infant*," *TLS*, Dec. 17, 1938, p. 802.

[2] *Astrophel*, 7-8.

[3] Hughes conjecturally puts the " Verses from the Commonplace Book " in the Saint Paul's period, and two other poems of unknown date, "Apologus de Rustico et Hero," and the translation from Horace, have been dated equally early by other scholars. See Donald Leman Clark, *John Milton at St. Paul's School* (New York, 1948), pp. 177-178.

[4] The second edition, 1621, was edited by Otto L. Jiriczek, *Quellen und Forschungen*, XC (Strassburg, 1903). Cap. xxi, " De figuris in sono," illustrates a dozen figures of repetition mostly by quoting from *The Faerie Queene*. As Clark, *op. cit.*, p. 70, points out, correcting the Columbia editors, XVIII, 656, there is no evidence that the book was actually " used at St. Paul's School," it having been designed for foreigners, but Milton surely was acquainted with it.

[5] *De ratione studii* (1511), translated by Clark, *op. cit.*, p. 216.

[6] See Sister Miriam Joseph, *Shakespeare's Use of the Arts of Language* (New York, 1947), who deals with the various figures of repetition on pp. 78-89, 305-307.

[7] See, besides the books by Clark and Sister Miriam Joseph mentioned above, Charles Sears Baldwin, *Renaissance Literary Theory and Practice* (New York, 1939), D. L. Clark, *Rhetoric and Poetry in the Renaissance* (New York, 1922), William G. Crane, *Wit and Rhetoric in the Renaissance* (New York, 1937), Veré L. Rubel, *Poetic Diction in the English Renaissance* (New York, 1941), T. W. Baldwin, *William Shakspere's Small Latine and Lesse Greeke* (Urbana, 1944), 2 vols. Only those with some classical education make contact with the art: for instance, Thomas D. Seymour's edition of *The First Six Books of the Iliad* (Boston, 1901) illustrates epanalepsis, as well as chiasmus, litotes, and periphrasis, with quotations from Milton (pp. xlii-xliii).

[8] Clark, *John Milton at St. Paul's School*, p. 183.

[9] Walter MacKellar, ed., *The Latin Poems of John Milton* (New Haven, 1930), p. 63.

[10] Ecl. V, 79-80.

[11] Masson, *Life of Milton* (reprinted New York, 1946), I, 136.

[12] Cf. VI, 331: " Tu multum dormis et saepe potas, quae duo sunt corpori inimica."

[13] *The Hill of Dreams*, quoted by Grierson, *op. cit.*, p. 92.

[14] *Works* (Oxford, 1825), VII, 119.

[15] Despite Keightley's suggestion of a possible model in *As You Like It*, II, vii, 113 ff., the interchange between Orlando:

> If ever you have look'd on better days,
> If ever been where bells have knoll'd to church,
> If ever sat at any good man's feast,
> If ever from your eyelids wip'd a tear
> And know what 'tis to pity and be pitied,
> Let gentleness my strong enforcement be;
> In the which hope I blush, and hide my sword,

and the Duke:

> True is it that we have seen better days,
> And have with holy bell been knoll'd to church,
> And sat at good men's feasts, and wip'd our eyes
> Of drops that sacred pity hath engend'red;
> And therefore sit you down in gentleness,
> And take upon command what help we have.

[16] *The Sofa,* I, 89 ff.:

> The nurse sleeps sweetly, hired to watch the sick,
> Whom snoring she disturbs. As sweetly he
> Who quits the coach box at the midnight hour
> To sleep within the carriage more secure,
> His legs depending at the open door.
> Sweet sleep enjoys the curate in his desk,
> The tedious rector drawling o'er his head,
> And sweet the clerk below: but neither sleep
> Of lazy nurse, who snores the sick man dead,
> Nor his who quits the box at midnight hour
> To slumber in the carriage more secure,
> Nor sleep enjoy'd by curate in his desk,
> Nor yet the dozings of the clerk are sweet,
> Compared with the repose the Sofa yields.

[17] " Desire," 3rd stanza (*Poetical Works,* ed. G. I. Wade, London, 1932, p. 77).

[18] See Friedrich Buff, *Miltons " Paradise Lost " in seinem Verhältnisse zur "Aeneide," " Ilias," und " Odyssee "* (Munich, 1904), p. 40.

[19] But see F. X. M. J. Roiron, *Étude sur l'Imagination Auditive de Virgile* (Paris, 1908), a difficult and fascinating study in " l'influence de Virgile sur lui-même."

[20] In Darbishire, *Early Lives,* p. 179.   Repeated by Richardson, p. 211.

[21] Ants Oras, *Milton's Editors and Commentators from Patrick Hume to Henry John Todd (1695-1801)* (Tartu, 1931), p. 43.

[22] C. M. Bowra, *Tradition and Design in the " Iliad "* (Oxford, 1930), p. 88.   There are, of course, German dissertations on the subject: W. Christ, *Die Wiederholung gleicher und ähnlicher Verse in der " Ilias "* (Munich, 1880) ; E. Pfudel, *Die Wiederholung bei Homer* (Liegnitz, 1891) ; K. Sittl, *Die Wiederholung in der " Odyssee "* (Munich, 1882).

[23] Also ii, 162-163; 787-791; 1021-1022; iii, 153-164; 178-180; 190-191; 298-301; 446-448; 566-570; 601-602; 645-646; 663-665; 668-670; iv, 27-29; 73-75; 482; 467-468; v, 146; 289-290; 317-318; 617; 679-680; 791-792; vi, 41-42; 289-290; vii, 184-187; ix, 422-424; 605-606; 708-710; x, 97-99; 668-672; 857-858; 995-997; xi, 95-96; xii, 202-203; 282-283; 447-449; 464-465; 580-581.

[24] "A Note on the Verse of John Milton," *Essays and Studies by Members of the English Association,* XXI, 1935 (Oxford, 1936), pp. 37 ff.; " Milton," *Sewanee Review,* LVI (1948), 199.

[25] *James Joyce: A Critical Introduction* (Norfolk, 1941), pp. 216 ff.

[26] Such as the participial " So saying " thirteen times (iv, 536, 797; v, 82, 331; vi, 189; viii, 300, 644; ix, 179, 780, 834, 990; x, 272, 410), varied by " Thus saying " four times (ii, 466, 871; ix, 385; x, 85). In the last two books there is " To whom thus Michael " eight times (xi, 334, 466, 603, 683, 787; xii, 79, 285, 386), and " T'whom Michael thus " once (xi, 453). We get " He ceased " six times (ii, 43, 845, 1010; viii, 412; xi, 126; xii, 372), " He ended " nine (ii, 106; vi, 496; viii, 452; ix, 733; x, 641; xi, 72, 238; xii, 552, 606), " She ended " twice (x, 937, 1007), " So having said " thrice (ix, 917; x, 157, 504), " He scarce had ended when " twice (iv, 874; vi, 569). " But say ... what " comes from inquiring Adam (xi, 879; xii, 479) (another time " But say " introduces a condition, x, 808), as does " thus ... gratefully replied " (viii, 4; xi, 370). Other expressions occurring twice are " answering spake " (vi, 450, 722), " (S)he scarce had said " (vii, 313; ix, 664), " So spake the false " (iii, 681; v, 694), " To whom thus ... replied " (iv, 440; ix, 342), " He said, and " (v, 872; vi, 719), " silence broke " (ix, 895; x, 353), " answered mild " (vii, 110; x, 67; cf. " mild answer," ix, 226). Analogously, when Michael shows rather than describes, the formula is, for Adam, " He looked and saw " (xi, 556, 638, 712, 840).

[27] And the previously cited (p. 15) " Heaven's King "—in other places with an intervening adjective (i, 131; ii, 851; v, 220; x, 387)— and " Eternal King," besides " the King of Heaven " (ii, 229, 316).

[28] A problem: see Hanford's *Handbook*, p. 194.

[29] There is ample promise " that thy seed shall bruise " (x, 1031; xi, 155), " shall bruise the Serpent's head " (x, 1031; xii, 149). So the Serpent is cursed in the garden: " Her seed shall bruise thy head " (x, 181). Satan reports back to the council: " His seed—when is not set—shall bruise my head " (x, 499). The prophecy " of that destined Seed to bruise the Serpent " (xii, 233) is not finally clear, however, to Adam until the latter part of the last book, when Michael describes the sacrificial act which " Shall bruise the head of Satan, crush his strength, Defeating Sin and Death " (xii, 430). By way of slight variety, Adam asks, " What stroke shall bruise the Victor's heel? " (xii, 385). He is told in what sense " death shall bruise the Victor's heel " (xii, 433). It is but too plain that in making the point, against the preponderant gloom of Books xi and xii, that the " culpa " has a " felix " issue, the poet resorts, almost desperately, to repetition. Every mention of Abraham brings with it the prophecy of Genesis, xxii, 18:

that in his seed
All nations shall be blest.   (xii, 126)

that all the nations of the earth
Shall in his seed be blest.   (xii, 147)

in whom all nations shall be blest (xii, 277)

So in his seed all nations shall be blest.   (xii, 450)

All this had, to be sure, been prepared for in Book iii.   In heaven
the edict had gone out, " Man ... shall find grace " (iii, 131), and
this " gracious ... word " (iii, 144) (another instance of the Miltonic
pun) of the Father was twice echoed by the Saviour (iii, 145, 227) in
offering Himself as the means.   But those who find the last two books
inferior can say, among other things, that the repetition is inferior,
not at all up to Milton's standard.   He has put a merely mechanical
trust in the letter of Scripture.

[30] For further instance, " loud was th'acclaim " before Satan's
victory speech in Book x, 455; Abdiel is " received with joy and
acclamations loud," vi, 23, in heaven.

[31] There is a variety of application also in " dominion given "—to
Christ in heaven (vi, 887); to Adam on earth, " Over all other
creatures " (iv, 430), " O'er other creatures " (viii, 545); to Sin, given
freedom to prey (x, 244), thanks to her " great author " (236), a very
different personage from " the World's great Author " of v, 188.   Likewise " Powers ... Dominions " is the mode of address for angels fallen
(ii, 11) and unfallen (iii, 320).

[32] See the table in Josephine Miles, *Major Adjectives in English
Poetry* (Berkeley, 1946), p. 317.

[33] The most elaborate study of this subject (whatever one may
think of the albino theory which it introduces) is Heinrich Mutsch-
mann's *The Secret of John Milton* (Dorpat, 1925).

[34] " In the firmament of heaven " (vii, 344, 349) (" on the open
firmament of heaven," vii, 390), " through (the) midst of heaven "
(iii, 358; v, 251), " our native heaven " (v, 863; x, 467), " heaven('s)
first-born " (i, 510; iii, 1), " heaven('s) high towers " (i, 749; ii, 62),
" the wall of heaven " (iii, 71, 427, 503), " fame in heaven " (i, 651;
ii, 346; x, 481), "(up, in=) to the heaven of heavens " (vii, 13, 553).

[35] Heaven shares with earth " circuit wide " (vii, 301; viii, 304), or
" wide circuit " (viii, 100), " flaming mount " (v, 598; xi, 216), "(the)
neighboring hills " (v, 547; vi, 663; xi, 575), " ground " that is " firm "
(vi, 242; vii, 443) (*terra firma*), " crystal wall(s)" (vi, 860; vii, 293;
xii, 197), and " charming symphony " (iii, 368; plural, xi, 595).   More

peculiarly heaven is the place below which or in which planets or angels move in " mystic(al) dance " (v, 178; 620), and cherubim have " four faces each " (vi, 753; xi, 128). There angels play on " their golden harps " (iii, 365; vii, 258), send forth " sacred song(s)" (iii, 29, 148, 369).

The inhabitants of heaven and hell are exercised over " new world(s)" (i, 650; ii, 403, 867; iv, 34, 113, 391; vii, 209; x, 257, 377), " another world " (ii, 347, 1004; v, 569; vii, 155; xi, 877), " the (this) new-created world " (iii, 89; iv, 937; vii, 554; x, 481), which, as previously noted, is linked to the floor of heaven " in a golden chain " (ii, 1005, 1051). Populated with " fair creatures " (iv, 790; viii, 276), the scene of " joy and love " (iii, 67, 338; cf. iv, 509), it is a place good enough for the angels: " down to the earth " (iii, 528, 651) they are wont to go, " to visit oft " (iii, 532, 661; vii, 570; cf. xii, 48). " God saw ... that it was good " (vii, 337, 352; cf. 249, 395). We get its topography in such combinations as " firm land " (ii, 589; iii, 75), " hill and dale " (iv, 243; vi, 641; cf. ii, 944; iv, 538; viii, 262), " hill and valley " (ii, 495; vi, 784; ix, 116), " rivers, woods " (viii, 275; ix, 116), " in sea or air " (vii, 629; viii, 341), " rapid current(s) (iv, 227; xi, 853); the sense of passing days in " even and morn " (vii, 252, 338, 550), " usher . . . evening " (iv, 355; x, 94), mists or the stars " rising . . . or falling " (v, 191; x, 663), and the moon " With borrowed light " (iii, 730), " borrowing her light " (vii, 377). For " the blissful seat " (i, 5; iii, 527) not yet become " a world of woe " (viii, 333; ix, 11), for " the seat of man (men)" (iii, 724; vii, 623), of " mortal men " (i, 51; iii, 268; xii, 248) (a Homeric expression), for the " happy ... seat " (ii, 347; iii, 632; iv, 247; vi, 226; xii, 642), " this happy place " (iv, 562; xi, 303) ("those happy places," v, 364), man's " native seat " (vi, 226) (to be lost as the devils lost theirs, i, 634; ii, 76, 1050), " native soil " (xi, 270, 292), recurring epithets abound, especially in testimony to its light and its fruitfulness. Satan addresses his allies; Eve, Adam; Milton, light, as " offspring of Heaven " (ii, 310; ix, 273; iii, 1). This is, literally, " enlighten(ed) earth " (iii, 731; viii, 274); there was no greater stage in creation than the separation of " light from darkness " (vii, 250, 352). It is " the eastern gate " (iv, 542; xi, 190; xii, 638) that gets all the emphasis, whence " the morning shine(s)" (v, 20; vii, 108) with the " rising sun " (iii, 551; iv, 651). The sun, even before it was lighted, was of "ethereal mould " (vii, 356), like God (ii, 139): heaven is " this ethereous mold " (vi, 473). There are " bright luminaries " (vii,

385; viii, 98), "sacred light" (ix, 192; xi, 134), light's "sacred influence" (ii, 1034; ix, 107), "orient beams" (iv, 644; vi, 15). This
is not to deny the use of "thick(est) shade" (iv, 532; viii, 653; ix,
1110) at high noon, and so we pass to the fruitfulness, the "nuptial
bower" (viii, 510; xi, 280), the "sweet recess" (ix, 456; xi, 304), a
"shady bank" (viii, 286; ix, 1037), "branching palm" (iv, 139; vi,
885), "among the trees" (vii, 459; viii, 313), "high overarch'd" (i,
304; ix, 1107). The command, "be fruitful, multiply" (vii, 396, 531),
"fill the earth" (iv, 733; vii, 531), has been overwhelmingly obeyed
by "living creatures" (iv, 287; vii, 413, 455; viii, 370; ix, 228), "living
soul(s)" (v, 197; vii, 388, 528; viii, 154) ("soul living," vii, 392, 451),
including "insect or worm" (iv, 704; vii, 476), "creeping thing(s)"
(vii, 452, 523). In this teeming of "various forms" (iii, 717; v, 473)
of creation ("In narrow room Nature's whole wealth," iv, 207; cf. i,
779), it is the "wanton growth" (iv, 629; ix, 211) of a vegetable
paradise, the "fruits and flowers" (viii, 44; x, 603), of which we are
most conscious, bedewed and fresh: "among . . . dews and flowers" (i,
771; v, 212), "with fresh flowerets" (v, 636; vi, 784), "a fresh fountain" (iv, 229, 326), "fresh dews" (i, 771; xi, 135), "tender stalk"
(v, 337; ix, 428), "grateful smell" (iv, 165; ix, 197), "gentle airs"
(viii, 515; x, 93). "Of grassy turf" Adam can have a table (v, 391)
or an altar (xi, 324); all around is stuff for "sweet repast" (v, 630;
viii, 214; ix, 407). The eye rises to "tree(s) . . . loaden with (fairest)
fruit" (iv, 147; viii, 307; ix, 577), "goodliest trees" (iv, 147; viii,
304). But "new delight(s)" (v, 19, 431) have their danger, and
"such pleasure" (viii, 50; ix, 455, 596, 1024) too quickly passes from
the licit to the illicit. To give Adam and Eve an opportunity to
exercise their free will over what they "as lords possess" (viii, 340),
"possess as lords" (x, 466) (but it is Adam rather than Eve who
should "bear rule," viii, 375; x, 155), stands the "forbidden tree"
(i, 2; x, 554), with its "false fruit" (ix, 1011; xi, 413), "the sacred
fruit" (ix, 904, 924) (in the Latin sense of having a curse on it),
which it is wrong, under whatever temptation, "to pluck and eat"
(viii, 309; ix, 595). "Send . . . from the garden forth" is the edict
twice pronounced in Book xi (97, 261). Not here will rise "proud
cities" (ii, 533; singular, xii, 342), and that in itself spells their doom.
In paradise it was flowers that "reared high" (iv, 699). Among
fallen men Dagon "had his temple high Reared" (i, 463). The
tragedy comes full circle. In Book i the problem for the devils is to
have "scaped the Stygian flood" (239). In Book xii the problem

for man is to have " scaped the flood " (117) which is likewise the
creation of a justly angered God. We find Satan desperately " Wandering this darksome desert " (ii, 973) outside hell. We find doomed
men " Wandering that wat'ry desert " (xi, 779).

Then there is that which is " neither sea, nor shore " (ii, 912),
" neither sea, Nor good dry land " (ii, 939; cf. ix, 117; xi, 749), where
dwell " Night and Chaos " (ii, 895; x, 477), " old Night " (i, 543;
ii, 1002), " ancient Night " (ii, 970, 986). As we shall have more
reason to suspect in a moment, " the wasteful deep " (ii, 961; vi, 862)
is perhaps modeled after Homer's " barren sea " (" ἁλὸς ἀτρυγέτοιο," Il.,
I, 316, 327; etc.), though Milton does not mean the sea by it. At a
distance the world is like a " continent, Dark, waste, and wild " (iii,
424), which recalls the " frozen continent ... dark and wild " (ii, 588)
to which the damned are brought to feel " the bitter change of fierce
extremes." Hell is " The dismal situation waste and wild " (i, 60).
This is true also of the kingdom of Chaos, " the vast immeasurable
abyss, Outrageous as a sea, dark, wasteful, wild " (vii, 212). At last
the Homeric epithet has got near its original noun. " Wild uproar "
(ii, 541; iii, 710) Chaos and Hell have in common.

There are adverbial expressions like " from all the ends of " (v, 586;
xi, 345), " from pole to pole " (iii, 560; ix, 66), " on either side " (ii,
649; vi, 221, 844; x, 415), " far and wide " (iii, 614; iv, 579; vi, 773),
" hither side " (iii, 722; xi, 574), " far off " (ii, 582, 636, 643), " in
mid air " (ii, 718; iv, 940; vi, 536), " distant far "—" far distant " (iii,
428, 501, 621; iv, 453; vi, 551; ix, 576), " height and (or) depth " (ii,
324; viii, 413), " through (in) mid heaven " (iii, 729; vi, 889; ix, 468;
xii, 263). Superhuman creatures soar with " winged ... speed " (i,
674; vi, 788; v, 744; cf. ii, 700) through " the ... air sublime " (ii,
528; iii, 72; vii, 421), " the buxom air " (ii, 842; v, 270), " the ...
ethereal sky " (i, 45; v, 267), " many a league " (ii, 929; iv, 164; x,
274), over " moist and dry " (ii, 898; iii, 652), on the " polar winds "
(v, 269; x, 289). If they walk, it is with " nimble tread " (vi, 73),
" tread of nimble feet " (iv, 866). " Discover wide " (i, 724; ii, 571)
refers to hell, " sudden view " first to chaos (ii, 890), then to earth
(iii, 542). Adam as well as Uriel sees far: " whose eye pursued him
down The way he went " (iv, 125); " Mine eye pursued him still "
(iv, 572); " Her long with ardent look his eye pursued " (ix, 397).
Satan's object, the first time we see him, is to get off the burning lake
onto " yon dreary plain ": " ' Thither let us tend ' " (i, 183). His
ultimate object is to do damage on earth: " ' Thither let us bend all

our thoughts ' " (ii, 354), says his spokesman. " Forth rushed " (vi,
749; x, 456) and " forth issuing " (ix, 447), " issuing forth " (x, 533,
537), " issued forth " (viii, 233), " forth issued " (ii, 786) cover activity blest, unblest, and, in one lovely " L'Allegro "-like simile (ix,
447), even human.

War is a category which gathers to itself " edge of battle " (i, 277;
vi, 108), " din of war " (i, 668; vi, 408), " a numerous host " (ii, 993;
vi, 231, 830), " highest deeds " (v, 865; vi, 112), " dreadful deeds "
(i, 130; iv, 990), " fought in heaven " (ii, 45, 768), the threat " expect
to feel " (iv, 972; v, 892), "(both) spear and shield " (i, 565; iv, 990;
x, 542), " flaming sword(s)" (i, 664; xii, 592), " the sword of Michael "
(ii, 294; vi, 250, 321), " flying march " (ii, 574; v, 688), " under spread
ensigns " (ii, 886; vi, 533), " to right and left the front " (vi, 558, 569),
" part curb the(ir) ... steed(s)" (ii, 531; xi, 643), and " foaming
steed(s)" (vi, 391; xi, 643), if not invariably " fiery ... steed(s)" (ii,
531; iii, 522; vi, 17, 391), " trumpet's sound " (i, 754; xii, 229),
" strictest watch " (iv, 783; ix, 363), " fear no assault " (ii, 343; iv,
190), and " vaulted ... with fire " (i, 298; vi, 214). The last corroborates General Sherman by linking war with hell.

This examination of recurrences in *Paradise Lost* can draw to a
close with those that have to do with the plot or the thought of the
poem. It is the story of a transition, not absolutely sudden fall, from
a " state of bliss " (v, 241, 543), " joy ... and bliss " (xi, 43; xii, 551),
" happy state " (i, 29, 141; iv, 519; v, 234, 504, 536, 830; viii, 331;
ix, 337, 347), " happier state " (ii, 24; iv, 775), " full of peace " (ix,
1126; xi, 815), to " endless misery " (i, 142; x, 810). (" Former
state," ii, 585; iv, 94; viii, 290, and " upright ... and pure," i, 18;
iv, 837, refer once to Satan.) It was not a " glorious trial " (ix, 961,
1177): only the fallen and still deluded Adam and Eve can call it
that; neither they nor the erring angels (" far the greater part," vii,
145; cf. 359; xii, 533, stood) operated under " strict necessity " (v, 528;
x, 131). They were amply warned (better warned, in this issue of
" weal or woe," viii, 638; ix, 133, than " by experience taught," v,
826; viii, 190): " If ye be found obedient " (v, 501, 514), " sole command " (iii, 94; vii, 47; viii, 329—all in connection with " transgress "
or " transgressed "), " well thou know'st " (iv, 426; cf. iii, 276; iv, 926)
(a formula like " as ... thou sawst," ii, 796; viii, 446; xi, 707, and
" was known in heaven," i, 732; x, 5), " the law of God " (xii, 397,
402), " God ordains " (iv, 636; vi, 175), " God made thee " (x, 760,
766), " honour due " (iii, 738; v, 817). " ' Nature ... hath done her

part; Do thou but thine!'" (viii, 561) "'God towards thee hath done
his part: do thine'" (ix, 375) (Adam passes on to Eve Raphael's
admonition). Satan speaks sophistically of "just right" (ii, 18), but
God and Eve use the words "just and right" (iii, 98; iv, 443) straight-
forwardly of Adam in his original state. These are not, in the correct
and final view, "strict laws" (ii, 241; xii, 304): "equal over equals"
(v, 820, 832) do not "reign."

The tree of the "knowledge of good and evil" (vii, 543; ix, 697,
723; cf. iv, 222; viii, 324; xi, 87), "knowledge forbidden" (iv, 515),
"forbidden knowledge" (xii, 279), is kept constantly before us in such
expressions as "forbids ... to taste" (v, 61; ix, 753), "the day thou
eatest" (vii, 544; viii, 329), "eaten of the tree" (x, 122, 199), "hunger
and thirst" ("Powerful persuaders," ix, 586; "constraining," x, 568).
It works a "strange alteration" (ii, 1024; ix, 599), gives a deceptive
"power ... within" (ix, 96, 681, 836). Those who taste find they
have "good lost and evil got" (ix, 1072; xi, 87), "utter loss" (ii, 440;
iii, 308; ix, 131). It is "death denounced" (ix, 695; x, 49, 210, 962),
death "cold and dry" (x, 294; xi, 544), "to dust return" (x, 208,
770), "in(to) my (thy) mother's lap" (x, 778; xi, 536), "mortal
sting" (ii, 653; iii, 253), besides "guilty shame" (iv, 313; ix, 1058)
leading to "with ... skins of beasts" (x, 217, 221), "together sewed"
(ix, 1095, 1112), and ultimately "idols" or "idolatries" that are
"foul" (i, 446; xii, 337): in three words: "all our woe" (i, 3; ii, 872).

A further stage in justifying "the ways of God" (i, 26; viii, 226)
is to show the mixture of "mercy and justice" (iii, 132, 407; cf. x, 59,
78) (the problem is ever one of keeping to the right proportions:
"within ... bounds," vii, 120, 167, "fully ... satisfied," viii, 180; x,
79, "enjoy ... fill," iv, 507; v, 503) that renders men (in contrast to
the fallen angels) not lost "without redemption" (iii, 222; v, 615).
Certain temporal expressions refer to this future of salvation or
damnation, as the case may be: "without end" (i, 67; ii, 870; iii, 142;
v, 165, 615; vi, 137; vii, 161, 542; x, 797), "future days" (vi, 502;
xi, 114, 357, 764), "to show thee what" (xi, 357, 709), "what shall
come in future days" (xi, 114, 357), "ere long" (ix, 172, 246), "first
and last" (ii, 324; iii, 134; x, 831), "final hope" (ii, 142; xi, 493).
Adam, a mortalist, decides that his "breath of life" (x, 784, 789) will
altogether perish, this against the doubt "lest all I cannot die" (x,
783). "All of me, then, shall die" (x, 792). This is opposite to,
yet curiously like, the Saviour's remark when he offers himself "for
man's offence" (iii, 355, 410): "All that of me can die" (iii, 246).

It will be " good out of evil " (vii, 188; cf. i, 163; xii, 470), " heaven and earth renewed " (x, 638; xi, 66), thanks to " supernal grace " (vii, 573; xi, 359). To the world's history as Michael unfolds it (or as anticipated elsewhere) are connected " just man (men)" (vii, 570; xi, 577, 681, 818, 890), Moses' " potent rod " (i, 338; xii, 211), " works of faith " (xii, 306, 536), " impose(d) (new) law(s)" (xi, 227; cf. ii, 241; v, 679; xii, 304, 397), " evil turn " (verb, xi, 373; xii, 471).

[36] " Fierce desire " (iv, 509; vi, 201) can be good as well as bad, just as " so minded " (iv, 583; viii, 444) can refer to either good or evil purpose. " Peculiar grace(s)" (ii, 183; v, 15) Eve shares with the elect. " One man except " (ix, 545; xi, 808) can be the words of the Serpent or of Michael. The devils and man are equally armed with " strength entire " (i, 146; x, 9). Death and Adam receive a " death's wound " (iii, 252; xii, 392). Gabriel looks at Satan " with stern regard " (iv, 877). So Adam looks at Eve (x, 866), as he bursts out with his long misogynistic tirade. " Bowing low(ly)" can be idolatrous (i, 434), hypocritical (iii, 736), or honest obeisance to a superior creature (v, 360). " Great potentate " (v, 706; xi, 231) can apply to Lucifer or to Michael: so with " by his gait " (iv, 870; xi, 230) as a method of judging rank. Within the same book " in ... sea tossed " (x, 287, 718) can be literal or figurative. " Wild work " (v, 112; vi, 698) refers to the fantasies of dreams or to the imminent damage to heaven of war among the angels. But " bulk " that is " huge " has the consistency of always applying to something floating—Satan on the burning lake (i, 196), monsters of the deep (vii, 410), Noah's ark (xi, 729).

[37] If we have " To whom ... thus ... replied " twice in *Paradise Lost* (iv, 440; ix, 342), we get it five times in *Paradise Regained* (1, 406; 2, 378, 432; 3, 43; 4, 285). (Other expressions common to both poems will be considered in Chapter III.) " To whom thus Jesus " starts four lines (2, 317, 378, 432; 4, 560), " To whom our Savior " seven (1, 406, 493; 3, 43, 121, 181, 386; 4, 285), in this contest with " the Tempter proud " (4, 569, 595) (called that at the moment of his downfall).

[38] A. H. Gilbert, " Is *Samson Agonistes* Unfinished? " *PQ*, XXVIII (1949), 105.

[39] *Ibid.*, p. 85.

[40] *Milton* (London, 1900), p. 205.

[41] (Cambridge, Mass., 1922), p. 80.

[42] *Ibid.*, p. 85.

[43] Pp. 295 ff.

[44] *New Memoirs of the Life and Poetical Works of Mr. John Milton* (London, 1740), pp. 105, 122-123. The two examples given are x, 1086 ff. and *Samson Agonistes*, 960 ff.

[45] *Poets and Playwrights* (Minneapolis, 1930), p. 248.

CHAPTER III

[1] " He added not " (xi, 263; 1, 497), " He ended, and " (vi, 496; ix, 733; x, 641; xi, 72, 238; xii, 552, 606; 1, 106, 346), " He ceased " (ii, 43, 845, 1010; viii, 412; xi, 126; xii, 372; 2, 235), " So saying, he " (v, 82; viii, 644; x, 410; 4, 394, 541), likewise " He looked and saw " (xi, 556, 638, 712, 840; 3, 310). " But say," in two of its four appearances (x, 808; xi, 879; xii, 479; 3, 357), introduces a condition.

[2] See Merritt Y. Hughes, " Milton and the Sense of Glory," *PQ*, XXVIII (1949), 107-124.

[3] " issue(d) forth " (viii, 233; 3, 305; cf. ii, 786; 4, 276), " summon all " (ix, 374; 2, 143), " far removed " (i, 73; ii, 211, 321; vii, 272; 4, 87), " which . . . most excel " (viii, 542; 3, 307), which can refer to figurative struggles as well.

[4] See the quotation in Douglas Bush, *Mythology and the Renaissance Tradition in English Poetry* (Minneapolis, 1932), p. 278, note 80. One of Milton's earliest commentators, James Paterson, connected Paradise with " the Fable of Adonis (which in the Greek signifies Pleasure) who had Golden Apples under the Custody of a watchful Dragon." *A Complete Commentary, with Etymological, Explanatory, Critical and Classical Notes on Milton's " Paradise Lost "* (London, 1744), pp. 10-11.

[5] See Brooke, *Milton*, p. 28; George F. Sensabaugh, " Milieu of *Comus*," *SP*, XLI (1944), 238-249.

[6] *The Miltonic Setting* (London, 1938), pp. 1-28. See the objection to this method of dating by A. S. P. Woodhouse, " Notes on Milton's Early Development," *University of Toronto Quarterly*, XIII (1943), 85 ff.

[7] *Poetical Works*, III, 8, note 1.

[8] Satan's son, Death, is " the dear pledge Of dalliance " (ii, 818). There is only a verbal connection with Camus's mourning Lycidas as " my dearest pledge " (107). (And it is a very slight verbal connection: " pledge " is the Latin *pignus*: in fact Milton has " pignora

cara " (El. IV, 42) ; " pledges dearer " can be found in *Titus Andro-*
nicus, iii, 1, 292, " dearest pledges," meaning offspring, in Bacon's
essay " Of Marriage and Single Life," the third sentence; see the
Oxford English Dictionary s.v. " pledge," 2d, and Jerram's edition of
"Lycidas," p. 68, for examples other than these.)

[9] A commonplace phrase like " various objects " (viii, 609; *Samson
Agonistes*, 71) need detain us still less.   Others in this neutral or
merely idiomatic class are: "(to) part . . . hence " (iv, 872; *S.A.*, 1229,
1481), " wedded maid " (Nativity Hymn, 3; v, 223) ; " inform(ed)
feet " (*Comus*, 180; *S.A.*, 335), " utmost end " (*Comus*, 136; x, 1020),
" heave . . . head " (" L'Allegro," 145; *Comus*, 885; *S.A.*, 197), " I hear
the tread of " (*Comus*, 91; iv, 866; *S.A.*, 111), " and . . . stretched out
all the " (" L'Allegro," 111; " Lycidas," 190), " little reckoning made
(make)" (*Comus*, 642; " Lycidas," 116), "(and) I . . . persuade me "
(" Death of a Fair Infant," 29; *S.A.*, 586, 1495), the combination of
" fears " with " grief " (*Comus*, 565; *P.R.*, 1, 110), " sea " with
" shore " (ii, 912; ix, 117; xi 750; *P.R.*, 2, 344; *S.A.*, 962), " (o'er)
hill " with " dale " (" Song on May Morning," 8; ii, 944; iv, 243,
538; vi, 641; viii, 262; *P.R.*, 3, 267), " his (thy) father's house "
(xii, 121; *P.R.*, 3, 175; 4, 552; *S.A.*, 447, 1717, 1733), " What boots
it? " (" Lyc.," 64; *S.A.*, 560), " Thrice (s)he assayed " (i, 619; *S.A.*,
392), " bring to my remembrance "—" to my remembrance bring "
(iv, 38; *S.A.*, 277).   " Radiant light " (*Comus*, 374; iii, 594) may be
figurative or literal.

[10] The Lady's song is associated with " smoothing " and a bird and
night in *Comus*:

> How sweetly did they float upon the wings
> Of silence, through the empty-vaulted night,
> At every fall smoothing the raven down
> Of darkness till it smiled! (249)

[11] John A. Himes, *Miltonic Enigmas* (privately printed, 1921), p. 16.
[12] See John S. Smart, editor, *The Sonnets of Milton* (Glasgow, 1921),
pp. 89 ff.; Grierson, *Milton and Wordsworth*, pp. 66 ff.
[13] Like " yet . . . remains " (Son. xvi, 9; *S.A.*, 433, 649) or " oft . . .
heard " (*Comus*, 252; x, 119; *P.R.*, 1, 270; cf. i, 275), or " strew . . .
hearse " in elegies (" Epitaph on the Marchioness of Winchester,"
58, noun first; " Lyc.," 151).
[14] Another persistent association is " truth and peace " (" On Time,"
16; xi, 667) or " peace and truth " (Son. xvi, 4).

¹⁵ The " fame " of " fame in heaven," " Lycidas," 84, is used, like *fama*, to mean rumor in *Paradise Lost* (i, 651; ii, 346; x, 481).

¹⁶ " Bold emprise " (*Comus*, 610; xi, 642), " high exploit(s)" (ii, 111; *S.A.*, 525, 1492), " great exploits " (xi, 790; *S.A.*, 32), " great acts " (*P.R.*, 2, 412; *S.A.*, 243), " acts " which are " heroic " (*P.R.*, 1, 216; *S.A.*, 527). There is awe of the great: " This, this, is (s)he " (*Arc.*, 5, 17; *S.A.*, 115), " stood . . . aloof " (i, 380; *S.A.*, 135), " with amaze " (Son. xv, 3; *S.A.*, 1645). From " quell the might(y)" (*Comus*, 613; *S.A.*, 1272), " quell(ed) their pride " (v, 740; *S.A.*, 286), and " hostile deeds " (xi, 796; *S.A.*, 893) we are led to battle: " endless war(s)" (Son. xv, 10; ii, 897), " war . . . cease(d) to roar " (" Vac. Ex.," 86; xi, 713), "(his) death's wound " (iii, 252; xii, 392; *S.A.*, 1581), " spear and shield " (Nat. Hymn, 55; i, 565; iv, 990; x, 542), " Both horse and foot " (xi, 645; *S.A.*, 1618), " trophies hung " (" Il Penseroso," 118; *S.A.*, 1736). Then there is the ignoble or unfortunate " heinous . . . fact " (*S.A.*, 493; cf. ix, 929; x, 1), " sad event " (iv, 716; *S.A.*, 1551), " experience of (from) this great event " (i, 118; *S.A.*, 1756), " cruel death " (*P.R.*, 4, 388; *S.A.*, 1198).

¹⁷ Darbishire, p. 32.

¹⁸ See Sigmund Spaeth, *Milton's Knowledge of Music* (Princeton, 1913), pp. 26, 90 ff.; Eleanor G. Brown, *Milton's Blindness* (New York, 1934), p. 136; Banks, *op. cit.*, pp. 124 ff.

¹⁹ This is the phenomenon that Roiron in his *Étude sur l'Imagination Auditive de Virgile* calls " la contamination phonético-sémantique " (pp. 65 ff.).

Chapter IV

¹ " Milton's sharpest impressions seem to be disagreeable rather than agreeable." Banks, *op. cit.*, p. 50.

² *Life*, II, 253. This has been disputed, as by Kathleen E. Hartwell, *Lactantius and Milton* (Cambridge, Mass., 1929), pp. 19 ff.

³ As everyone knows, he abounds in allusions to "heathen writer(s)" (III, 181, 273; IV, 312), "heathen authors " (IV, 302; VI, 63; cf. V, 8), " ethnicis auctoribus " (XV, 40); of them, Plato is " divine," (III, 293, 305; " divinus Plato," XII, 264; VII, 350).

⁴ To speak the learned languages, is it to speak "in an unknown tongue " (IV, 312), " in a tongue unknown " (VI, 11; " in lingua ignota," " Canzone," 3)?

[5] Edward Phillips in Darbishire, p. 72.

[6] *Op. cit.*, p. 55, note 29.

[7] Compare: " How should then the dim taper of this emperor's age that had such need of snuffing, extend any beam to our times wherewith we might hope to be better lighted than by those luminaries that God hath set up to shine to us far nearer hand " (III, 24). Cf. " great luminary," p. 92.

[8] Just as " the ready way " (III, 53; VI, 251; X, 253) (compare " readiest way," VI, 104, 247) in its first use looks forward to a much later title, as does " of true religion " (VI, 3), but these were all standard combinations: indeed the first and third turn up in non-Miltonic portions of the *Works* (IV, 21; VI, 229: cf. X, 359).

[9] " the vehemence of this our Savior's sentence was chiefly darted against Herod and Herodias " (IV, 143), " this vehemence of our Savior's sentence was chiefly bent against Herod, as was cited before " (IV, 209). (The most repetitious pamphlet, however, is the small *Treatise of Civil Power in Ecclesiastical Causes*, with its *bête noire*, " outward force," putting in an appearance eight times, VI, 20, 22 four, 23, 35, 37; cf. 47, and " profane and licentious " five times, 34, 35, 36, 37, 38, not to mention lesser repetitions.)

[10] See Irene Samuel, " Milton on Learning and Wisdom," *PMLA*, LXIV (1949), 708-723.

[11] III, 277; V, 37, 66; cf. 258; 126, 127, 165, 217, 260, 302 twice, 303 twice; " evil counsel(s)," V, 94, 154, 166.

[12] Nor is the lover of music fond of the " din of bells " (III, 34; X, 346).

[13] " un(at)tainted honor " (III, 61, 374), " fundamental . . . laws " (III, 476; V, 91; quotation, VI, 158), " fair deduction(s) " (III, 478; IV, 88), " earnest expression " (III, 316; VI, 27), " powerful preaching " (III, 156; IV, 251), " Christian prudence " (III, 413, 491; IV, 78, 136, 151, 191, 195), "Christiana prudentia " (XIV, 20), " heavenly gift(s)" (III, 92; V, 224), " gift(s) of God " (pp. 100-101), a " heavenly power " (III, 245; IV, 16). " The duty and the right of an instructed Christian calls me through the chance of good or evil report to be the sole advocate of a discountenanced truth " (III, 369). " God hath now joined with me necessarily in the good or evil report of this doctrine which I leave with you " (IV, 19). (Compare: "And thus do they raise an evil report upon the expected reforming grace that God hath bid us hope for," III, 214; " bring an evil report upon the land which God gave," IV, 154.) He

invokes "divine vengeance" (III, 279; V, 272, 275; X, 151), "divinam ultionem" (VIII, 90; gen. XV, 102) or "the sword of Justice" (V, 7, 272) on the enemies of truth.

He associates "peace and unity" (III, 212, 220), "just and equal" (III, 503, 504; V, 203) or "equal (and) just" (III, 428; IV, 44), and, more individually, "just(ly)" and "magnanimous(ly)":

their just and magnanimous actions (III, 341)

I call therefore a complete and generous education that which fits a man to perform justly, skilfully, and magnanimously all the offices, both private and public, of peace and war. (IV, 280)

in those proceedings, which hitherto appear equal to what hath been done in any age or nation heretofore, justly or magnanimously. (V, 5)

justly and magnanimously abolished it. (VI, 112)

On the theological side, pains is taken to avoid " making [or some other form of the verb] God . . . the . . . author of sin " (III, 434, 440, 442; IV, 157; VI, 169). Other more or less set phrases are "high (higher, highest) dignity" (III, 79, 158, 201, 364; V, 63, 179, 227), "(our) ancient stories" (III, 101, 237; singular, X, 180), "ancient(est) fathers" (III, 84, 100, 123, 126; IV, 312, etc.), " hanging by a (the) twined thread " (III, 106, 432), " proper sphere " (III, 401; V, 81), " the general scope " (III, 178; VI, 27), " position . . . be . . . laid down (first)" (III, 195, 387), " rich presents " (X, 237, 355), " with great presents " (X, 255, 299), " a great purchase " (III, 361; V, 117), " token of . . . favor " (sarcastic, III, 116; V, 117), " human . . . frailty " (III, 209, 292, 400; IV, 125; VI, 168), " mean fortunes " (III, 273, 342), " a huge army " (V, 15, 126), " pagan enemies " (III, 170; X, 203), " send(s) ambassadors to treat of peace " (X, 38, 85) or " about another payment " (X, 254), " Picts . . . come (coming) out of Scythia " (X, 82, 90), " a strong castle " (X, 119, 214), " strong drink " (III, 276; IV, 132; VI, 52), " vexed " or " possessed with an evil spirit " (X, 151, 177; " vex him like an evil spirit," V, 96), " the author(s) of so foul a deed (fact)" (III, 232; X, 154), " so foul a deed " (V, 105; cf. Bucer, " foul deeds," IV, 28), " so foul a fact " (X, 62, 232; " fact . . . too foul," 275), " a nursing father of (to make) the church " (VI, 48, 82). Presumably the Icarus myth precipitated the following " fall headlong " image:

But they who made no reckoning of those wings while they had that power in their hands may easily mistake the wings of faith for the wings of presumption, and so fall headlong. (V, 169) the prayer . . . flying up in haste on the specious wings of formality, if it fall not back again headlong. (V, 223)

Then there is the common analogy of bending crooked things " the contrary way " to get " straightness ":

by a countersway of restraint curbing their wild exorbitance almost into the other extreme; as when we bow things the contrary way, to make them come to their natural straightness. (III, 430)

resembling it, as when we bend a crooked wand the contrary way, not that it should stand so bent, but that the overbending might reduce it to a straightness by its own reluctance. (IV, 174)

"(With) all . . . diligence " (III, 228, 493; IV, 163; V, 270; VI, 168), " summoque studio " (IX, 282)—fits either side in controversies.

[14] While on the subject of poetry, we may note the phenomenon of these two sentences, a generation apart in time, which end with the same four words. Milton published in 1645-46 at the end of " The Passion " this remark:

This subject, the author finding to be above the years he had when he wrote it, and nothing satisfied with what was begun, left it unfinished.

He wrote in the Preface to *Samson Agonistes*:

Augustus Caesar also had begun his *Ajax*, but unable to please his own judgment with what he had begun, left it unfinished.

CHAPTER V

[1] *On the Composition of " Paradise Lost "; " Is Samson Agonistes* Unfinished? " *PQ*, XXVIII (1949), 98-106.

[2] *On the Composition of " Paradise Lost,"* p. 27.

[3] A. W. Verity, in his edition of *Paradise Lost* (Cambridge, 1921), p. xxxviii, note 4, called attention to the resemblance between the beginning of "Adam Unparadised ": " The angel Gabriel, either descending or entering," and the stage direction at the start of *Comus*: " The Attendant Spirit descends or enters."

[4] Patterson Index, *s.v.*, singular and plural.

[5] *The Early Lives of Milton*, Introduction, p. lviii.

[6] Cf. Irene Samuel, *Plato and Milton* (Ithaca, 1947), pp. 142-143.

[7] Some of Milton's word associations can hardly be considered surprising, but are worth recording in passing. He associates " joints(s) " with "sinew(s)" (III, 18, 369; *Comus*, 615; *S.A.*, 1142),

" spot " with " blemish " (III, 284; cf. " unspotted . . . unblemished," IV, 66; Son. xxii, 2), " mist " with " vapour " (III, 348-49; ix, 159; x, 694). " Bulk " is " huge " (III, 140; i, 196; vii, 410; xi, 729), " attempt(s)" " vain " (IV, 314; i, 44), " reared " goes with " high " (III, 219; *Comus*, 798; i, 464; iv, 699), and " lovely " goes with " fair ": whether applied to Edwi of England (" his lovely person surnamed him the Fair," X, 241), or the church (" once fair and lovely in your eyes," III, 356), or Eve (" more lovely fair," v, 380; " so lovely fair," viii, 471). An " all-grateful mind " (III, 297), " a grateful mind " (iv, 55) is, needless to say, commendable. " Fresh dews " were in " Lycidas " (29) and *The Reason of Church Government* (III, 214) before contributing to the appeal of earth in *Paradise Lost* (i, 771; xi, 135). If the frenzied rout made a " hideous roar " in " Lycidas " (61), whales " roared hideously " in *A Brief History of Moscovia* (X, 371). " Bold emprise " (*Comus*, 610: xi, 642) has the prose form " bold enterprise " (X, 277). " Vain deluding " (" Il Penseroso," 1) has become " vain and delusive " (X, 198), " easy conquest " (X, 50) " easier conquest " (vi, 37). Followers " came flocking " (X, 108; i, 522; compare with the prose *P.R.*, 1, 21) to a leader's call, but this is as common to the language as " give(n) . . . (his) death's wound " (X, 136; xii, 392; cf. *S.A.*, 1581).

[8] Here, as elsewhere, we are reckoning with a commonplace that Milton made his. It can be found in that repository of commonplaces, Erasmus' *De Utraque Verborum ac Rerum Copia* (Amsterdam, 1645), p. 141: " Tot me pericula circumstant, circumsistunt, obsepiunt, cingunt, obsident, premunt, urgent." I have not seen it pointed out that Harington's Ariosto, Book I, Stanza 50 begins: " But being now with danger compast round."

CHAPTER VI

[1] Compare " the trample and spurn of all the other damned " (III, 79) ; " I fear yet this iron yoke of outward conformity hath left a slavish print upon our necks " (IV, 348), and other yoke images.

[2] *Poets and Playwrights*, pp. 191, 291, 293.

[3] Some of these involve proper names or modifiers, faintly shadow the consistency with which Milton, everywhere *except* in his Latin prose, referred to the Druids as " old ": " Where your old bards, the famous Druids, lie " (" Lyc.," 53), " gens Druides antiqua " (" Mansus," 42), " our ancient Druids " (III, 376), " our old philosophers the

Druids " (X, 2). He reiterates that More has been shown to be what
he reaches for a French word to describe: " Gallice *Altier(us)*" (IX,
66, 118). He was impressed by the fate of Ocnus, who was condemned
in hell to the futile twisting of ropes: " cum Ocno illo apud inferos
torqueant funiculos " (XII, 168); " consequentias torquere solet,
quales Ocnus funes apud inferos " (VII, 474). He goes on to complete this charge against Salmasius by adding, " quae nulli sunt usui,
nisi ut comedantur ab asinis," and that is what, as a student, he
thought logic was, at its worst—thorny, food for asses or finches:
" dumis et spinis asperum " (XII, 162); " inter dumos et spinas
logicae " (XII, 216), " Quid logica? . . . spinis vescuntur " (XII, 276).
By the same token he was wary of indulging in an Asiatic exuber-
ance of words, "Asiatica verborum exuberantia " (XII, 4), "At si
Asianam illam exuberantiam imitabor " (XII, 290). (This classification goes back to antiquity: see Ida Langdon, *Milton's Theory of
Poetry and Fine Art*, New Haven, 1924, p. 142, note 1.)

There are more or less standard references like " irae(que) divinae "
(XV, 304, 342), Christ's " propheticum munus " (XV, 290; oblique
cases, 288, 302), " honorem . . . divinum " (XIV, 236, 242, 302, 330;
ablative, 200; " divinum honorem," 216; " honores divini," 390) ; " de
antiquo jure," " jus patrisfamilias antiquum " (VII, 266, 394). The
blind and subordinate inditer of State Letters has formulae, even if
they are his own formulae, such as " id maluisse Majestatem Vestram
suis literis amicissimis " (XIII, 142), " Majestatis Vestrae literis
amicissimis " (XIII, 286), with which the earlier " hac amicissima
literarum provocatione " (XII, 48) and " sent as a friendly letter of
advice " (V, 5) are to be compared. He stresses the " cum Faederatis
Belgii Provinciis amicitiam pristinam " (XIII, 256, 258). He urges
peace and moderate counsels between the United Provinces and
Sweden: " ad moderata consilia," " ad pacem et moderata consilia "
(XIII, 242, 286). " Singulare studium " (XIII, 104), " nostrum erga
Majestatem Vestram singulare studium " (216) is returned for " tam
singulare erga nos studium " (144), " Singulare tuum erga me . . .
studium " (252), " singulari tuo studio " (146). (In private letters
there is "singularis animi mei gratitudo," XII, 4, " ex singulari animi
tui gratitudine," XII, 60.) A common wish is for " prosperis . . .
successibus " (XIII, 256, 408; accusative, 452, 476). Having epistles
on the Piedmont massacre to despatch to several princes, Milton can
naturally be caught stating the same facts in a similar way: " sub-
ditos suos Alpinarum quarundam Vallium incolas " (XIII, 164),

" subjectos sibi Alpinos incolas " (170), " subjectos sibi Alpinarum Vallium incolas " (440), " qui radices Alpium et valles quasdam in ditione vestra incolentes " (478). He stresses their suffering from " fame et frigore " (XIII, 168, 170, 174), and the " caede ac sanguine " (258, 286). " Rolled . . . infant down the rocks " says the famous Piedmont sonnet (7); " infantum autem alii in saxa contriti," says an oration Milton prepared (XIII, 480). Repetition carries over into a few other letters on common subjects, e.g., " graves ad nos allatae . . . querelae " (XIII, 122, 124), " multis ac variis negotiis summa fide, probitate ac solertia " (340, 342). Similarly, if it is a complaint about privateering, the words are " in navem quandam praedatoriam per insidias abducti essent " (XIII, 6), " eosque in navem praedatoriam abduxerant " (50). But it is remarkable how much variation there is, as if in this situation, as in that of the Arguments to the poems, it were a point of pride. In any case, these are not borrowings across the years, like " immodice laudantem," from the First Prolusion (XII, 142), which turns up in the *Second Defense* as " immodicis laudibus " (VIII, 80), " laudatores . . . immodicos " (VIII, 4). Day fled adulation; Salmasius welcomed it.

There is no denying that Milton derived a certain satisfaction from repeatedly knocking down adversaries in a language all civilized Europe could read (" Of which all Europe talks from side to side," Son. xxii, 12). He keeps dragging into the open More's nocturnal jaunts, etc.: " illa nocturna itinera quae toties Hagacomitis Leidam cucurristi; illi nocturni et furtivi congressus cum Pontia " (IX, 138); " nocturna illa nempe Haga Leidam " (IX, 190); " De illis nocturnis Haga Leidam itineribus, de illis cum Pontia clandestinis atque nocturnis congressibus " (IX, 270). He gave as good as he received, had a talent for this, as has been recognized by such diverse critics as Jonathan Richardson (in Darbishire, p. 282: "Many of his Choicest Years of Life were Employ'd in Wrangling, and Receiving and Racquetting Back Reproach, Accusation, and Sarcasm. Which though he had an Arm and Dexterity fitted for . . . ") and Professors French (who goes so far as to say, " Milton's mind . . . was essentially critical rather than creative . . . He was attracted by satire, an essentially critical art," *PMLA*, L, 1935, 476) and Parker (" Milton loved controversy not wisely but too well," etc., *Milton's Contemporary Reputation*, Columbus, 1940, pp. 32 ff., 61 ff.). If only a few specialists read what he gave, still fewer are those who read what he received, apart from Milton's own ample quotations. But, without seeking out the deservedly forgotten books of three centuries ago, one may learn something from the frequency with which Milton refers to the infamous libel he thought More the author of—" illius libelli famosissimi " (IX, 12), " libellus . . . famosus " (262), " famosis libellis " (144), " famosos libellos " (248; cf. 252), " libellum . . . famosum " (46, 292, 294), " libelli infamissimi " (36), " infamissimi libelli " (114), " infamis libelli " (52, 160) (compare " slanderous and seditious libel," VI, 258). The *Defensio Secunda* was written, as the title page announces, " Contra infamem libellum anonymum." It contains the demonstration: " Ex quo intelligi potest tuarum narrationum fides " (VIII, 170), " quae tua sit narrationum fides, jam aliquoties vidimus " (VIII, 202). Toward the beginning and toward the end of the *Defensio Prima* Milton speaks of Salmasius as a spitter of venom: " mitte virus illud tuum acerbitatis evomere " (VII, 30), " virus omne acerbitatis evomere cupiebas " (VII, 502). Salmasius is a great—critic (VII, 16; IX, 184) (but guilty of disgraceful solecisms).

On the autobiographical side, there are references to Milton's bad health—" adversa valetudo " (XII, 52), " adversa simul valetudine " (VIII, 68)—and indications, both in youth and during the time of civil troubles, of the importance he attached to literary leisure—" in otium alte literarium recedere " (XII, 12), " recessum otio literario " (XII, 50), " literato otio " (XII, 98), " otium illud literarum " (XII, 204).

⁴ " libertatem pristinam " (XIII, 160), " pristinam . . . libertatem " (XIII, 172) ; " ancient liberty " (Son. xii, 2; V, 117).

⁵ Like " in most esteem for virtue and generosity of mind " (VI, 142) (applied to those whom kings especially mistrust), of which " singularem benignitatem animique magnitudinem " (XIII, 382) (addressed to Louis XIV of France) can be taken as the Latin equivalent. Naturally there can be singled out connections between Milton's state letters in English and the majority that were written or translated by him in the other tongue, such as " vicinorum omnium principum " (XIII, 300), " all neighboring princes " (XIII, 504), and " Quapropter pro illa arctissima necessitudine " (XIII, 256), " fundamenta arctioris etiam necessitudinis " (XIII, 368), for which, we learn, Milton's English would be " a straiter bond of alliance " (XIII, 497). (The Latin is good for marriage as well as politics: " arctissima necessitudo," XV, 120, " necessitudinis illius arctissimae," XV, 122.) These are no more to be dwelt on than " jurisperitorum nostrorum sententias " (XIII, 276), " lawyers' opinions " (XVIII, 166), or

"grievous complaints" (III, 62), "non sine gravissima querela" (XIII, 28). "If we mean to inherit the great reward there promised" (III, 408), "in hope of great reward" (X, 279), "spe praemii cujusdam majoris" (VII, 398-400), have various meanings. There are allusions involving names, such as "Gildas, the most ancient of all our historians" (V, 26), "teste Nennio historicorum nostrorum post Gildam antiquissimo" (VII, 436); "this Pluto's helmet, as Homer calls it, of obscurity" (XII, 321; cf. *Iliad*, V, 845), "neque Plutonis ista galea diutius te teget" (VIII, 28).

[6] Other points of doctrine are "that not examples, but express commands oblige our obedience to God or man" (VI, 54), "praecepta enim nos, non exempla, ne Dei quidem, obligant" (XVII, 180). Hardness of heart is one of the final punishments, "had gone on sinning to an immeasurable heap, which is one of the extremest punishments" (III, 255), "extrema fere maximorum poena peccatorum est" (XIV, 164). Another punishment is asking for and being given a king: "If God afterward gave or permitted this insurrection of episcopacy, it is to be feared he did it in his wrath, as he gave the Israelites a king" (III, 211), "Exaudit etiam nonnunquam iratus: ut . . . petentes . . . regem" (XVII, 102), "Petentibus tamen iis dedit regem Deus quamvis iratus" (VII, 156; cf. 76, 84). Christ's words to the Pharisees on divorce are to be viewed in the light of the circumstances. "The occasion which induced our Savior to speak of divorce, was either to convince the extravagance of the Pharisees in that point, or to give a sharp and vehement answer to a tempting question" (III, 429), "Christ therefore having to answer these tempting Pharisees" (III, 455), "to quell and put to non-plus the tempting Pharisees" (III, 459), "Christus, tentantibus se Pharisaeis, respondit apposite quidem, . . . ad arrogantiam, ut fere solet, Pharisaeorum reprimendam" (XV, 158). It is basic that "God cannot contradict himself" (IV, 85), "how is God not made the contradicter of himself?" (IV, 130), "sibi contradicere videbitur Deus" (XIV, 68), "nec . . . Deus . . . potest . . . sibi contradicere" (XIV, 342).

[7] Concern with larger questions by no means precludes fine points, such as deportment, "Toward him they bend With awful reverence prone" (ii, 477), "prona corporis inclinatione" (XVII, 294).

[8] *Letters*, edited by M. B. Forman (Oxford, 1935), pp. 227-228. Quoted by Stoll, "Milton a Romantic," *From Shakespeare to Joyce* (New York, 1944), p. 404.

CHAPTER VII

[1] *Narragansett Club Publications*, edited by J. R. Bartlett (Providence, 1874), VI, 251.

[2] Quoted by Katherine John, Introduction to Louis Racine, *Life of Milton* (London, 1930), pp. 61-62.

[3] *Works* (Oxford, 1825), VII, 116.

[4] Boswell's *Life of Johnson* under date of July 31, 1763 (Hill-Powell edition, I, 463).

[5] *Letters of Samuel Johnson, LL.D.*, edited by G. B. Hill (Oxford, 1892), I, 287.

[6] W. Grinton Berry, *John Milton* (London, [1909]), p. 45.

[7] *Ibid.*, p. vii.

[8] *Gleanings of Past Years* (London, 1879), p. 305.

[9] *A History of Elizabethan Literature* (New York, 1887), p. 317.

[10] *Puritan and Anglican* (London, 1900), p. 136.

[11] " Milton on the Position of Women," *Modern Language Review*, XV (1920), 244 ff.

[12] Cf. *Flores Historiarum* (XCV in Rolls Series, Vol. I, 329): " sed indignantibus regni magnatibus expulsa est a regno, nolens sub sexu femineo militari."

[13] *De Gestis Regum Anglorum Libri Quinque*, edited by William Stubbs (London, 1887), I, 7.

[14] *Historia Regum Britanniae*, III, xiii.

[15] *Historie of England*, III, ch. v.

[16] Genuissa by acting as mediator stopped the war between Arviragus and Vespasian, according to Geoffrey of Monmouth (IV, xvi). On Hamo, see *ibid.*, xii-xiii.

[17] So previous historians had regarded her, as Sir Charles Firth notes in " Milton as an Historian," *Proceedings of the British Academy* (1907-1908), p. 247.

[18] Atque illi vinclis absoluti Agrippinam quoque, haud procul alio suggestu conspicuam, isdem quibus principem laudibus gratibusque venerati sunt. Novum sane et moribus veterum insolitum, feminam signis Romanis praesidere: ipsa semet parti a maioribus suis imperii sociam ferebat. (*Annales*, XII, 37.)

On the other hand, we see the civilizing effect of Rome on a woman in Milton's sentence:

Claudia Rufina, the daughter of a Briton and wife of Pudence, a Roman senator, lived at Rome, famous by the verse of Martial for beauty, wit, and learning. X, 81.

The poet Martial convinces, where the "monkish" chroniclers do not.

[19] *John Milton, Englishman*, pp. 130 ff.

[20] *Milton* (London, 1879), p. 58.

[21]___

The soberest and best governed men are least practised in these affairs; and who knows not that the bashful muteness of a virgin may ofttimes hide all the unliveliness and natural sloth which is really unfit for conversation? Nor is there that freedom of access granted or presumed, as may suffice to a perfect discerning till too late; and where any indisposition is suspected, what more usual than the persuasion of friends, that acquaintance, as it increases, will amend all? And lastly, it is not strange though many, who have spent their youth chastely, are in some things not so quick-sighted, while they haste too eagerly to light the nuptial torch; nor is it, therefore, that for a modest error a man should forfeit so great a happiness, and no charitable means to release him, since they who have lived most loosely, by reason of their bold accustoming, prove most successful in their matches, because their wild affections unsettling at will, have been as so many divorces to teach them experience. Whenas the sober man honoring the appearance of modesty, and hoping well of every social virtue under that veil, may easily chance to meet, if not with a body impenetrable, yet often with a mind to all other due conversation inaccessible . . . (III, 394-395).

With "freedom of access" compare "free access," p. 150.

[22] See III, 382, 388, 391, 393, 397, 403, 415, 423, 457, 492, 510; IV, 87, 89, 101.

[23]___

The truth is that Godwin and his sons did many things boisterously and violently, much against the King's mind; which not able to resist, he had, as some say, his wife Edith, Godwin's daughter, in such aversation as in bed never to have touched her: whether for this cause or mistaken chastity, not commendable; to inquire further is not material.

But it is material to note Milton's consistency. He had referred in the Cambridge Manuscript, presumably before his own marriage, to this same case of Edward the Confessor's "superstitious pretense of chastity" (XVIII, 244). His attitude gets final expression in *Paradise Lost*, iv, 741 ff.

[24] *De Officiis*, I, 4, 11.

[25] It is curious to find the exact sentiment proceeding from Boswell's actress friend, "Louisa." *London Journal, 1762-1763* (New York,

1950), pp. 95, 139. Copybook maxims will out, on the guiltiest occasions!

[26] IV, 97, 221, 227-228.

[27] ——

Spernuntur namque primae, post monachi votum irritum illicitae licet, tamen propriae conjugis praesumptivae nuptiae, alia viri viventis, non externi, sed fratris filii adamata. Ob quod dura cervix illa multis jam peccaminum fascibus onerata, bino parricidiali ausu, occidendo supradictum, uxoremque tuam, aliquamdiu a te habitam, velut summo sacrilegii tui culmine, de imis ad inferiora curvatur. Dehinc illam, cujus dudum colludio ac suggestione tantae sunt peccatorum subitae moles, publico et, ut fallaces parisitorum linguae tuorum conclamant, summis tamen labiis, non ex intimo cordis, legitimo, utpote viduatam, thoro; ut nostrae vero, sceleratissimo adscivisti connubio.

(*Epistola Gildae* in *Monumenta Historica Britannica*, 1848, p. 19.)

[28] J. Milton French, " Milton's Annotated Copy of Gildas," *Harvard Studies and Notes in Philology and Literature*, XX (1938), 79.

[29] *The Epistle of Gildas* (London, 1638), p. 91. The nineteenth-century translation of J. A. Giles, *Works of Gildas and Nennius* (London, 1841), has the identical phrase (p. 31).

[30] VIII, 136: " quatuor jam libros absolveram." This gives us a *terminus ad quem* of March, 1649 for the composition of the first four books. Firth (*op. cit.*, p. 229) and Hanford (*A Milton Handbook*, p. 116) conjecture that Milton began the writing at about 1646.

[31] He calls her " virtues more than female " (X, 236), but at least, and in contrast to his handling of Boadicea, he admits that she had them.

[32] *Donne's Sermons, Selected Passages*, edited by Logan Pearsall Smith (Oxford, 1919), p. 86.

[33] If the Malvezzi marginalia are Milton's, he implied that the Queen was astute in refusing to allow any discussion of who was to succeed her (XVIII, 494).

[34] *Milton*, p. 131.

[35] Quoted by Masson, *Life*, II, 595. A generation later, however, Mrs. Aphra Behn felt meet to deal with the fop who said " they were to expect a woful Play, God damn him, for it was a woman's." See her *Works*, edited by M. Summers (London, 1915), I, 224.

[36] Cf. William R. Parker, "A Word on ' Misogyny ' " in *Milton's Debt to Greek Tragedy in " Samson Agonistes "* (Baltimore, 1937), pp. 129-135, who points out that " we must not . . . confuse hatred of uxoriousness with misogyny." F. Michael Krouse in *Milton's*

Samson and the Christian Tradition (Princeton, 1949), pp. 57 ff., 72 ff., 102 ff., provides timely illustration of the moral severity with which medieval and Renaissance writers treated Dalila.

[37] See Chilton L. Powell, *English Domestic Relations, 1487-1653* (New York, 1917), Louis B. Wright, *Middle-Class Culture in Eliza-bethan England* (Chapel Hill, 1935), pp. 201-227, and Francis L. Utley, *The Crooked Rib, An Analytical Index to the Argument about Women in English and Scots Literature to the End of the Year 1568* (Columbus, 1944). See also Celeste Turner Wright, " Something More about Eve," *SP*, XLI (1944), 156-168. Extremely enlightening is the article by William and Malleville Haller, " The Puritan Art of Love," *Huntington Library Quarterly*, V (1942), especially pp. 247 ff., who well apply the adjective " patriarchal " to Milton's attitude. Even that first modern man, the mild and liberal Montaigne, flatly states in his essay " De l'Affection des Pères aux Enfants " (II, 8): " Mais, au dermeurant, il me semble, ie ne sçay comment, qu'en toutes façons la maistrise n'est aucunement deüe aus femmes sur les hommes, sauf la maternelle et naturelle "; and adds, very Miltonically, " si ce n'est pour la châtiment de ceus qui, par quelque humeur fieureuse, se sont volontairement soubmis a elles." *Essais*, edited by R. Dezeimeris and H. Barckhausen (Bordeaux, 1870), I, 329-330. The remark was too much for Montaigne's editor, Mlle. de Gournay, who altered it to: " il naist *rarement* des femmes à qui la maistrise soit deüe," etc. When a woman did rule well, it was cause for wonder, as to the author of a ballad " Upon the death of Queen Elizabeth ":

> O shee bore the Sway, & of all affaires,
>   & yet shee was but a woman;

and again:

> A wiser Queene never was to be seen
> For a woman, or yet a stouter.

Ballads from Manuscripts, edited W. R. Morfill (Hertford, the Ballad Society, 1873), II, 98, 99. Nor does the modern temper go all one way, as witness D. H. Lawrence's remark in a letter to Katherine Mansfield, " I do think a woman must yield some sort of precedence to a man, and he must take this precedence " (*The Portable D. H. Lawrence*, edited by Diana Trilling, New York, 1947, p. 584) and the drift of the same author's pamphlet, *Men Must Work and Women as Well* (*ibid.*, pp. 623-637), which anticipates a " reactionary " book that was a best-seller in 1947, Ferdinand Lundberg and Marynia Farnham, *Modern Woman: the Lost Sex* (New York, 1947).

[38] See C. S. Lewis, *A Preface to " Paradise Lost "* (London, 1942), pp. 72-80, the chapter on " Hierarchy."

[39] On the myth see Charles G. Osgood, *The Classical Mythology of Milton's English Poems* (New York, 1900), pp. xlvii and 34, and the quotation from George Sandys in Bush, *Mythology and the Renaissance Tradition*, p. 273, note 65.

[40] ——

The " marriage " of Yahweh and Israel meant that apostasy and false worship were adultery, whence the common phrase of " going a-whoring " after other gods. Sexual imagery was common among the sensuous and sensual Orientals, and the prophets condemn the sexual rites and ceremonial prostitution which expressed union with the god and also—as the gods were givers of fertility—were believed to promote the increase of nature and man. Physical union with the god or goddess could be actualized by the intercourse with " sacred " men and women dedicated to the service. (Milton knew this, XVII, 142.) Stanley Cook, *An Introduction to the Bible*, Harmondsworth, a Pelican Book, 1945, p. 90. Compare the sexual imagery of Ezekiel, Chs. xvi and xxiii.

[41] *Milton and the Puritan Dilemma*, p. 15.

[42] *Chariot of Wrath*, pp. 97-98.

[43] *Ibid.*, p. 98.

[44] Had he in mind Horace's " introrsum turpem, speciosum pelle decora " (*Epist.* I, xvi, 45), a line translated in *Tetrachordon*, " Sees his foul inside through his whited skin " (IV, 137), and referred to in *Pro Se Defensio* (IX, 224)?

[45] Banks, *Milton's Imagery*, p. 246, speculates that the following from the Fifth Prolusion, " Itaque nostrae nunc erit operae, ut nudatum, plumisque emendicatis exutum errorem deformitati nativae reddamus " (XII, 194), may derive from " the stripping of Duessa " (*Faerie Queene*, I, viii, 45-50). See Banks also on images " concerned with substances which conceal evil under a superficially bright and attractive surface," pp. 16 ff.

[46] 1634 edition, p. 54.

[47] *The Allegory of Love* (Oxford, 1936), p. 328.

[48] *Ibid.*, p. 337.

[49] For quotations and references see George W. Whiting, *Milton's Literary Milieu* (Chapel Hill, 1939), pp. 370 ff., and Audrey Chew, " Joseph Hall and Neo-Stoicism," *PMLA*, LXV (1950), 1138 ff. The latter says of Hall (p. 1138): " If a thing looked too good he feared

it could not be sound." For other points of agreement between the two opponents, see Miss Chew's " Joseph Hall and John Milton," *ELH*, XVII (1950), 274 ff. It is to be remembered that Hall was " a Bishop with a Puritan past." A. Davenport, ed., *Collected Poems of Joseph Hall* (Liverpool, 1949), p. v.

[50] A paradox dealt with by Knight, *Chariot of Wrath, passim*, and Ross, *op. cit.*

Chapter VIII

[1] Sandys here cites Masson's edition of the *Poetical Works* (London, 1890), III, 255.

[2] " The Literary Sources of Milton's ' Lycidas,' " *Transactions of the Royal Society of Literature*, 2nd Series, XXXII (1914), 234. James Reuel Smith, *Springs and Wells in Greek and Roman Literature* (New York, 1922), pp. 214-215, complicates the issue further by asserting that another Heliconian spring, Aganippe, " has every credential to prove it the ' Pierian Spring ' and the one to which Pope's directions for taking the waters may be applied." This is impossible if " Pierian " or " Pierius " is taken as locating the spring, but the adjective *may* mean " sacred to the Muses, who come from Pieria."

[3] Jerram, p. 51; William Vaughn Moody, ed., *Complete Poetical Works of John Milton* (Boston, 1924), p. 393.

[4] *Explanatory Notes and Remarks on Milton's " Paradise Lost,"* by J. Richardson, Father and Son (London, 1734), pp. 19-20.

[5] Oras, *op. cit.*, p. 80.

[6] *The Sonnets of Milton*, pp. 115-16 (quotations from Wordsworth and Tennyson).

[7] Fraser Neiman, " Milton's *Sonnet XX*," *PMLA*, LXIV (1949), 480-483; Elizabeth Jackson, *PMLA*, LXV (1950), 328-329. Northrop Frye, ed., *" Paradise Lost " and Selected Poetry and Prose* (New York, 1951), p. 584, also favors this interpretation.

[8] Thus I have answered Professor Jackson's points 1 and 2. As for her point 4, Horace throws no light on the crux. Point 3 (*op. cit.*, p. 328) reads: " *The climax.* Fire, food, wine, *music.* Milton's works give constant evidence of his delight in music, without containing, so far as I can remember, any warning against overindulgence." I am not sure that this point should be conceded, either. Why should music be exempted from the " aurea mediocritas " set up for the other

pleasures? Aristotle argued that a " right measure " was necessary for music as for other things, lest the practise and the skill be carried to the point of professionalism. *Politica*, VIII, 6. Milton knew the " giddy cunning " of music. Spaeth observes: " Milton only once refers to the Lydian mode, for its ἦθος evidently does not please him. Plato describes it as ' a soft or drinking harmony,' not fit for men of character, and it is significant that Milton's single reference occurs in the description of purely sensuous music (' L'A.,' 135-150)." *Milton's Knowledge of Music*, p. 67.

[9] Neiman, pp. 481-482. I must in all candor give my opinion, however, that the reaction against the " personal heresy " has been carried too far in some academic quarters, so that only autobiographies are allowed to contain autobiographical references. The small facts are easier to handle, but there comes a time when the large facts—and the veiled ones—must be faced. If a poem, published in 1671, has an overwhelming number of what have long been considered correspondences with—and allusions to—the condition of England, and the position of Milton, after the Restoration, it does not seem a very profitable skepticism to entertain at length a conjecture that the poem was written years before the Restoration since it cannot be proved —in the sense of having a date attached to it—to have been written after. (A by no means minor fact, which must be given due evaluation also, is the markedly *dramatic* quality of the poem which was published with *Samson Agonistes* and the position of which after *Paradise Lost* no one can question. To quote the latest commentary: " *Paradise Regained* is a debate, a debate over ends and means. But it is much more than a dry exercise in dialectics. It is dramatic, intensely so . . . " Brooks and Hardy, *op. cit.*, p. 279.)

[10] John Downame's tract, *The Christian Warfare*, was printed six times between 1604 and 1634. The figured title page of the 1634 edition is reproduced as the frontispiece of William Haller's *The Rise of Puritanism* (New York, 1938). Haller shows, pp. 142 ff., that wayfaring and warfaring are both common images in the literature of the Puritans.

[11] *Milton*, p. 76.

[12] *Studies in Literature, Second Series*, p. 103.

[13] *Milton*, p. 157.

[14] *The Seventeenth Century Background* (London, 1934), p. 244.

[15] *Chariot of Wrath*, p. 76.

[16] *The Modernity of Milton* (Chicago, 1927), p. 97.

[17] *Lactantius and Milton*, p. 30.

[18] Pitt Press Series (1918), p. 20. It is certain that Jebb, however, and probable that Verity—were not responsible for the text used in this edition. The same reading appears in Milton's *Selected Poetry and Prose*, ed. C. R. Bull (Melbourne, 1948), p. 21.

[19] *Prose Works*, II, 68. The association of " see " and " seek " is as old as *Beowulf*, " seon ond secean " (3102). The earliest repetition of the error I know of is in German: " ' Ich kann eine Tugend nicht preisen, die sich versteckt, die niemals hervorbricht um ihren Gegner aufzusuchen.' " Gustav Liebert, *Milton, Studien zur Geschichte des englischen Geistes* (Hamburg, 1860), p. 153. The Bohn edition must be used with great caution. James Goode, " The Bohn Edition of Milton's Prose," *TLS*, August 1, 1929, p. 608, pointed out three textual errors, including one in *Areopagitica*. A third error in this *Areopagitica*, this one brought to my attention by Professor Haller, occurs in the last sentence, where " a sumptuous bribe " has become " a sumptuous bride." This reading is followed in one well-known modern edition.

On the other hand, the original text of *Areopagitica* has been questioned in other places. Should it not be " newing her mighty youth " (IV, 344)? See R. S. Loomis, *MLN*, XXXIII (1917), 437-438. Should it not be " endowments haply not the worse for two and fifty degrees of northern latitude " (IV, 296)? As John W. Hales (ed. *Areopagitica*, Oxford, 1904, p. 66) observes, " It is possible *worst* may be a misprint for *worse*; but there is no authority for saying that it is so." This emendation has been silently adopted by Robert P. Tristram Coffin and Alexander M. Witherspoon, editors, *Seventeenth-Century Prose and Poetry* (New York, 1946), p. 409, and by Roberta F. Brinkley, ed., *English Prose of the XVII Century* (New York, 1951), p. 483. The former also have (p. 414) " attendant minorities " instead of " attendant minorites " (IV, 305).

[20] Compare Milton's statement as to what a satire should do:

strike high and adventure dangerously at the most eminent vices among the greatest persons, and not to creep into every blind taphouse that fears a constable more than a satire. (III, 329).

[21] The editors of Volume XVIII of the Columbia Milton dismiss Candy's argument abruptly (601-602), but I am inclined to agree with Clark: " It seems possible to me that the Ovid verses are by the boy Milton. But case not proved." *John Milton at St. Paul's School*, p. 202.

[22] *Life of Milton,* V, 188, note 1; cf. n. 3 and p. 391.

[23] I take it that it outdistances the most famous crux in Shakespeare, "runaway's eyes" (*Romeo and Juliet,* III, ii, 6), which, as Harley Granville-Barker, *Prefaces to Shakespeare* (Princeton, 1947), II, 328, noted with awe, gets twenty-eight pages in the Furness Variorum. In any case, that is very likely a textual problem, which the "two-handed engine" is not, though we get a small variant in the 1638 text, "smites no more" instead of "smite no more."

[24] "'That Two-Handed Engine' and Savonarola," *SP,* XLVII (1950), 589-606; also "Supplement," *SP,* XLIX (1952), 548-550. If Milton *did* read Savonarola's sermon on Psalmus lxxiii—a conjecture on which my explanation of the crux by no means depends—we can understand how it would have impressed one who so strongly felt himself that the decorated was the false and who had himself so eloquently much to say against "embezzling the treasury of the Church on painted and gilded walls of temples wherein God hath testified to have no delight" (III, 74). I quoted III, 47, observing that the key word "ruin" (on this word and its derivatives in Milton's poetry, see Elizabeth Holmes, "Some Notes on Milton's Use of Words," *Essays and Studies by Members of the English Association,* X, 1924, pp. 115-117) introduced a similar train of imagery. In 1641 the author was still a constitutional monarchist. But in *Eikonoklastes* he turns similar imagery against the King: "Yet here, like a rotten building newly trimmed over, he represents it speciously and fraudulently to impose upon the simple reader" (V, 98); and his sardonic answer to the charge of the author of *Eikon Basilike* that the Puritans "think all is gold of piety that doth but glister with a show of zeal" is: "We know his meaning, and apprehend how little hope there could be of him from such language as this, but are sure that the piety of his prelatic model glistered more upon the posts and pillars which their zeal and fervency gilded over, than in the true works of spiritual edification" (V, 147).

[25] The point I am making is that, under the doctrine of divine providence, men were accustomed to see, or to expect, the hand of God, or the sword of God, whenever anything extraordinary happened or catastrophic punishment of conspicuous sinners was hoped for. I have illustrated this (see the last footnote to my original article, and the article's Supplement, point 3) in connection with the "Blackfriars Fatal Vespers," the collapse of a popish place of worship in London October 26 (which was noted to be November 5 by continental reckon-

ing), 1623, fatal to almost one hundred persons. I might here move
on to the year of "Lycidas." The prevalence of the plague in 1637—
which Tillyard calls " a fact to be remembered in reading 'Lycidas'"
(*Milton*, p. 80)—moved young Andrew Marvell at Cambridge to
express himself as follows, in his "Ad Regem Carolum," a " Parodia "
on Horace (*Carm.* 1, 2) (published in *Sunodia Musarum Canta-
brigiensium*, 1637). First he referred to God's hand:

> Jam satis pestis, satis atque diri
> Fulminis misit Pater, et rubenti
> Dextera nostras jaculatus arces
>   Terruit urbem.

Then, in the sixth stanza, he referred to God's sword:

> Audiit caelos acuisse ferrum
> Quo graves Turcae melius perirent;
> Audiit mortes vitio parentum
>   Rara juventus.

[26] If not from Elegia III (1626), 5-8:

> Dum procerum ingressa est splendentes marmore turres
> Dira sepulchrali Mors metuenda face,
> Pulsavitque auro gravidos et iaspide muros,
> Nec metuit satrapum sternere falce greges.